JACKSON SCHOOL PUBLICATIONS
IN INTERNATIONAL STUDIES

JACKSON SCHOOL PUBLICATIONS

IN INTERNATIONAL STUDIES

Senator Henry M. Jackson was convinced that the study of the history, cultures, political systems, and languages of the world's major regions was an essential prerequisite for wise decision making in international relations. In recognition of his deep commitment to higher education and advanced scholarship, this series of publications has been established through the generous support of the Henry M. Jackson Foundation, in cooperation with the Henry M. Jackson School of International Studies, and the University of Washington Press.

The Crisis of Leninism and the Decline of the Left: The Revolutions of 1989, edited by Daniel Chirot

Sino-Soviet Normalization and Its International Implications, 1945–1990, by Lowell Dittmer

Contradictions: Artistic Life, the Socialist State, and the Chinese Painter Li Huasheng, by Jerome Silbergeld with Gong Jisui

The Found Generation: Chinese Communists in Europe during the Twenties, by Marilyn A. Levine

Rules and Rights in the Middle East: Democracy, Law, and Society, edited by Ellis Goldberg, Resat Kesaba, and Joel S. Migdal

Can Europe Work? Germany and the Reconstruction of Postcommunist Societies, edited by Stephen Hanson and Willfried Spohn

Marxist Intellectuals and the Chinese Labor Movement: A Study of Deng Zhongxia (1894–1933), by Daniel Y. K. Kwan

Essential Outsiders: Chinese and Jews in the Modern Transformation of Southeast Asia and Central Europe, edited by Daniel Chirot and Anthony Reid

Days of Defeat and Victory, by Yegor Gaidar

The Production of Hindu-Muslim Violence in Contemporary India, by Paul R. Brass

Modern Clan Politics: The Power of "Blood" in Kazakhstan and Beyond, by Edward Schatz

MODERN CLAN POLITICS

The Power of "Blood"
in Kazakhstan and Beyond

EDWARD SCHATZ

UNIVERSITY OF WASHINGTON PRESS

Seattle and London

This publication was supported in part by the Jackson School Publications Fund, established through the generous support of the Henry M. Jackson Foundation and other donors, in cooperation with the Henry M. Jackson School of International Studies and the University of Washington Press.

The book also received support from the Donald R. Ellegood International Publications Endowment.

University of Washington Press PO Box 50096, Seattle, WA 98145
www.washington.edu/uwpress

Library of Congress Cataloging-in-Publication Data
can be found at the back of this book.

The paper used in this publication is acid-free and recycled from 10 percent post-consumer and at least 50 percent pre-consumer waste. It meets the minimum requirements of American National Standard for Information Sciences-Permanence of Paper for Printed Library Materials, ANSI Z39.48-1984. ♾♺

Parts of chapters 4 and 6 have been published in slightly different form as "The Politics of Multiple Identities: Lineage and Ethnicity in Kazakhstan" in *Europe-Asia Studies* 52(3):489–506; chapter 4 has also appeared in part in "Framing Strategies and Non-Conflict in Multi-Ethnic Kazakhstan," *Nationalism and Ethnic Politics* 6(2):70–92. Thanks to *Europe-Asia Studies* (*www.tandf.co.uk*) and *Nationalism and Ethnic Politics* for permission to use the material.

Contents

Preface   ix

A Note on Transliteration   xiv

Introduction: Modern Clan Politics   xv

Part One: The Reproduction of Clans

1 / Kinship and Modernity   3

2 / Nomads, Diffuse Authority, and Sovietization   21

3 / Two Faces of Soviet Power   46

4 / Continuity and Change after the Soviet Collapse   72

Part Two: The Political Dynamic of Informal Ties

5 / Clan Conflict   95

6 / Clan Metaconflict   113

Part Three: Managing Clans

7 / A Vicious Cycle? Kinship and Political Change   139

Conclusions: Kinship and "Normal" Politics   163

Appendix: Methods   175

Notes   185

Bibliography   223

Index   245

Preface

I began to study clan politics because of what I found in the political world: clan divisions continue to animate power relations in a wide array of contexts. This is true not only across the southern tier of the ex-USSR, which is the empirical focus of this book, but also in broad parts of the Middle East, East and North Africa, and Southeast Asia. Moreover, such kinship-based divisions are not simply residual factors of limited political import but often lie at the center of politics. In this book, I explore the relationships between clans and the paramount power in the contemporary world, the modern state.

What sparked my initial interest in these issues was the sense that dominant theories were out of sync with empirical developments across the southern tier of the former Soviet Union. Although they were criticized, modernization and neomodernization paradigms continued to inspire background thinking on identity politics, permitting no conceptual space for clan politics. In these approaches, the political significance of clans was understood to be restricted in two ways: spatially, to the remote margins of the state system where traditional and diffuse authority patterns prevailed, and temporally, to historical periods before the emergence of modern state structures.

But kinship divisions have both broader and more lasting significance for politics than we normally recognize. Of course, their significance changes across space and time; it is a variable, not a constant. What is surprising, from the perspective of our usual theoretical concerns, is how important clans continue to be. The former Soviet southern tier offers an array of cases through which to study this relatively underexamined phenomenon.

This book also tells a story about the persistence and transformation of clan politics in Kazakhstan. The exercise is largely one in induction. That is, I move from an empirical phenomenon to theory construction, although in no sense did I approach the issue with a theoretical blank slate. Tipping the balance toward induction seemed warranted, given the lack of attention paid to the issue. As a practical matter, this meant that I gathered data using intensive, rather than extensive, strategies. I felt that it was important first to capture accurately the issue through close study of a single country (Kazakhstan, in this case) rather than rushing to broad comparison. We should not avoid generalization; we should, however, ground our comparative enterprise in the specifics of time and place.

Intensive focus on a single country makes good sense for another reason. It can highlight actual causal mechanisms, where studies that cover a large number of country cases can only find correlations. Moreover, the coding strategies that undergird cross-case statistical evaluation capture certain factors better than others. Identity politics—which necessarily involves perceptual variables, discourses, and symbols that inform group behavior and self-understandings—benefits from an intensive, rather than an extensive, perspective.

This book is not a story about Kazakhstan for its own sake. Ex-Soviet Central Asia tells us much about the encounter between clan-based societies and modern state institutions. Kazakhstan, Kyrgyzstan, Tajikistan, Turkmenistan, and Uzbekistan all experienced a heavy-handed state push for modernization that included coercive attempts to root out clan relationships. Yet, clan networks remain central to political life. Among these cases, Kazakhstan stands out further; it felt the state effort most dramatically. Whereas the populations of the other parts of Central Asia and the Caucasus were geographically more remote and could more easily resist the Soviet effort, the same cannot be argued for Kazakhstan. The latter felt the brunt of Sovietization. Why clan politics persists in a most unlikely case is the central puzzle that inspires this research.

To undertake a study of clan politics is to rely on the widest array of methodological strategies available. Eclecticism is the best way to sort through biases and attempt to minimize their impact on the final product. In addition to using Western and Soviet secondary sources, I examined newspapers, magazines, scholarly journals from across the region, conducted elite interviews in several cities, led in-depth interviews, ran focus groups in three regions, engaged in ethnographic observation of events of cultural and political relevance, and examined documents of particular importance from the Central State Archives of the Republic of Kazakhstan. The appendix provides detail on these strategies.

To undertake a study of clan politics is also to tax one's sense of humor. Because this is a phenomenon that many individuals prefer to conceal rather than reveal, I cannot count the number of false leads generated by innocently offered misinformation. With good cheer, many local scholars steered me away from dangerously unproductive fates, sorting through raw data and the somewhat alien perspectives of a Western social scientist. Particular thanks go to Gulnara Dadabaeva, Igor Savin, and Serik Aidossov, each of whom modeled intellectual integrity and a manifest willingness to exchange ideas globally. They also became true friends as I spent many months away from home.

Nurbulat Masanov offered trenchant, incisive, and thoughtful analysis, as well as unparalleled access to important data. His hospitality was incredible—rivaled only by his love for sport. Meruert Abuseitova and the Institute of Oriental Studies provided an excellent institutional connection in Almaty. Bulat Zhanaev of the Central State Archives of the Republic of Kazakhstan was kind enough not only to facilitate access to documents on the 1920s and 1930s, but also to provide an insider's view on how I might best use the collection. Raushan Muserova and Gavin Helf at the International Research and Exchanges Board made Kazakhstan a home away from home for most of 1998. Bhavna Davé modeled the kind of work, and the kind of intellectual and personal integrity, that I admired. Steve Sabol, Saulesh Esenova, and Sean Roberts showed me that extended field research and sanity preservation are compatible—even complementary—processes. Saule Moldabekova at the Kazakhstan office of the American Councils provided tremendous logistical support for a return stay in 2002.

Alma Qunanbai and Uli Shamiloglu (both of the University of Wisconsin–Madison) made learning the Kazakh language a joy; without their talents, my ability to grasp the complexity of the issues would have suffered. I activated my knowledge of Kazakh by living with the Zhatqanbaev family in 1997 under a predissertation grant from the Social Science Research Council. SSRC's project, which led a ten-year existence, is a model of how funding agencies can successfully train social scientists to study the developing world. Deep thanks go to Natalia Shurygina and Vanya Shurygin, who became good friends as they began in 1989 to cultivate my interest in the ex-USSR, always with humility, humanity, and intelligence.

Countless others in Central Asia—many whose names appear in the pages that follow, either directly or pseudonymously—showed classic Kazakh hospitality not only by letting me into their lives, but also by allowing me to glimpse how they view their lives. I hope that I have been true to their voices.

Beyond Central Asia, I owe a huge debt of gratitude to a range of institutions and people who allowed me the creative space to work and cultivated the tools for doing so. In an environment that combined analytic rigor with intellectual freedom, the Political Science Department at the University of Wisconsin–Madison proved the perfect place to cultivate tools for pursuing a sometimes untraditional research agenda. Mark Beissinger epitomized the patient mentor, always finding the time to listen and take seriously his students' intellectual journeys. I have internalized more of his outlook than he would be comfortable to admit. Crawford Young and Michael Schatzberg forced me to be self-conscious about the comparative enterprise, always suggesting that students of Central Asian politics are wise to consider the paths that African states and societies have traveled. Far from Wisconsin, Jorge Domínguez provided support, professional socialization, and analytic insight through all stages of the project.

On the institutional end, the International Research and Exchanges Board generously funded my field research in 1998 and a return trip in 2002. The Social Science Research Council provided funding through its International Predissertation Research Program in 1997–98 and its Eurasia Program in 1999–2000. I am grateful to have spent a year as a postdoctoral fellow at the Davis Center for Russian Studies at Harvard University, working on this project. In Cambridge, the intellectual enthusiasm of Lucan Way was addictive. I am also thankful for a semester spent at the Kellogg Institute for International Affairs at the University of Notre Dame and to Scott Mainwaring and his staff for providing an unrivaled work environment.

I finished writing the book while at Southern Illinois University at Carbondale. Special thanks to Uday Desai for creating the conditions in which I could complete the project. Thanks to Anna Gregg for her research assistance.

Michael Duckworth at the University of Washington Press expressed an interest in this project and ushered it through the review process. Thanks to him, three anonymous reviewers, Marilyn Trueblood, and Julie Van Pelt for making it a better book. They are absolved, of course, of any responsibility for remaining shortcomings.

My biggest thanks are reserved for my wife, Lara Dominguez, whose support has made the project possible and the experience of creating it a meaningful one. Grateful that she agrees that neither matrilineal nor patrilineal descent is adequate, I dedicate this book to her.

A NOTE ON TRANSLITERATION

Transliterations from the Russian are based on the Library of Congress standard. Transliterations from Kazakh are based on the standard developed by the Central Eurasian Studies Society (http://cess.fas .harvard.edu/cesr/CESR_trans_cyr.html), although diacritical marks have been removed to make the English versions less awkward. Many of the places and people referred to in the text have both Russian-language names and similar, but not identical, Kazakh-language equivalents. I have tried to be sensitive to context in identifying the language that is most appropriate. For example, if an interviewee preferred to speak Kazakh, I transliterate from Kazakh when referencing her name. If she preferred to speak Russian, I transliterate from Russian.

Introduction:
Modern Clan Politics

> The role of kinship ties and kinship rivalries is not merely a curious anachronism. It has important consequences for the political system as a whole. —*Carl H. Landé*

One way to spot a foreigner visiting ex-Soviet Central Asia is to look at his shoes. Like that of his local counterpart, his footwear may be expensive or cheap, polished or scuffed, fashionable or ordinary. Given worldwide commerce, moreover, it may have been produced anywhere across the globe. What distinguishes his shoes is that he ties his laces tightly, while his counterpart ties them loosely or opts for laceless varieties.[1]

How Central Asians tie their shoes is a clue about the significance of kin ties. Since so much of a Central Asian day is spent visiting relatives and friends, and since shoes are doffed at the entrance to each home, it is a matter of some significance to learn to wear one's shoes in the proper, local way. The alternative—continually to lag behind—eventually becomes tiresome.

Patterns of political life often reveal themselves in the mundane, implicit, and unspoken. They are rooted in everything ordinary—in that which requires no remark. In Central Asia, kinship ties are like the loosely laced shoes that give them away; they are a silent reality that pervades everyday life. What role they play for political and social actors and why they play a political role—when dominant approaches expect them not to—is the subject of this book.

We seldom expect kinship-based divisions to occupy a prominent place in modern political life. In the era of the nation-state, we expect

Figure 1.1. Map of Kazakhstan and Central Asia
Source: Central Intelligence Agency, *The World Factbook,*
http://www.odci.gov/cia/publications/factbook/geos/kz.html.

that national-level allegiances and statewide bureaucratic structures
supersede local attachments and marginalize local institutions. How
can these attachments stand up to the pressures of nation and state
building, let alone to the more recent transformative powers of globalization? The general assumption is that they do not. From this perspective, this chapter's title—"Modern Clan Politics"—seems a
contradiction in terms. We expect that the more complete the coercive apparatus of the state, the less likely clan politics would survive
into modernity.

One of the most coercive regimes ever witnessed, however, was
unable to eliminate clan divisions and preclude their role in political
life. Since the Soviet collapse in 1991, we have caught glimpses of clan
relationships in politics. In Chechnya, subethnic *teips* became
ensnared in Moscow's decision to launch a bloody invasion in 1994;
some groups were more closely allied with Russia and others more
staunch supporters of independence.[2] In Uzbekistan, attachments to
kin and locale that permeated everyday life even during the Soviet
period continued to dominate a predominantly rural society.[3] In Kyr-

gyzstan, a north–south divide that had its roots in segmentary divisions helped to define the bases for political appointments.[4] Subethnic clans were likewise the major actors in Tajikistan, which descended into a protracted civil conflict that defied easy resolution.[5]

On a superficial level, the persistence of clan politics seemed to represent one of many failures of the Soviet state; it appeared that Moscow, in spite of its proclamations to the contrary, had simply failed to transform the building blocks of identity along a vast southern periphery. Indeed, many of the newly independent state apparatuses that inherited Soviet structures were weak enough that it was difficult to imagine that the Soviet experiment represented anything less than a failure to penetrate its far-flung populations.[6]

But this was only a surface appearance. Today's challenges of state weakness should not color our understandings of Soviet-era processes. Far from failing to transform the southern periphery, the Soviet state effected radical social and cultural change. The question then becomes: in what ways, and with what consequences, were the Soviets able to transform the populations that inhabited these regions? To ask such a question is to recognize the unusual scope and capacity of Soviet power, although it does not mean accepting the terms of debate about whether the Soviet Union was "totalitarian" or not.[7]

How do we square the transformative power of the Soviet state, on the one hand, with the outcomes we witness across the former USSR, on the other? Why did the profound social changes set in motion by an unusually powerful state result in politically salient subethnic divisions? This general question is germane to the entire region; it is all the more relevant for Kazakhstan. On the one hand, Kazakhstan underwent radical socioeconomic and cultural changes in the Soviet period. The Soviet state undermined the nomadic economy of extensive pastoralism, replacing it with large-scale, mechanized agriculture, extractive industries, and manufacturing. By the end of the Soviet era, the republic was predominantly urban, industrialized, and held up as a model of socialist development. Near-universal literacy, broad-based education, and an extensive communications and transportation infrastructure added further impetus to change traditional social structures and identities. Observers debate whether or not these transformations were necessary, coercive, beneficial, or detrimental to the population of Kazakhstan; whatever else they were, they were profound.

On the other hand, a vibrant politics based on subethnic clans that had predated Soviet rule (what Kazakhs call *zhuz* and *ru*[8]) emerged in post-Soviet Kazakhstan. The first president of the independent state hinted at the breadth of the problem, decrying the attempts of local elites to establish "tribal" ideology and clan-related "protectionism."[9] One scholar wrote in a semiofficial publication:

> All the pressure groups in the power structures of Kazakhstan are exposed to the spirit of tribalism and clanness, which always hovered in the political life of the republic on a negative level [*sic*], but which had a second birth with the period of sovereignty and the crisis that enveloped the economy, education, and culture, in a country where rural residents comprise 60 percent of the population with [their] agrarian-patriarchal mentality, where the influx of marginals with their unchanging [*stereotipnoe*] consciousness acquired threatening proportions.[10]

In the 1990s, the subethnic pedigree of political actors in Kazakhstan became a critical factor in the allocation of political resources (especially posts in the state bureaucracy) and economic resources (especially access to revenues from extractive industries). Among nation- and state-builders, the role of subethnic divisions became the subject of a hot political debate.

In light of seventy years of the Soviet state-building project, these developments seemed surprising. In addition to providing the engine for modernization, the Soviet state had dedicated itself to the eradication of these divisions from political and social life; Moscow fully expected that progressive modernization and ethnicization would bring with it the marginalization of these identities from politics. Why did politicized expressions of subethnic identity persist in Kazakhstan?

I begin by posing two questions. First, why do subethnic clan divisions persist, thereby animating political competition, in a context where they were targeted for elimination? Second, what kind of political competition do they generate, as a result? That is, what is distinctive about clan politics that distinguishes it from identity politics based on other divisions such as ethnic, racial, religious, gender, or class differences? These issues—the persistence of identity categories and the particular forms that identity-based competition assumes—are crucial to our ongoing efforts to sort out the ways in which group solidarities and power relations intersect.

OBJECTIVES

The story of clan politics in Kazakhstan is important because it helps us to pursue several objectives. First, it serves as an analytic point of departure from which to conceptualize the distinctiveness of clan politics. Much discussion of "identity politics" implies, even if it does not supply evidence to support the claim, that a fundamental logic underlies all forms of group-based competition. For this reason, Horowitz subsumes religious, ethnic, and racial cleavages under the single taxonomic canopy of "ethnicity."[11] And yet, we know that religious divisions inspire a politics rooted in supernatural justifications for behavior; we know that gender politics interrogates the public-private dichotomy; we know that racial politics begin with scientistic ideologies about phenotypical differences. By charting out a distinctive clan politics, this book helps us to unravel the variety of competition that we facilely label "identity politics."

If in the West, clan politics is the subject of an academic discussion, for many populations across Central Asia, the Caucasus, the Middle East, Africa, and Southeast Asia, clan politics propels real-world challenges to governance, economic performance, and, in some cases, stability. In Weber's perspective (to be taken up more directly in the next chapter), kinship groups inspire irrationality in the legal system and fuel patrimonialism in governance.[12] A second objective is therefore closely related to the first: to understand the distinctive dynamic of clan politics is to come closer to understanding the challenges that it poses.

A third objective is to use the Kazakhstan case to suggest a way to bridge the gap between primordialism and constructivism. These two scholarly perspectives on identity politics begin with opposite premises about change and continuity in collective identities. Primordialists take group identities as a given that is scarcely changeable. Constructivists contend that groupness is a sociological artifact—a human creation that must be problematized and historicized. The sometimes shrill tenor of the debate aside, most scholars recognize that group solidarities change and evolve over time (per the constructivists), but they do so within identifiable limits (per the primordialists). This book suggests that we need not choose between radical transformation and essential stasis; in fact, to choose sides obscures important aspects of the problem.

A final objective is classically empiricist: to study a geographic region about which we know strikingly little. The Central Asian cases raise theoretical issues directly, but I consider them not as the servant of theory. Central Asia is again tied to the outside world, after a long hiatus that began when the steamship suddenly marginalized overland trade routes. Its economic links, security concerns, and state-building prospects are intertwined with our own and recommend that we learn more. I focus on identity-related issues, emphasizing subethnic clan ties and paying considerable attention to their interrelationships with ethnic divisions. This is a topic of critical importance not only for addressing theory, but also for discovering the reality that people face as a matter of daily life.

APPROACH

Scholars of identity politics assume either that groups are given and change little over time (primordialists) or that groups are fluid and change much (constructivists). Constructivism has been ascendant of late, since it posits that identity is open to various social, economic, and political influences that can be closely examined. Constructivism falls short, however, in explaining the *persistence* of some identity categories. In a world of fluidity and change that constructivism emphasizes, persistence becomes a puzzle. The theoretical leverage offered by constructivist approaches needs to be improved to account equally for stasis and persistence as for fluidity and change.

The approach taken here offers constructivism a way to account for both change and persistence. Borrowing a page from historical institutionalism, I assume that if an identity persists over time, we should be able to locate a mechanism that propels this persistence.[13] Just as historical institutionalists contend that change and stasis in institutions can be traced to mechanisms that underlie the institutions themselves, the same can be argued for collective identities. Groupness does not survive merely by definition; rather, it survives (if and when it does) because of identifiable *mechanisms of identity reproduction*. Consequently, if such mechanisms are disrupted or changed, we can expect concurrent changes in the shape, meaning, and salience of associated group identities.

This focus on the mechanisms of identity reproduction fits not just with the constructivist's concern with historicizing and problematizing group identities. It also helps those who would view groupness as an independent variable with causal significance. By learning the extent and type of social transformations that occur to identity relationships, we better specify the nature of the identity to which we seek to attribute causal weight. That is, by pinpointing the mechanisms that underlie group affiliations, we better identify changes to the character of those affiliations and, therefore, what impact they have on politics.

The approach used here also takes emic (i.e., insider) perspectives seriously. This goes against the trend in many studies of identity politics. Many analysts understand groups as unproblematic and therefore take their causal significance to be straightforward. As a result, while they may agree with constructivists about the changing nature of identities, they find analytic reasons to retain primordialism's assumptions. Identities certainly are constructed, the argument goes, but by viewing them rather as given, we identify their impact.[14] This step is to be applauded for its opportunism. Social scientists make the assumptions that they do because doing so helps to solve concrete research problems. These analysts are primordialists by convenience rather than by conviction.

On the other hand, we lose something critical when we ignore emic perspectives. It comes to matter little what meanings are attributed to group solidarities. Being a Palestinian in 1949 is assumed to have the same social and political implications as being a Palestinian in 2004, notwithstanding all that we know about a turbulent political history that intervened. Being Palestinian entails different meanings in different contexts, so we can be sure that it will help to generate a different political dynamic in each time and place. Of course, insiders have no monopoly on truth, but lurking behind consistency in nomenclature may be profound changes that insider perspectives can begin to unravel.

THE ARGUMENT OUTLINED

When social systems collide—as they did when Russian imperial expansion met Central Asian populations in the nineteenth century—the new order necessarily changes preexisting patterns of local authority and customary identity. But traditional relationships do not disappear, nor do traditional identities and indigenous categories evaporate. As the imposed order penetrates more deeply into the everyday life of the population, it circumscribes the legitimacy of traditional identities and categories, redefining their role in contemporary social and political life and changing their meaning. "Institutional syncretism" is the result, even if that is not the outcome that elites would prefer.[15]

The architects of an imposed order are often self-conscious about their transformative efforts. That is, they are not content to let a new hybrid architecture emerge naturally from circumstances. Just as subjects view the imposed order as illegitimate, these agents view local populations as manifesting behaviors, identities, and institutions that are themselves illegitimate. Transforming society to new dictates is viewed as a political imperative. The Soviet state stands out for the scope and ambition of its transformative campaigns, and the willingness to combine raw coercion with pervasive propaganda in the effort. Branding traditional practices as illegitimate, Moscow expected that the vestiges of the traditional order would lose their social and political import. The effort was unusual in its extent, but it was not unique.[16]

But, with regard to clan-based systems, these campaigns to undermine traditional practices have unintended consequences. Whether waged in clearly coercive ways as during the Soviet period or pursued more subtly as in the post-Soviet context, they activate the most important inherent quality of clan divisions: their concealability. Kinship divisions are not rooted in visible markers that establish identity and difference, but rather in an exchange of genealogical information that can occur privately. Thus, the attempt to remove clan from legitimate public space gives the subject population reasons to hide its traditional practices and affiliations. By driving these behaviors and identities underground, the state infuses clan divisions with explosive potential. If, as James Scott suggests, state-led campaigns of this sort seek to make traditional practices more "scrutable" in order to control them better,[17] the result in this case is a tragedy for the state: clan divisions become less visible and therefore less prone to state control.

The irony of unintended consequences goes further. Moscow's drive to bring state control to the exchange of goods (social, economic, or political goods) willy-nilly provided a mechanism for clan divisions to reproduce themselves. Underground networks allowed access to scarce goods in the all-pervasive "gray market" that developed under Soviet rule. Kin-based networks, concealable and less likely to be detected by agents of state surveillance, provided such access across much of the Soviet southern tier.

Clan identity thus became an asset when manifested in private but a liability when expressed in public. This is the enduring legacy of state socialism and the imprint it left upon clan politics that is evident in post-Soviet Kazakhstan. The mechanism that unintentionally fueled clan identities into the 1990s also gave shape to the particular kinds of clan-based politics that we witness. First, we see networks that occupy illicit social niches vying for control over scarce resources. Second, we see a broad discursive battle that plays on the ongoing public stigma attached to clan divisions.

From the perspective of former Soviet Central Asia, the usual image that modern statehood and clan identities are mutually exclusive must be considered incomplete. State-led coercion and modernization do not necessarily dissolve clan divisions; in fact, such processes may lend them import. Moreover, the particular ways in which these processes play themselves out leave a profound imprint on the shape of the ongoing identity dynamic. As ideal types, states and clans may operate by deeply divergent logics. When they collide in real-world contexts, such different logics produce syncretic outcomes that become the hybrid stuff of contemporary social and political life.

This has important implications for cases beyond the former USSR where kinship and power continue to intersect. If state-led campaigns to root out clan divisions may in fact enhance their political role, then finding ways to reconcile the diverse logics of states and clans in unified institutional settings becomes the task of the day. Locating the means by which subethnic kin-based identities can be accommodated through institutional "crafting" may prove to be a more effective means of preserving stability, enhancing state performance, and ensuring representative government than trying to crush clans and undercut tradition. If the goal is to create a Weberian state in which "loyalty is devoted to impersonal and functional purposes," rather than to kin ties, the means to achieving this goal is—in a seeming paradox—to relegitimate clans as an acceptable part of political and social life.[18]

STRUCTURE OF THE BOOK

To develop this argument, I divide the book into two parts. In the first, I treat clan persistence as something that requires explanation.

I document how state socialism was implicated in the production of clan divisions as networks. The state both transformed clan divisions (by limiting their salience to illicit and private niches) and reproduced them (by providing impetus for their private expression). In the second part, I treat clan relationships as a factor contributing to political outcomes. I examine how clans (both as networks and as contests over identity categories) affect state-building efforts. This part treats the persistence of clan divisions as having political significance of its own.

Chapter 1 offers a framework for considering kinship divisions in an array of contexts. It shows that while kinship divisions often remain below the researcher's field of vision (since they are less observable than other identity categories to which states give positive sanction), they may be more politically important than more visible divisions. It then elaborates why Central Asia provides a window into the study of clan politics. In Central Asia, state structures were a Soviet creation; the region is an unusual opportunity to see how the imposition of statehood reshapes and constructs clan identity politics. Kazakhstan sharpens the question further, since it experienced social, demographic, and economic transformations that were even more dramatic than those its neighbors experienced. Kazakhstan is a chance to view how state actions affected—and unintentionally fueled—kinship-based political competition.

Chapters 2 through 4 document the encounter between the diffuse authority patterns of a nomadic population and state structures. They cover the onset, consolidation, maturation, and legacies of Soviet rule. I first establish a conceptual and empirical baseline in the pre-Soviet period as a way to identify transformations. I show that kinship-based divisions were the glue of social and political relations before the onset of Soviet power. A harsh steppe environment placed critical limits on the scope of capital accumulation, thereby minimizing social stratification and privileging horizontal kin-based ties. The nomadic pastoral economy was the mechanism that reproduced the kinship system.

Soviet power transformed the identity dynamic, but not in the ways intended. Building on secondary sources in Russian and Kazakh, I examined documents from the Central State Archives of the Republic of Kazakhstan to learn why early Soviet efforts to eradicate clan divisions did not succeed. Until Stalin dealt a powerful blow to the economy of nomadic pastoralism in the early 1930s, the clan remained the basic functional unit of society.

This section argues that Stalin eliminated the traditional basis for clan organization, but he replaced it with a novel mechanism: the shortage economy. Clan-related behaviors were broadly criminalized and removed from the public sphere, but kin links nonetheless flourished privately in the shortage economy. Networks of access to goods proliferated along the former Soviet southern tier. The state-led effort unintentionally tapped a critical, inherent quality of subethnic clan divisions: their concealability. Clan networks were valuable because they were elusive: they could be hidden from the agents of Soviet surveillance.

As Soviet power receded in the 1990s, continuities with the Soviet era remained strong. Chapter 4 covers these legacies, highlighting first how the structure of the political economy had changed little for ordinary people. Access to hard-to-get goods (consumer wares, capital, and political power) remained restricted, as a hierarchically built polity and economy created privileged nodes of access. In such a context, clan identity was a resource. A powerful second legacy lay in the public discourse on identity groups. I show that a modernist discourse continued to stigmatize clan relationships and to drive them from legitimate public space into private niches.

In chapters 5 and 6, I consider the imprint that Soviet rule (and its residue in the post-Soviet period) had on the social meanings and practical utility of clan relationships. First, as a result of the Soviet political economy and its notable legacies in the post-Soviet era, clan became and remains important as the basis for access networks. Using data on political appointments and clan background, chapter 5 discerns the lines of competition at the national, regional, and local levels among clan-based networks. In particular, it critically evaluates the widespread assertion (made by journalists both in Central Asia and abroad) that President Nursultan Nazarbaev's clan-based network dominated political and economic life in the republic. It finds empirical support for this assertion, but within limits.

Second, if the jockeying among clan-based networks might be called "clan conflict," chapter 6 covers the discursive battles surrounding clan politics, which might be understood as clan "meta-conflict." Because kin-based divisions continue to be removed from public space, political and social actors often possess quite sketchy knowledge of the background of other actors. But this sketchiness of knowledge is an opportunity for political entrepreneurs to speculate grandly and use the language of clans to discredit their political opponents. Thus, the modernist discourse that stigmatizes clan divisions as "regressive" or "primitive" means that political actors must find ways to deny acting in a "clannish" fashion.

Is Central Asia stuck in a closed cycle where the state constructs clans as inimical, which in turn drive clan networks further underground, potentially destabilizing the state? Chapter 7 considers this question, focusing specifically on the impact that changes in economic and political institutions in the 1990s had on social networks, and the salience of kin-based networks and other types of ties. Based on focus-group research and ethnographic data, it finds that the state's role remains prominent, and an array of other factors.

In the book's conclusion, I ask whether or not clan divisions can be reconstructed as a "normal" part of political life. Are kinship ties inherently incompatible with modern politics? Without minimizing the difficulty, I argue that they are not. Since much of the challenge that clans pose for states is the product of state policies themselves, there is considerable room for state elites self-consciously to "craft" solutions to the problems facing kinship-rich societies.

PART ONE

The Reproduction of Clans

1

Kinship and Modernity

[K]inship in these settings is not merely a logical apparatus consisting of complicated rules for terminology and marriage; it is
instead a way of apprehending and ordering the world, replete
with implications for the evolution and organization of political
life. —*Charles Lindholm*

WHAT IS THE PLACE OF SUBETHNIC IDENTITIES IN MODERN
politics? How do lower-aggregate affiliations—to tribe, clan, village,
or locale—affect the mechanisms by which the contemporary state
exercises power?[1] How does this exercise of power in turn shape expressions of these local identities? We rarely ask such questions, but perhaps we should. Subethnic politics occurs broadly across space and
time, and it has serious consequences in a variety of contexts. I cover
some of these consequences in greater detail below; for now, the disintegration of the Somali state into kin-based units in 1990 is reminder
enough of the importance of subethnic ties.

In this chapter, I first illustrate how the problem of kinship and
power lies at the interstices of academic disciplines and therefore
largely goes unaddressed. I then elaborate the significance of the problem. Finally, I develop the book's argument (summarized in the introduction), situating it vis-à-vis alternative approaches and laying the
groundwork for the empirical chapters that follow.

THEORIZING AT THE DISCIPLINARY MARGINS

Clan politics lies at the interstices of disciplines, occupying a conceptual blind spot. Leaving lower-aggregate group identities for anthropologists to study, political scientists perhaps assume that nothing so microlevel could have an important effect on political life. I question this assumption. If it results from a division of labor forged for professional convenience, it is one that has ontological consequences. By leaving explicit conceptualization of these identities to other disciplines, political science may misread their literatures and misunderstand the role these group solidarities play in the contemporary world.

The picture of identity politics that prevails among political scientists is this: the forces of modernization (urbanization, industrialization, mass literacy, and education) dissolve group boundaries. Studies of nationalism in particular imply that subnational divisions (ethnic groups or kinship-based clans) progressively fade from social and political importance. When outcomes deviate from this core expectation — that is, when subnational identities remain important — this is usually explained to be a result of incomplete homogenizing pressures. The logic is that institutions or processes that generally dissolve lower-aggregate divisions may fail to do so in particular instances, for idiosyncratic reasons.[2] While the implied teleology of progressive homogenization of populations has come under fire,[3] the assumption that identity divisions generally fade away has received new life with discussions of the cultural homogenization expected to accompany globalization.

Rooted in once fashionable theories of modernization, this perspective might be called "identity modernization." The core idea is that powerfully transformative pressures are brought to bear on societies that fundamentally alter social structures and the bases for group affiliations. Because the moral logic at play is viewed as essentially different for the state and for subethnic attachments, the latter succumbs to the former. Alternatively, subethnic divisions are seen to reside beyond the reach of the state apparatus — in what Moroccan authorities called the "zone of dissidence," over which the state has little control, as distinct from a "zone of control," in which the state was able to tax and conscript.[4] In this line of thinking, either these affiliations gradually disappear as state apparatuses consolidate, or they remain outside the purview of the state.

From the perspective of identity modernization, the persistence of subethnic divisions produces a theoretical tension. Gellner sets out the puzzle in the strongest terms, suggesting that the state functionally requires the elimination of lower-aggregate cultural and political attachments. He argues that with the creation of the modern state,

> [c]ulture is no longer merely the adornment, confirmation and legit-imation of a social order which was also sustained by harsher and coer-cive constraints; culture is now the necessary shared medium, the life-blood or perhaps rather the minimal shared atmosphere, within which alone the members of the society can breathe and survive and produce. For a given society, it must be one in which they can *all* breathe and speak and produce; so it must be the *same* culture. More-over, it must now be a great or high (literate, training-sustained) cul-ture, and it can longer be a diversified, locality-tied, illiterate little culture or tradition.[5]

For the Gellnerian perspective, where the modern nation-state and Weberian rationality eventually triumph, lower-level affiliations are eclipsed as obsolescent. In his work on the Middle East, Gellner under-stands tribes as separate from the state apparatus; evidence of their existence is considered tantamount to state ineffectiveness. Histori-cal attempts to create mercenary (*mamluk*) armies in the Middle East, he explains, met with failure due to the "temptations of honor, kin-ship, and wealth."[6] Education plays a central role in homogenizing previously differentiated cultures, leaving little room for alternatives: "Time was when education was a cottage industry, when men could be made by a village or clan. That time has now gone, and gone for-ever. . . . Exo-socialization, the production and reproduction of men outside the local intimate unit . . . is unavoidable. That is what nation-alism is about, and why we live in an age of nationalism."[7]

Other central figures in modernization theory likewise leave lit-tle space for subnational and subethnic identity politics. Deutsch, for example, argues that a "nationality" emerges as a functional requirement of the modern state: since statehood required social inte-gration and assimilation to be effective, communication became increasingly effective and dense among its networked individuals.[8] This may be a useful heuristic, but it downplays the possibility that communicative networks can be concentrated in or be largely coter-minous with subgroups, and thus may not play the integrative func-tion that he envisions.

We know that nations are, in Anderson's felicitous phrase, "imagined communities" and that these communities are no less powerful for being the product of the imaginative act. But the question remains: why have the factors that Anderson isolates — print-capitalism, the census, the museum, and the map — not had the same transformative value in later nationalist movements that they appear to have had in European cases? Why do communities continue to be "imagined" on levels other than the national one, and why does the national one not supplant lower-level affiliations? In short, there is good reason to examine what Anderson relegates to parentheses: "In fact, all communities larger than primordial villages of face-to-face contact (*and perhaps even these*) are imagined."9

Modernization theory is not in intellectual fashion the way it once was, but its assumptions linger.10 They find an unusual source of ongoing support: the structural-functional paradigm of early cultural anthropology. The tendency within this paradigm was to treat locale and tribe as closed systems, that is, as constellations of institutions and practices that perpetuated themselves to meet certain "needs" — usually understood as rooted in environmental conditions. This approach undertheorized links to forces and actors external to the locale and its environment.11 When such links were considered, they were often depicted as deviations from a "normal," a mode of existence centrally related to an observed, or imagined, "ethnographic present."12 For example, a focus on the effects of colonial rule encouraged scholars to locate a precolonial social and cultural baseline, from which all deviations emerged as a result of influences defined a priori as alien.

By underestimating the vibrancy of external links, these approaches overestimated the transformative properties of state-led modernization projects. The more the realm of the "traditional" appeared to be discrete and closed, the greater the contrast with the "modern" appeared. The result was a stark traditional-modern dichotomy that presented the possible trajectories for local groups as dichotomous: either they would accept, succumb, or assimilate to the overwhelming pressures of state-driven modernization, or they would resist the same, to some uncertain fate. Either such identities were smothered by the state, or they remained outside its reach. The possibility of syncretic outcomes was downplayed.

It is becoming increasingly clear — *contra* the assumptions of modernization perspectives — that low-aggregate identities such as clans remain very much a part of the modern political condition. These are affiliations that are neither slated for social oblivion nor doomed to political insignificance. Moreover, we should not understand the ongoing political expression of subethnicity in the modern period as evidence of failed or incomplete modernization. This is one theoretical possibility, but the Kazakhstan case points to an alternative: that the specific mechanisms of modernization may *themselves* preserve and even strengthen—rather than render obsolescent—these lower-aggregate attachments. This possibility becomes apparent if we retain a broad definition of modernization as "the growth and diffusion of a set of institutions rooted in the transformation of the economy by means of technology."[13]

One final perspective on the problem should be addressed. If there is a tension between usual approaches to identity and the ongoing significance of clan politics, perhaps this results innocently from a difference of focus. Maybe students of nationalism simply train their lenses on the coincidence (or lack thereof) of cultural and political boundaries, while students of clan relations examine lower-aggregate divisions and the dynamic they produce. But a difference of focus is only a part of the story. Clan politics is typically a quieter, and less visible, politics than the noisy contention of nationalist groups.[14] Walker Connor once commented, "There is an understandable propensity . . . to perceive the struggle in terms of its more readily discernable features."[15] We should remember that the most visible divisions and the most politically important ones might not be one and the same.

THE PROBLEM

Subethnic clan politics deserves attention because it poses critical challenges to nation-building efforts, state-building programs, and battles over the nature of legitimate authority. In sometimes vivid form, its significance plays itself out across the Middle East, East and North Africa, Southeast Asia, and the former USSR. Particularly evident with decolonization, the questions of how to build viable state institutions and how to secure popular allegiance to new administrative apparatuses preoccupy political actors. These challenges lie at the center of politics through much of the world.

Consider nation-building processes, in which elites seek to foster allegiance to a higher-aggregate community (i.e., a community that goes beyond face-to-face interaction). In their efforts, elites typically confront culturally plural societies whose loyalties are directed not toward the state and its agents, but rather toward the locale and local authorities. In such circumstances, local populations adhere to local customs, participate in and support local (and often informal) institutions, and behave with purposes that are typically local in scope. Such populations invoke kinship and kinlike affiliations that are built on profound and often exclusive group solidarities based on trust;[16] they hold all extralocal symbols, constructs, or authorities not related by blood to be inherently suspect.

If populations feel bound to the ties of place or of tight-knit locale, reconciliation between local and national allegiances becomes difficult. This is especially true if a local group views "nation-building" efforts as merely the smoke screen behind which cliques from other local groups seek to impose an alien, illegitimate, or unrepresentative order. The contests are seldom zero-sum; the successful construction of national identity does not require a concomitant destruction of local attachments. Nonetheless, reconciliation remains a formidable challenge.

Similar challenges present themselves with state-building efforts. How can territory-wide institutions perform well if local practices and kin-based behaviors represent an alternative institutional order to that which the state seeks to create? Clans and other "clublike affiliations" have a profound effect because they provide advantages to members.[17] Clan organizations generate clear rules by which members interact, thus lowering transaction costs for the in-group. Nonmembers, who may not know the "rules of the game," confront higher transaction costs for their ignorance. What is a boon to individual members is a burden to the larger social unit. Thus, as a whole, society experiences a proliferation of nonproductive activities, such as rent seeking. Even in some advanced industrial contexts, the performance of formal, state-introduced institutions suffers in those areas where kinship networks remain vibrant.[18]

In this sense, there is a trade-off between what the ideal-type state prizes (public goods–provision, anonymous transactions, technical expertise, formal equality) and what subethnic groups seek to preserve (connections to kin or locale). The Weberian legal-rational state that elites claim to want to create excels at providing public goods; lower-aggregate networks provide goods to more limited populations. This may also complicate attempts to create markets and democratic institutions. Profound interpersonal trust, on the one hand, and anonymous transactions, on the other, are competing principles in the functioning of markets.[19] Likewise, if political parties have a subethnic basis, this represents an alternative to a system of mass, interest-based parties.

In the extreme, if efforts at nation- and state-building fail, subethnic divisions can become part and parcel of violent conflict and the dialectic of state collapse. Thankfully, such an outcome is a rarity, but when it does occur, kin ties may be implicated. Although not *the cause* of state breakdown, strongly drawn blood relationships can make conflict more intractable once it has begun. Descent ideologies are easily mobilized by political actors with narrow goals and agendas, as blood ties are widely understood as immutable;[20] calls to arms based on kinship meet with profound effect. Moreover, where kin lines are well defined, the memory of acts committed by ancestors quickly becomes a personal matter. Tragically, while many of those societies that traditionally had strongly drawn kin divisions also enjoyed informal institutions that successfully mediated conflicts, in the modern context these institutions may have been weakened or eliminated.[21] State breakdown in places like Somalia, as well as Lebanon, therefore, has protracted and especially deleterious consequences.[22]

The problem of clans and states usually falls short of state collapse. In some cases, subethnic ties appear to play a positive role. Laitin, for example, has demonstrated that attachment to ancestral town crosscuts religious divisions within Nigeria, thus tempering religious tensions. In a similar vein, Collins has shown that clan divisions play a stabilizing role in a Kyrgyzstan and Uzbekistan, where conflict along ethnic lines might otherwise have been expected. These lines of research are encouraging; clearly, zero-sum thinking on the problem of clans and states obscures the possibilities for their reconciliation.[23]

Far more often, however, subethnic divisions leave their mark. At minimum, they help to define the modus operandi of the state's exercise of power. For example, ruling parties may follow the outlines of kinship divisions, as has the Baath Party in Iraq.[24] Outside of the formal institutional architecture of the state, informal politics often turn on these divisions. In Morocco, subethnic networks help to distribute political and social goods, generating something close to a stable equilibrium by which the state conducts its affairs.[25]

All of these challenges to nationhood and statehood erupt from the collision of alternative conceptions of legitimacy. Rather than accommodate those local institutions, identities, and modes of behavior that enjoy broad societal resonance, state elites typically view them as threatening. The logic is that subethnicity is built on an edifice that is by its nature *local* and not amenable to appropriation by *national-state* structures. State elites thus turn the problem of legitimizing their own authority into a problem of delegitimizing long-standing, society-wide practices. Thus, in Somalia, Siad Barre organized state-led campaigns against "tribal" identity and the accouterments of tribal culture.[26] Much rarer are those cases, such as Jordan, in which state elites seek to absorb and appropriate similar subethnic identities and ideologies to legitimize their rule.[27]

Weber's *problématique* captures much of the significance of clans. Following Weber, particularistic (rather than national) identities, institutions, and sources of legitimacy create a traditional dynamic that foils attempts to create an effective, modern bureaucracy. He considered a state bureaucracy successful to the extent that individual bureaucrats did not privatize the physical assets of administration or the services it provided.[28] Properly, a bureaucrat would not even claim ownership over his or her own labor.[29] The rules that governed bureaucracies were to be hierarchical, applied impersonally, and thereby capable of creating a "goal-rational" apparatus (i.e., one that was effective in pursuing a particular end); at least in theory, the provision of public goods could be that particular goal.[30] By contrast, premodern societies were dominated by individuals with nonrational orientations (traditional, charismatic, or affective, in Weber's language)—orientations that undermined attempts to create such an apparatus.

While most recognize, as Weber did, that bureaucracy is no panacea, but instead produces a potential "iron cage" that undermines human freedom, the danger for post-Soviet states was not that they possessed too much ideal-typical bureaucracy but rather too little. As the sanguine expectations of early-1990s scholars of democratic and market "transitions" came to seem more blithely hopeful than realistic, both observers of the ex-USSR and practitioners working in the region shifted their perspective. By the first years of the twenty-first century, they seized Weberian language about the need for international actors to foster the "rule of law" in the region—efforts that achieved few results for a variety of reasons.[31]

From the Weberian perspective, cultural ties are generally expected to thwart the efforts of would-be state builders. Affective bonds generate "social closure" that undermines the drive to create efficient practice based on specialized labor and impersonal relationships. Cultural groups foster particularistic identities that work to generate *private* goods. If this is true of any cultural connection, clans are ties of even more limited scope, typically incorporating fewer individuals than do their higher-aggregate counterparts (such as ethnic groups). For a Weberian, clans epitomize the subversiveness of traditional society in the face of attempts to construct modern institutions. If ethnicity and Weberian states are in tension, clans and states generate even greater contradictions.

But if Weber expertly outlines the challenges that kinship-rich societies present, he does so without providing guidance for a solution. Instead, he proposes an evolutionary "march of bureaucracy," implying that there is nothing distinctive about such societies; they are merely understood to be "earlier" in their historical development.[32] Although a strong critic of the teleology inherent in Karl Marx's work, Weber nonetheless posits a teleology of his own in suggesting that kinship divisions would eventually lose their utility. This is not a theoretical impossibility, but the perspective does require our asking why such an outcome has not yet materialized.

PRIMORDIALISM: A FIRST CUT

If modernization-based approaches have little to say about subethnic clan politics, what analytic leverage does the rest of the identity politics literature offer for a study of subethnic politics? I first examine how well primordialism addresses the issue.[33]

To students of identity politics, the suggestion that primordialism offers analytic leverage arouses immediate suspicion. It has become a mantra in the literature to confirm that group identities are constructed, not biologically or culturally primordial. We have learned that the collectivities involved in political competition are not given and unchanging, but rather are influenced by a potent array of political and social forces.[34] Among its other benefits, this theoretical shift keeps in check the ever-present analytical temptation to reify difference and create static, categorical cultural amalgams with the appearance of mutual exclusivity.[35] Constructivist approaches highlight how the contours and content of groupness change over time—an issue that otherwise remains in shadow.

But can constructivism explain continuity as well as change? Even if the nature of identities is continually contested, and even if their dynamic is subject to secular pressures and sudden shocks, groups are nonetheless not infinitely changeable. We need an approach that can provide insight into the staying power that identity categories, once created, potentially enjoy.

In spite of a torrent of criticism, primordialism provides a first-cut explanation. Unlike national identities, clans seem not to require common abstractions to link the members of a national group; rather, they appear based in iterated, day-to-day social interaction based in deep-seated feelings of trust and loyalty.[36] Accordingly, the primordialist's explanation might be very simple: profound emotional attachment prevents the members of a group from challenging the assumption of groupness. Clan cleavages persist because they are the emotional building blocks of identity. As Collins suggests, trust lies at the heart of this attachment: "Once trust is established, kinship is an organizing device for stabilizing social ties across time and space. A pattern of frequent interaction—dense interaction—over time leads to the social embeddedness of kinship and clan relations."[37] Such an approach would explain the upsurge in clan politics as Soviet power receded in Central Asia. As a coercive regime receded, powerfully emotive clan relationships naturally reemerged.

Indeed, this should be an easy case for primordialism to make. After all, if the "constructedness" of national and ethnic attachments is widely recognized, kin-based divisions are believed to be something more elemental. So, the argument would go, in spite of the policies of the twentieth century's most coercive regime, these seemingly rock-solid, essential building blocks of identity survived.

A comparative perspective points up the limits of primordialism's explanatory power. Scotland—to take one example—had a strong clan social organization from the fourteenth to the seventeenth centuries. Extended families advanced chiefs who were seen as the authoritative representatives of common ancestors. These clans were engaged in constant rivalries, such that Scottish clan warfare achieved legendary status. Eventually, however, the clan system went into demise. After the Jacobite Uprising in 1745, Charles Edward Stewart favored certain chiefs over others, granting them titles and the opportunity to increase their personal land ownership and wealth, rather than that of the clan. The expanding state gradually supplanted clan authority. If clan ties are primordial, why do they fuel resurgence in some cases and not in others?

Since a focus on the assumed emotional "stickiness" of identity divisions cannot account for this variation, we are left wanting an approach that can reconcile continuity and change in clan relations. Moreover, we are left wanting a perspective that can identify causal mechanisms that propel continuity (or disruptions) in clan relations. To look for causal mechanisms is to seek to avoid primordialism's core tautology: that collective identities persist because they are persistent.

MECHANISMS OF IDENTITY REPRODUCTION

On the surface, constructivism appears to fare no better. Well attuned to change and fluidity in identity relations, it has less to say about the conditions under which collective identities persist over time. Yet, a modified constructivism could say much on this count.

If an identity persists, we should be able to locate a mechanism that propels this development. What Thelen suggests for institutions might be argued for group identity as well: "Institutions rest on a set of ideational and material foundations that, if shaken, open possibilities for change."[38] If we can identify the *mechanisms of identity reproduction*, we gain exceptional purchase on both identity persistence and identity construction. If, in turn, we have a better sense of continuity and change, we better specify group identity as a variable in ways that make social-scientific sense.

This is a different way to think about identity relations. It suggests that if groups survive, this is not the product of emotional "stickiness" that is understood to be the glue of group membership. If, by contrast, groups go into demise, this is not the outcome of processes (such as those associated with modernization) that inexorably dissolve group boundaries. Emotional stickiness and the transformation from traditional to modern may play a role in the fate of identity cleavages, but I argue that whether clan divisions persist or not hinges on identifiable mechanisms of identity reproduction.

The mechanisms that lurk behind identity dynamics involve causal chains that can be linked to specific temporal and spatial contexts and contingencies. The particular mechanism that I highlight has much to do with the nature of the Soviet state, but these mechanisms vary widely in their form and scope. Some are intimately tied to the state; in other contexts, they may not be. As Thelen suggests with regard to institutions, "different institutions rest on different foundations, and so the processes that are likely to disrupt them will also be different, though predictable."[39]

When the mechanism that sustains identity relations encounters an exogenous shock, identity relations shift and recombine. These newly recombined forms, in turn, may be sustained by new mechanisms. The demise of identity divisions occurs when the mechanisms that sustain particular group affiliations are undermined and no alternative emerges to replace them. When an alternative mechanism does emerge, it may be substantially different from what preceded it and therefore leave its imprint on the identity dynamic. There need not be a conscious intention to fuel identity relationships for such mechanisms to be operative. Quite to the contrary, the Kazakhstan case shows that the intention to eradicate clan identities can translate into the practice of sustaining them.

Different mechanisms that underlie identity relations produce different types of politics. This makes intuitive sense: the foundations of group relations lend structure to identity politics. We therefore need to ask two questions of any given group solidarity. First, what makes this identity category resonant? To put it differently, what mechanism contributes to its ongoing appeal? Second, how does what makes this identity category resonant in turn affect its relationship to power? In other words, how does identity politics emerge from the forces that propel identity relations? I suggest that a focus on the mechanisms of identity reproduction gives us leverage on both questions.

CLANS AND THE STATE IN KAZAKHSTAN

The Soviet drive to modernize a traditional landscape in fact had the opposite effect of increasing the import of kinship by tapping its most important inherent quality: its concealable nature.

This causal link between the Soviet regime and clan-identity persistence is not what primordialists would generally expect. Soviet authorities set out to "modernize" Central Asia, loudly trumpeting their campaigns for cultural transformation. Given the often brutal nature of these efforts, a primordialist might expect that the persistence of clan divisions occurred in spite of the state effort. To address Kazakhstan, she would be forced to suggest that clan survival had almost nothing to do with one of the most coercive regimes in modern history. For a primordialist, the Soviet state and its transformative capacity would seem irrelevant.

It is difficult, however, to ignore the degree to which Kazakhstan was transformed under Soviet rule. It moved from an economy dominated by nomadic pastoralism to one based on large-scale mechanized agriculture and extractive industry. Even rural residents encountered dramatic pressures from Soviet modernization and the infrastructure it provided. Bureaucratization, electrification, the mechanization of agriculture and animal husbandry, near-universal literacy and education, as well as the palpable presence of state and Communist Party agents all contributed to a diminished rural-urban divide. The regime spared little brutality to make such transformations possible, but it ultimately did not eradicate clan divisions in Central Asia and the Caucasus. Thus, while some scholars offer a picture of Central Asia as on the whole untransformed by Soviet rule, this is misleading if we include Kazakhstan in the picture.[40]

To the extent that the Soviet state enjoyed uncontested power, the argument is state-centric. Moscow was unusual in this effort, but it was hardly unique in driving the mechanisms of identity reproduction. The state is the engine behind both the persistence and particular manifestations of identity politics. Examining the top-down impact of state-generated political processes seems especially warranted for the study of the former socialist bloc, with its hypertrophic coercive and bureaucratic structures and unusual degree of attempted control over civil society.

But in orienting this study to the state, I seek to go beyond the *intentions* of state actors to consider the *realities* of state action. Rational-choice institutionalism tells us that when the state creates institutions for particular purposes (e.g., social transformations, economic equalization, administration of populations), it generates a series of incentives that affect the behavior of participants.[41] Following this logic, elites who seek to initiate behavioral transformations are wise to "get the incentives right." Without denying the central fact that institutions affect behavior, I wish to make the picture a bit more complicated. First, institutions often create incentives other than those intended by actors. Second, what the state creates in one policy area may have profoundly unintended consequences in another area. Unintended consequences flow across policy areas and are the hallmark of state action.

But, one might object, since the Soviet state ultimately proved fragile, why choose a state-centered approach? The Soviet cultural engineering project failed to produce the intended outcomes; a huge gap separated the actual accomplishments of the project from its aims. In this sense, the Soviet experience was one among many failures of high modernism to "improve the human condition."[42] But failures, too, have profoundly transformative value. A runner who stops three miles before the marathon's finish line has failed to complete the race. From a failure of this sort, can we conclude that the runner's grueling and time-consuming training regime had no significant effect on her physical well-being? In the Soviet case, the failure of state-led cultural engineering should not imply that cultural and political identities were untransformed by state practices. The resulting transformations simply confounded the expectations of project designers.

State-centrism is relatively common among specialists on this region, but the approach I take is at some odds with usual treatments. Studies on the state's role in identity politics show how Soviet institutions served to construct ethnonationalist identities.[43] Where ethnic divisions predated Soviet rule, Soviet institutions lent them additional salience; where ethnic divisions were absent before state socialism, Soviet institutions served to create them.[44] This occurred because an ethnic logic pervaded Soviet life. Passports and other state documentation emphasized ethnic background; political appointments and professional advancement often centered on ethnic criteria; ethnically defined working classes were created; ethnic languages received state support; ethnically defined elites enjoyed distinctive privileges from Moscow; and, an ethnoterritorial principle defined the federal administrative structure.

These practices etched ethnicity deeply onto the plate of Soviet and post-Soviet politics, but state influence on identity politics should not be reduced to promoting ethnicity. If we expand our understanding of what states do (deliberately or not), we develop a fuller appreciation of their role in social and cultural transformation.

Shortage Economy and Other Mechanisms

The Soviet modernization effort vis-à-vis clan relations was multifaceted. On the one hand, it replaced traditional authority with Soviet power and created on a traditional landscape a more complex society. Key (though less obvious) processes moved in the opposite direction, however, promoting the use of clan divisions. This second face of the modernization project began with a political economy of shortage.[45] Shortages of goods, services, and access to power that were endemic to the state socialist economy encouraged access networks to proliferate. Across the southern-tier regions, these access networks often followed kinship lines.

By constraining access to political and economic goods (political power, industrial inputs, consumer wares), the command system produced opportunities for the proliferation of access networks. Across the southern tier of the USSR, ordinary people mobilized preexisting cultural links along subethnic lines as a means of gaining access to such goods. Clan networks were not the only kind of network that could provide such access, but they did have certain advantages. Specifically, subethnicity was not rooted in *visible* markers (as ethnic divisions tend to be) but rather in an exchange of genealogical information that defines identity and difference. Clan background could thus be *concealed* from the agents of Soviet surveillance who prosecuted network behavior as illegal. Subethnic networks came to occupy illicit and private social niches because the state edged them from public life while promoting their utility as an underground phenomenon.

At the same time, the Soviet cultural engineering project viewed clan attachments as "backward" and therefore anathema to the efforts at "socialist construction." State campaigns targeted clan divisions not only to eliminate them from people's behavior, but also to eradicate them discursively from people's consciousness. By singling out subethnic divisions for removal, Soviet propaganda moved these divisions from legitimate public space. They pushed underground and made private. Whereas before the Soviet period, clan identity and difference were freely established through relatively unencumbered flows of genealogical information, in the Soviet period most Kazakhs kept their background private—at least from state agents.

By edging these categories from the public sphere but simultaneously providing opportunities for their reproduction, Soviet state action helped to re-create clan identities over time. Thus, the political and social salience of clan divisions in the post-Soviet period is a consequence of this mechanism that reproduced clans as access networks.

If this shortage economy helped to promote clan identity relations, what earlier mechanism had it replaced? In the pre-Soviet period, the Kazakh steppe lacked state structures, notwithstanding a creeping Russian colonization of the region before Soviet rule. The harsh ecology of the steppe environment placed limits on capital accumulation (which was typical of nomadic and seminomadic contexts), thus stalling one of the prime engines of social stratification and change. Nomadic pastoralism and the clan system were well suited to this severe environment, as it provided the glue of diffuse authority in the absence of a central state apparatus.[46]

In the early Soviet period, Moscow did not deal a fundamental blow to the economy of nomadic pastoralism that lay at the root of the clan system. Rather, it relied on local authority structures to consolidate its rule in the Central Asian periphery. With forced collectivization and sedentarization of the early 1930s, the mechanism that had previously propelled clan identities was fundamentally undermined.

A resource scarcity that played an important role even under Stalin became systemic after his death. With Brezhnev's trust-in-cadres policy that entrenched republican elites, the previous systemic dynamism predicated in great measure on Stalin's ever-changing preferences vanished; "stagnation" set in, in which patronage networks crystallized and the rules of social and political life became more predictable. Everyday affairs centered on questions of goods procurement, and access networks became increasingly important, useful, and reliable for ordinary people and elites alike. In the Soviet south, these networks often followed blood lines.

In the 1990s, the command nature of the political economy was scrapped, but the essential problem remained the same, notwithstanding President Nazarbaev's portrayals of Kazakhstan as a developmental state that would exploit its natural resources and become the next Kuwait or Saudi Arabia. A sharp economic decline produced acute scarcity that intensified resource-competition. With the real GDP declining precipitously through the mid-1990s, politics in Central Asia was based on distribution of scarce goods. The utility of subethnic access networks did not evaporate with the Soviet collapse.

An Imprint on Clan Politics

As a mechanism of reproduction, this shortage economy was responsible not only for promoting subethnic clan divisions; it was also responsible for the particular *forms* in which they were reproduced. It left a distinctive imprint on the identity dynamic. By the end of Soviet rule, clan divisions were no longer the paramount wellsprings of social, cultural, and political identity that they had been in the nineteenth century. The Soviet shortage economy had made their function more specific: they were brought closer to essentially political questions of goods distribution. Clans emerged into the post-Soviet period *as access networks* to goods in short supply. These access networks jockeyed for control over increasingly lucrative resources in a process that might be called "clan conflict."

A second type of subethnic politics occurred on the discursive plane. The clan-based access networks were not merely private; they were also contested. As chapter 2 introduces, social discourse — rather than outwardly visible markers of difference — established the contours of clan identity and difference before Soviet rule. Soviet modernization transformed these identities, but it did not change their centrally discursive nature. Driven from legitimate public space by an ongoing stigma, subethnic identities remained largely in the private realm. The flow of genealogical information that once established identity was no longer free and open. In the modern context, subethnic relations became opaque, opening a wide berth for imagination in their social construction and in the political contests that surrounded them. Myriad political actors exploited this opacity to their own ends, challenging given categories, suggesting new ones, infusing old ones with new meaning, and engaging in battles over the legitimacy of power holders.

This is what a number of scholars mean when they discuss "metaconflict" over identity relations; conflict over the nature of the identity-based conflict is a contest over the shape and nature of the identities that animate politics.[47] Who the actors are, where their interests lie, and what might represent just solutions to political problems are not exogenously given (except in the minds of remote analysts) but rather endogenously produced, transformed, and contested by iterations of conflict. Identity politics is not simply driven by group solidarities that can be understood as static, but rather invariably include contests about the groups themselves. The assertion and denial of groupness becomes a central tool of the trade. For example, when a state conducts a census in some senses it *records* existing identity divisions, but in a more central way it *shapes* the politics of cultural identities. A census is a political, as much as a demographic, issue. And if such metaconflict is present in all identity politics, it is present all the more for clans. Their legitimacy called into question by the very nature of modernity, subethnic divisions give life to a politics that necessarily involves this discursive, metaconflictual moment.

I do not intend to focus exclusively on the discourse, ideas, and intellectuals involved in identity politics. As Stevens observes, "To hear a practice called discursive may prompt the inference that it follows from the merely whimsical, playful qualities of language, that who one is might be a matter of 'mere words,' and not the necessary pulls of life and death many find in their forms of being."[48] Not all politics recommends a focus on discourse. For some politics, however, the discursive element is too central to be ignored, even in the interest of analytic parsimony.

Clan politics occupies a conceptual blind spot, since it occurs at the juncture of disciplines. While less visible than above-ground forms of identity politics (such as ethnicity- or religion-based contests), it drives important developments in a broad array of contexts. In particular, it generates challenges to nation- and state-building efforts, since clans often bring the pull of locality and the proposition of alternative institutional orders to the political game. Moreover, the usual perspectives fail us on the subject. The identity-modernization approach cannot account for persistent clan politics. Primordialist approaches can account for persistence, but they say little about the causal process by which this persistence occurs.

Taking a page from historical institutionalism, I propose that a stronger theory of identity politics identifies the mechanisms by which identities are reproduced. To do so is to suggest a way to improve radically our conceptual purchase both on clan politics and on identity politics more generally.

2

Nomads, Diffuse Authority, and Sovietization

> The assumption of inertia, that cultural and social continuity
> do not require explanation, obliterates the fact that both have to
> be recreated anew in each generation, often with great pain and
> suffering. —Barrington Moore

MODERN HISTORY IS A STORY OF STATE EXPANSION — EXPANSION
not into empty space but over inhabited territory. The rapid conquest
by tsarist Russia into Central Asia has many parallels — notably in the
feverish scramble for African colonies — but even in Africa, rare is the
case in which a stateless population so radically and so quickly suc-
cumbed to alien state institutions.

In this sense, Kazakhstan is terra firma for examining the influence
of states on indigenous identity patterns. Apart from the institutions
of Russian colonial expansion, the steppe nomads had minimal expo-
sure to the apparatuses of state before the consolidation of Soviet rule.
This affords an unusual opportunity to trace how states produce identity politics.[1]

To understand the collision of clan and Soviet authority patterns,
we require a step backward. Conceptually, we must first cover terminological issues. Chronologically, we need clarity on what lay at
the heart of the traditional, pre-Soviet clan dynamic. As I will show,
nomadic pastoralism generated an entire social system built on kinship ties. Readers who skim this chapter will miss the presentation
of key evidence, but the logic of the book's argument should not
suffer.

CONCEPTUAL BACKGROUND

Some definitional clarity makes analysis possible. As Hobbes wrote, "A man that seeketh precise truth had need to remember what every name he uses stand for, and to place it accordingly, or else he will find himself entangled in words, as a bird in lime twigs, the more he struggles the more belimed."[2] To avoid such a messy fate, I consider the use of three key terms: identity, ethnicity, and clan.

Identity

"Identity" is a term whose utility as empirical descriptor and analytic category may be uneven. The postmodern turn in the social sciences in the 1980s and 1990s harkened to the social psychology of Mead and the strategic interactionist sociology of Goffman in contending that any given person has multiple, overlapping relational identities, the expression of which is situation-dependent.[3] Together with the post–Cold War ascendance of liberal democratic norms, these insights powerfully suggested the individual as the unit of analysis for research in identity politics.

This was useful as a corrective to previous primordialist theorizing, but it suggested an oversight: identity involves more than the irreducible and elusive individual singularity suggested in both postmodernism and liberal democratic theory. Identity entails a sameness that links individuals in a group. The recognition that groups are unstable, contested, and overlapping should not obscure the fact that identity is a social phenomenon that on some level must be described in Durkheimian terms.[4] In the extreme, a postmodern lens that focuses attention on various, ever-changing multiple identities loses sight of the coercive power of groups by depicting them as mere paper tigers. Identity is at root about group behavior and group self-understandings.

By the same token, there is an opposite pitfall in studies of identity: the assumption that group identities remain discrete and constant. Invoking the need for parsimony, some analysts reify difference and create static, categorical cultural amalgams with the appearance of mutual exclusivity. In extreme form, this practice is clear in the "Clash of Civilizations" argument, wherein Huntington essentializes and homogenizes world "civilizations" and expects that conflict will result from these divisions.[5] To be sure, cultural differences are important for politics, but the political significance of difference does not inhere in the difference itself.[6] Rather, it is continually constructed through social interaction and can therefore take on a variety of forms. Any scholarship that imbues entire cultural groups with unity and agency can fall prey to this practice.

Avoiding the reification of group boundaries, on the one hand, and recognizing social behaviors, on the other, is an ever-present challenge for identity research. With this in mind, I understand identity as a minimal set of characteristics that an individual is recognized to share with others in a group.

Ethnicity

"Ethnicity" is a term that students of the former USSR rapidly embraced to describe the primary cultural categories that appeared in Soviet censuses. There is little conceptual difference between what Sovietologists had referred to as "nationalities" and what scholars of other world regions referred to as "ethnicities," but the shift in vocabulary to the latter signaled an ambition among specialists on post-Soviet identity politics to engage cross-case comparisons. It is worth asking what we mean by the term.

Ethnicity is generally understood to encompass differences in language, dress, religion, customs, cuisine, family patterns, and other cultural diacritica. Many such factors operate in the setting of cultural boundaries. Conceptual messiness ensues, however, since some of these factors understood to define ethnic difference do not always do so. For example, religion is a marker of ethnic difference between Orthodox Russians and Muslim Chechens in the North Caucasus, but common religion unites Russians with many Ukrainians across ethnic lines, as Islam unites Chechens with Pashtuns and Uyghurs. To say that religious difference makes ethnic difference is wrong for these cases. Likewise, dress, custom, and cuisine have crossed cultural frontiers as long as there has been commercial exchange and migration. As markers of ethnic difference, these also are inadequate. Recognizing this, Barth suggests that ethnicity is less about the substance of cultural difference than about the maintenance of group boundaries itself.[7]

In former Soviet space, language is often identified as the fulcrum of identity relations. This may result from Stalin's well-known theoretical preoccupation with language issues, but for some scholars this focus is practical. Discussing linguistic "tipping games" in four post-Soviet republics, Laitin suggests that language use has the social scientific advantage of being easily measured and monitored. By using language as a proxy for culture, he shows that a new identity emerged among diaspora Russians—an identity that distinguishes them from homeland Russians, as well as from the non-Russian titular population.[8] But, *of what* is language an indicator? Whether this language base can be considered "ethnic" remains unclear even at the conclusion of a well-executed, empirically grounded study. Indeed, Serbs and Croats are united in a common language, notwithstanding the feeling of ethnic difference that became palpable in the late 1980s.

The question whether or not diaspora identities are distinctive in an *ethnic* sense might be moot, but it touches on important conceptual issues. Is there a common substance to ethnic identity that distinguishes it from other identity formations? I follow Horowitz in suggesting that the defining aspect of ethnic affiliation is the myth of kinship, which contributes to the emotional charge that may accompany it. As Horowitz states, "To call ethnicity a kinlike affiliation is thus to call into play the panoply of rights and obligations, the unspoken understandings, and the mutual aspiration for well-being that are so characteristic of family life. . . ."[9] Ethnicity is based on the conflation of kin and group, on the blurring of lines between identifiable kin and those assumed to be kin. The expression of this myth occurs in various ways: through language, dress, custom, cuisine, and/or religion. In other words, one is marked as kin-related if one demonstrates native fluency with the language, customs, and traditions of a given group.

In this sense, the ethnic groups that inhabit Central Asian territory are Kazakhs, Russians, Ukrainians, Uyghurs, Tatars, Chechens, Greeks, Jews, and others. Some of them (Ukrainians, Russians, Uzbeks, Germans) are co-ethnics with the titular population in independent states; some (Tatars, Bashkirs, Chechens, Ingush) are co-ethnics with the titular population in neighboring substate administrative units; and some (Kurds, Uyghurs) are co-ethnics with populations of stateless minorities in other states. Twentieth-century Kazakhstan had such a culturally variegated landscape that ethnic Kazakhs became a minority in their "own" republic, beginning with forced collectivization and famine in the late 1920s and early 1930s, to recover to demographic predominance only in the middle of the 1990s.

Subethnicity and Clan

Divisions *within* ethnic groups are the primary focus of this book. To discuss such subethnic divisions is to choose among terms with normative baggage.

Consider "tribe." Consensus over a definition is elusive even among anthropologists who confront the question frequently. Khoury and Kostiner contend that "a single, all-encompassing definition is virtually impossible to produce."[10] Inductively derived definitions are equally problematic, since "the ethnographer has often only managed to discern the existence of *a* tribe because he took it as axiomatic that this kind of cultural entity must exist."[11]

At the core of many understandings of tribe is its presumed conceptual opposition to modern institutions and identities. Many assume that tribes exist at an evolutionary stage before the emergence of modern national states. That is, tribes are ipso facto understood as primitive and backward. Christie echoes a common perspective when he contends, "[T]ribes are an early form of human organization, preceding that of nation or state. Tribes, presumably, can be found hundreds, perhaps thousands, of years before the latter forms of human organization appear."[12]

From the teleological perspective of presumptive developmental end points, to invoke the term "tribe" is to make a normative claim. To highlight the social significance of tribal divisions is all but to suggest the immanence of violence; to claim that "tribalism" animates politics is to imply that particularistic interests dominate a patrimonial polity. Thus, various forms of culture-based mobilization against an existing political order are often glossed as tribalism, even for societies lacking in actual tribes.[13] This is possible because of the negative connotations that the term tribe has come to carry.

The term "clan" also carries unfortunate connotations. Before the Asian financial crisis in 1998, Westerners routinely referred to the Suharto "clan" in Indonesia to depict a plutocracy that enriched members of the former ruler's family. In the Russian context, *klan* became a rough equivalent of "faction," but with the added implication of exclusivity and the in-group trust assumed to accompany family rela-

tions.[14] The underlying contention is that clans are entities that operate in ways fundamentally opposed to the principles of market democracies. This metaphorical usage of "clan" is not analytically helpful.
While certain entities do acquire the properties described, they cannot be considered clans in Durkheim's sense of a politico-familial
organization in which "affinities produced by sharing a blood kinship
are mainly what keeps [members] united."[15]

A definition of clan that emphasizes kinship may help us to recover
its dynamic: clan divisions are those that exist within an ethnic group
and in which demonstrable common kinship is understood to underlie membership. This understanding of clan begins with segmentary
lineage theory.[16] In segmentary societies, groups divide into smaller
units and coalesce into larger ones, depending on the vagaries of climate and external military threat. Fissure and fusion occur along
genealogical lines, with the smallest referent groups based most
clearly upon common descent and larger ones based on the assumption of common descent. The members of such societies understand
kinship as definitive, even if lineages can be fictitious.

With clans, precise genealogical knowledge is understood to define
membership. Of course, such knowledge can be created or manipulated by elites to justify their rule, just as it can be shaped or altered
by secular influences. Nonetheless, descent—both fictive and real—
is the central operative principle of subethnic clan identity. The
higher one moves in the model of segmentary lineage, the more an
assumption of descent prevails over a need to actually demonstrate
genealogical ties. At the level of the ethnic group, demonstrating actual
descent is usually unnecessary; it is axiomatic.[17]

Subethnic ties vary; they may be rooted in kin relations or in attachment to physical place. Kin ties are more portable than place-linked
affinities. For the former type of tie, the physical distance between
members that is generated with migrations may stretch the fabric of
group relations, but not to the point of tearing; group identity does
not require physical proximity. Thus, nomads, seminomads, and former nomads often use regular and ritualized oral communication to
reiterate their genealogical bonds. By contrast, migration may be a
more disruptive development for sedentary populations; group identity travels less well when it is rooted in place.

Nonetheless, there are certain family resemblances between subethnic clan identities and subethnic attachments to place. In both

cases, the presumption is that they are subcategories within larger cultural units that receive positive political sanction. Both types of sub-ethnicity are divisions that the modern state often renders illegitimate—a fact that centrally shapes their political dynamic.

IDENTITY RELATIONS IN THE PRE-SOVIET STEPPE

This section elaborates a specific vocabulary for understanding the particular forms that subethnic clan and ethnic attachments took in the Kazakh steppe.[18] Before the changes that accompanied Russian colonization, five identity forms intersected in the steppe: local clan divisions, a limited class stratification, umbrella clans, ethnic difference, and a nomad-sedentary divide. I take each of them in turn. Underlying the logic of these identities is the mechanism that propelled them: the political economy of nomadic pastoralism.

Amidst considerable variety and local complexity, the primary locus of identity before the onset of Russian colonial rule was local clans (*ru*), which resembled the constituent divisions in other nomadic societies.[19] As Evans-Pritchard illustrates for the Nuer of the Anglo-Egyptian Sudan, nomadic societies exhibit a segmentary lineage structure, in which members claim common descent (understood patrilineally, in the Kazakh case, as in most cases) from a single progenitor.[20] At the top of Kazakhs' genealogical tree sits Alash, the mythical founding father. Moving from the apex to the base, descent lines proliferated and became more complicated. At any given level in the descent structure, common agnatic kin could be invoked (or invented) to define the contours of a given segment.

Segmentary divisions among precolonial nomads were flexible and scaled at multiple levels. Contingent on prevailing ecological conditions and constellations of external threats, groups would coalesce at different taxonomic levels at different times. Clans were a moving target. It was a rather complicated undertaking to establish a static picture of segmentary divisions, as Evans-Pritchard attempted. Aleksei Iraklievich Levshin, known for his seminal ethnography of the steppe nomads, encountered the same difficulties among Kazakhs.[21]

Genealogical knowledge played a critical role among these nomads in determining the boundaries between segments. Unlike ethnic divisions, divisions between segments were defined not by a myth of kinship played out in the form of various cultural diacritica, but by demonstrable knowledge of kin relations. Each nomad was expected to know his or her genealogical background (*shezhire* or *zheti ata*) at least to the seventh generation. This cutoff point was critical, since the society placed a proscription on endogamous marriage (within seven generations of common descent). Given regular migrations and mass illiteracy, this information was transmitted orally before the forced sedentarization and literacy campaigns of the Soviet period.

After inquiring into the health of one another's livestock, nomads meeting in the steppe would typically ask, "What clan do you come from?" (*Qai rudan keldingiz?*), or more generically, "What people do you come from?" (*Qai eldensiz?*). The answer was couched by recounting ancestry; genealogical knowledge was thus reiterated with every new interaction and comprised a dense discursive exchange that helped to establish the widely recognized contours of clan at various levels. Thus, identity and difference were built upon a societal discourse that later would become fundamentally altered with the imposition of a Soviet state apparatus that edged it from legitimate public space.

Since local clans were the primary site of group identity in the pre-Russian period, a number of related families would inhabit a single mobile encampment (*aul*).[22] The steppe environment was the limiting factor on the size of the encampment. Great distances, a strongly continental climate (harsh winters and hot, dry summers), and scarce water and fodder restricted its extent. During the winter migration (*qystau*), pasturage was found near rivers, and encampments were more widely dispersed, thus reducing intergroup contact and increasing vulnerability to outside threat. During the summer migration (*zhailau*), several encampments would settle in closer proximity. This was a time for weddings, games, festivals, and competitions.[23]

A symbiotic relationship emerged between the steppe environment and Kazakh social structure. Because of the harsh steppe ecology, Nurbulat Masanov argues, "nomadism is an ecologically determined way of life."[24] Indeed, with the exception of areas along the Syr Darya River on the Mangyshlaq Peninsula and in the desert of central Kazakhstan, most of contemporary Kazakhstan is better suited for extensive pastoralism than for agriculture. Many areas can also support some degree of cultivation; in those areas, ecological severity influenced but did not determine whether pastoralism or agriculture prevailed in any given period; rather, specific social and political processes appear to have been critical.[25] Indeed, the Soviet period witnessed a massive changeover from pastoralism to cultivation, an undertaking that was difficult and ecologically suspect but possible.

The Kazakh nomadic pastoralists had a loose, but still notable, attachment to territory. While we often expect agriculturalists to harbor strong ties to particular places, the same can occur among nomads, as climatic variability produced stable migrations along regular routes. Ishchenko and coauthors suggest, "For a nomadic household migrating many hundreds of kilometres from north to south, it is very important for there to be fodder crops along the entire migration route at a stage when they are nutritionally valuable. The arrival of a nomad in July in the North with his livestock still scraggy after winter is tantamount to jute [a huge loss of stock] because the grass begins to dry out at this period and is almost two times less nutritious than it is in May and June."[26] The pastoralist valued his livestock first and foremost as property and thus branded them with group symbols or emblems (*tamga*). What is more surprising is that such emblems were also used to mark claims to pastureland. Ties to territory were clearly not irrelevant to nomads.[27]

Authority was vested locally. Primary among authorities were elders (*aqsaqaldar*) and judges (*biler*). The elders were the male heads of each encampment who would select a judge to adjudicate disputes among a number of encampments. During times of peace, the elders would select a judge to govern relatively fewer encampments; during times of external threat, the elders would select a judge at a higher level to govern more encampments. Customary law (*adat*) provided guidance in the absence of an ultimate authority.[28] So critical were many of these local authorities that clan divisions were often named in honor of the judges who governed them, especially if efforts at governance proved effective.[29]

Until the twentieth century, socioeconomic stratification remained minimal. The steppe climate imposed important physical limitations on the accumulation of material wealth, and therefore on the emergence of stable class divisions. As one traveler to the region observed, "They experience very rapid rises and downturns in material well-being, depending almost exclusively on the weather and harvests. . . . A few extra degrees of cold that suddenly overtake winter pastures can in the shortest of time-spans turn a rich Kyrgyz [i.e., Kazakh][30] into a poor man."[31]

To the extent that there was much social stratification in the precolonial steppe, it favored the so-called whitebone (*aq suiek*) aristocrats, who formally were considered separate from the segmentary
divisions of ordinary nomads. The whitebone was composed of two
groups. First was a class of sultans (*tore*), who claimed descent from
Genghis Khan himself and enjoyed some governing authority over
the clan structure. Based largely on their charisma, these sultans chose
khans who ruled the separate umbrella clans (discussed below), as
well as the Kazakh Khanate, during those periods of unity among
the three umbrella clans. The second part of the whitebone elite consisted of those who claimed special social standing on the basis of
presumed descent from the Prophet Muhammad (*hozha*). These aristocrats enjoyed social status that set them apart from the so-called
blackbone (*qara suiek*) commoners. But, given the limitations of the
steppe environment, material plenty was elusive; aristocrats were thus
distinguished largely by the legitimacy derived from privileged
descent.[32]

The blackbone elite could claim no special standing, and the forces
limiting its status were profound and pervaded Kazakh lore. One
Kazakh proverb attests, "If a Sart [agriculturist] gets rich, he builds a
home; if a Kazakh gets rich, he accumulates wives."[33] Or, as one
Kazakh song put it: "I was riding to the pitch when my horse-yoke
broke / I tossed a coin, and it came up tails / Oh, if I only had a lot of
money / I would get myself four wives."[34] Progeny was a preferred
resource, since it produced a web of kin-related supporters who could
consolidate authority and provide labor. Material wealth, by contrast,
was ephemeral.

While the local clan was the locus of identity before Russian colonization, the subethnic level of horde or umbrella clan (*zhuz*) also
achieved considerable resonance.[35] In the middle of the sixteenth century, the Kazakh Khanate disintegrated into three subunits led by three
separate khans. This tripartite division is usually explained by the existence of three natural climatic zones that gradually forged stable migration routes for identifiable clusters of mobile encampments.[36] A
minority view holds that the umbrella clans began as military formations, presumably the institutional residue of Genghis Khan's Mongol army.[37]

In the fluid political and social context of the precolonial steppe, the umbrella clans were notable for their relative political stability. Within each umbrella clan a meeting of sultans, judges, and elders elected a khan.[38] Each khan ruled by virtue of charismatic authority, and periods of unity among the Kazakh umbrella clans occurred because authority was vested in a single khan whose personalistic rule succeeded in commanding respect.[39]

The relative political stability of the umbrella clan allowed identity to be expressed in broad-based regions. These regions, in turn, were subjected to varying political and cultural influences, owing largely to their physical location. The Younger Umbrella Clan (*kishi zhuz*) governed a region roughly framed by the Aral Sea, the Caspian Sea, and the Ural River. The Middle Umbrella Clan (*orta zhuz*) occupied the northern and central regions. The Elder Umbrella Clan (*uly zhuz*) dominated in the eastern and southeastern portions of the territory. As a consequence of this geography, before the colonial presence, proximity to the Khivan Khanate and Turkmen groups influenced the Younger Umbrella Clan. Russian traders, Bashkirs, Tatars, and Kalmyks shaped relations with the Middle Umbrella Clan. Pressures from Uyghurs, Uzbeks, and the oasis cultures affected the Elder Umbrella Clan. The result was the production of cultural difference at the level of the umbrella clan.

Unlike umbrella-clan attachment, ethnic identification remained weak before the twentieth century. Notwithstanding the drive of ethnonationalist scholars to rewrite the region's history with an ethnic pen, the term *qazaq* (Kazakh) makes its earliest documentary appearances only in the fifteenth century.[40] Kazakh identity is best dated to the emergence in this period of the Kazakh Khanate on the ruins of the Mongol empire.[41] The northward migration of the khans Girei and Zhanibek from the Shibanid-ruled Uzbek Khanate of Abulkhair was the spark for popular identification with a new political entity. The terms *qazaq* and Uzbek "assumed such a meaning that they served not only to define the followers to the old nobility of the Shibanids, Girei, Zhanibek and their descendents, but also to distinguish among kinspeople by their place of residence, as now delimited by the frames of certain political borders."[42]

How far the designation *qazaq* went beyond a circumscribed elite in the fifteenth century is not clear. *Qazaq* could not have been broadly used as an ethnonym for ordinary people for three reasons. First, it was easier to become a *qazaq* than one would normally expect of an ethnic group. The term itself carried the meaning of "wanderer" or "vagabond," leading some scholars to propose a linguistic link between *qazaq* and the Cossacks, the Slavic descendants of runaway serfs who lived at the periphery of the Russian empire.[43] Residence at the margins of centralized state authority, rather than any group characteristics assumed to be immutable, underlay them both.

Second, the boundaries between what today are recognized as ethnic groups were quite porous; in a number of cases, subethnic clan divisions crossed boundaries. To take a few examples: the Naiman clans are found among both Kazakhs and Kyrgyz; the Adai are found among both Kazakhs and Karakalpaks; the Qangly subdivision is found among both Kazakhs and Uzbeks; and the Arghyns are found among both Kazakhs and Turkmen.[44] Moreover, Russian colonial ethnographers with great difficulty distinguished between Kazakhs and Kyrgyz, calling the former "Kyrgyz-Kaisak"[45] and the latter "Kara-Kyrgyz." In the region as a whole, identity was scaled at different levels under different circumstances.[46]

Third, the primary axis of alterity before the Russian colonization was mode of economy (nomadic pastoralist versus sedentary agriculturalist). When people would meet on the steppe, the first ritualized question asked was about the health of the other's livestock. As with their sedentary counterparts, internal cultural divisions were less socially important than a common identity as nomad. While nomadism would become a central facet of the later crystallization of a Kazakh ethnic identity, to be a nomad in the precolonial steppe did not imply ethnic belonging.

For the present purposes, the most important point from the foregoing description of identity relations is the centrality of nomadic pastoralism. Indeed, nomadic pastoralism was the sustaining force behind such identity relationships and one that left a deep imprint on the identity dynamic. Specifically, nomadism privileged genealogical knowledge, diffuse authority patterns, and a segmentary social structure. It resulted from a harsh steppe environment that made the local-level encampment and associated clan(s) the most salient social division.

When subsequent, exogenous forces exerted pressure on this mechanism of identity reproduction, the identity dynamic would shift and transform.

RUSSIAN COLONIZATION: IDENTITY TRANSFORMATION?

Putting identity formations into historical motion is no mean task. The imposition of a colonial apparatus usually brings with it greater documentation of social change, but more written evidence does not mean that social change was absent before colonialism. Nomadic societies present particularly formidable challenges in this regard. A paucity of written material forces researchers to rely on the accounts of outsiders—travelers and colonial ethnographers—accounts which can smuggle in particular ideologies. Moreover, a wealth of orally transmitted information has remained generally underutilized as historical evidence, and the passage of time may erode its reliability.[47]

But the record is far from silent on identity-related issues, and a picture emerges of the limited extent of social transformation that occurred with Russian colonization.[48] Russian colonization introduced two central changes to identity politics. First, it brought the locus of authority increasingly to the level of the local clan. Second, it intensified identity divisions by raising the political stakes involved in claims to group membership.[49] Nonetheless, identity relations remained relatively stable even in the late nineteenth century. As long as nomadic pastoralism dominated life in the steppe, clan retained its prominence.

Of course, the architects of colonial policy sought not to transform identity relations but rather to secure for Russian traders the overland caravan routes across the steppe as prelude to the conquest of the khanates of Khiva, Kokand, and Bukhara, with their access to Silk Road commercial opportunities. Russian industry sought new markets where its goods could compete, and Asia offered much promise. Moreover, securing the region offered geopolitical advantages vis-à-vis an expanding British presence in the region, and tsarist army officials may have sought to conquer Central Asia to reestablish the prestige of their beleaguered institution after the Crimean War debacle.[50] Finally, overpopulation in European Russia, exacerbated acutely by the emancipation of Russian serfs in 1861, fueled a continuing search for arable land that brought Slavic migrants to the steppe.

Indigenous populations were not incorporated into the Russian empire all at once. First, Abulkhair Khan of the Younger Umbrella Clan swore fealty to the Russian empire in 1730, giving rise to a series of anticolonial uprisings that forestalled the Younger Umbrella Clan's total capitulation to Russian rule until 1824. The Middle Umbrella Clan came under similar pressures and concluded treaties of loyalty to Russia in 1732 and 1740. Abylai Khan of the Middle Umbrella Clan resisted fuller Russian encroachment by playing Russian, Zhungar, and Manchu Chinese interests off each other. Ultimately, after Abylai's death in 1781, rule by khans in the Middle Umbrella Clan was greatly weakened, leading to the annexation of the Middle Umbrella Clan in 1822. Finally, in the Elder Umbrella Clan, some groups acceded to Russian rule in the 1820s, but others remained under the rule of the Kokand Khanate. Only with the ultimate conquest of the khanates at Bukhara, Samarqand, Khiva, and Kokand were the remaining Elder Umbrella Clan groups brought under Russian control.[51]

The introduction of a colonial administrative apparatus brought the locus of authority to a local level by eliminating the khans. Administrative units were created first among the Middle Umbrella Clan nomads with the 1832 Regulations on the Siberian Kyrgyz.[52] Designed to be inviolable, notwithstanding the fact that they crosscut migratory routes, boundaries were created in a territory that had not previously seen them. Eliminating rule by khans, the regulations established sultans as the primary legitimate local authorities. The administrative structure began with a kin-based unit (*rodovaia uprava*) that consisted of about fifteen extended families and was represented by a local elder. About ten to twelve such units comprised a region (*volost*) that was governed by a sultan. Eighty-seven regions comprised four districts (*okrug*), each of which was ruled by a committee of a sultan, two other Kazakh representatives, and two Russian emissaries.[53]

Additional administrative reforms localized authority even further. In 1867 the creation of three governor-generalships (Orenburg, West Siberia, and Turkestan) for the steppe populations—administrative divisions that elided traditional authority patterns—provoked profound anticolonial sentiment.[54] The result was a weakened position for the whitebone sultans and a privileging of the blackbone elites. Land was declared the property of the Russian state. Kazakhs who tried to sell or rent land were contravening imperial law, as in the Syr Darya region (*oblast*), where one tsarist official complained in 1909 that "in one of the *uezds* (districts) . . . the selling of state lands by Kyrgyz nomads is practiced on quite a wide scale."[55]

Privileged relative to the sultans, the blackbone elite quickly found its power circumscribed by the colonial apparatus. By 1880, one observer would remark about the relative standing of the blackbone elders: "The elders still recall those times when, before the introduction by our government of well-known orders [*poriadky*], the many tribes [*plemena*] and family units [*semeistva*] enjoyed special meaning and did what they desired."[56] Instead of flexible group boundaries that shifted in accordance with prevailing ecological conditions and circumstances of outside threats, segmentary identities were made more local, more clearly defined, and more closely tied to specific territories.

As Russia's colonial frontier gradually moved southward, diminishing pasturage intensified competition for land, and the *barymta* (punitive raid on neighboring groups) became more widespread.[57] Slavic peasants supported by colonial structures continued to arrive, and a simple lack of land for extensive pastoralism forced some nomads and seminomads to adopt agricultural practices; maintaining a sufficient herd became more difficult without supplementary fodder produced through agriculture.

Further impetus for sedentarization came in a number of forms. With the 1867 reforms that had, among other things, legally appropriated all land as imperial property, any imperial subject's claim to land stewardship required settlement and the erection of permanent structures. Some indigenous nomads themselves advocated sedentarization, seeing in it prospects for the consolidation of popular resistance. Such was the case with Kenesary Kasymov, the leader of the most widespread Kazakh revolt against Russian rule (1837–47).[58]

If sedentarization was largely the product of colonial encroachment, it was a product that created commercial opportunities for some former nomads.[59] As the volume of trade with Central Asia, Persia, India, China, and Russia increased, subsistence-based animal husbandry gave way to the more specialized trade of livestock (particularly beef) and related products. In addition, microclimatic variations rendered certain areas more amenable to cultivation and neighboring sedentary groups could put pressure on indigenous populations to "acquire a taste for settled life [*osedlost*]."[60] Perhaps not surprisingly, poor peasants tended to support sedentarization, since they often lived on the brink of subsistence in any case.[61] Some scholars consider that full sedentarization was already inevitable by the end of the nineteenth century, when a tsarist decree forcibly confiscated lands used for extensive pastoralism, thus exacerbating the land shortage further.[62]

Identity divisions lay at the heart of competition over land resources that had become more acute with decreasing pasturage—a political competition that occurred along the lines of clans, umbrella clans, and ethnic divisions. In some cases, tsarist authorities were asked to adjudicate disputes between claimants that were local clans. In other cases, umbrella clan divisions entered the written record of disputes. In still others, Kazakhs demanded in ethnic terms that authorities restore to them high-quality indigenous lands that had been confiscated for use by Cossacks.[63]

Ethnically marked competition for land resources became more frequent, given the broad-scale introduction of an ethnic "other." According to estimates based on the first imperial census in 1897, 18.3 percent of inhabitants of what today is part of Kazakhstan were non-Kazakhs. By 1903 the northern regions of this territory witnessed a non-Kazakh population of 26.4 percent, almost all of whom were Russians.[64] Enjoying the political support of the tsarist administration, these colonists were a particularly visible population with which indigenous nomads could contrast themselves.

This growing colonial presence fueled political and intellectual movements of an ethnonationalist bent. However, the popular resonance of ethnic identity was still limited. Even during the most widespread anticolonial rebellion, Kenesary Kasymov was unable to keep at bay interclan rivalries.[65] As Sabol underscores, to call Kasymov's rebellion a "national-liberation endeavor" (as many post-Soviet ethnonationalist historians do, thus projecting ethnic identity where it does not belong) "bestows a level of national consciousness upon the man and the rebellion which was still many years away."[66]

The first decade of the twentieth century witnessed still-nascent ethnonationalist sentiment. Compared to that in neighboring territories, a Kazakh-language press emerged relatively late and likely enjoyed limited appeal given broad illiteracy. By 1916, a decree to conscript Central Asians into the tsarist army engendered widespread resistance expressed in ethnic terms; several years of quasi independence followed as the crisis of Russian tsardom deepened and led to civil war. But the movement was neither well coordinated nor broad based. On the eve of Soviet rule, ethnic divisions were becoming more salient. Soviet institutions would crystallize ethnic attachments much more profoundly.

As important as these changes to identity relations were in the pre-

Soviet steppe, they were in fact limited in the light of changes that followed. After all, the central organizing principle of nomadic pastoralism remained largely intact, notwithstanding pressures to sedentarize. Even with the gradual Sovietization of the steppe, we see that local clan identities remained the primary site of identity politics.

SOVIETIZATION AND SUBETHNICITY

Early Soviet rule acutely politicized subethnic identities. Competition among clans manifested itself most clearly during the cadre-development efforts of the Soviet state and in land-use debates. As we shall see, initial Soviet governance did not fundamentally disrupt identity relations; rather, it ensnared them in a series of political contests. In addition, it lent clan relationships a public stigma that further shaped their dynamic.

While some scholars classify Soviet rule as the epitome of coercive governance and thus "totalitarian," this state also was predicated on effective local-level administration.[67] Effective administration required administrators, and by the mid-1920s a strategy of nativization (*korenizatsiia*) of the regional administrative apparatus emerged. Promoting non-Slavic indigenous groups through broad-based "affirmative action" policies in cadre development,[68] the new state set out to address two problems at once: (1) the widespread illiteracy and sporadic resistance that had limited Central Asians' involvement in administration, thus casting doubt on the popular legitimacy of nascent Soviet institutions, and (2) the legitimacy of alternative patterns of authority in the form of local rule by blackbone elites.

Developing Cadres

The main mechanism for cadre replacement was "elections" (*perevybory*) to the local councils (*soviets*). Conducted in 1926, 1927, and 1929, these events involved a modicum of competition over posts, but Soviet authorities strongly promoted preferred local candidates over others. By 1929, official endorsement had become prerequisite for standing for office; those lacking sanction were slowly purged from the apparatus. Thus, elections were at root a means by which to develop cadres for Soviet governance.

The language that Soviet authorities used for this sea change of cadres was one of class warfare. As in attempts to consolidate Soviet rule in Slavic regions, in Central Asia relatively well-to-do peasants (*kulaks*) were assumed to be the agents of capitalist exploitation and were accordingly targeted for political or physical extermination. In Kazakhstan the *bais* (rich ones) were declared to be the equivalent of the *kulaks* of the Slavic areas, and their stubborn attempts to cling to socioeconomic privileges by entering local state organs were declared equally reprehensible. Authorities consistently described these elections as the most effective weapon against the *bais*.[69] The ostensible beneficiaries of this cadre replacement were to be the poor nomads— officially, the Kazakh equivalent of poor peasants among Slavs.

If it required a feat of Leninist creativity to imagine that Marx's proletarian revolution could occur in primarily agrarian Russia, the language of class warfare was particularly ill suited to describe the steppe nomads.[70] To be sure, a nascent rise of class divisions was evident. The increasingly dense commerce across the steppe that accompanied tsarist-era colonization had begun to disrupt long-standing social dynamics among nomads by the end of the nineteenth century, but class stratification was still far less significant than segmentation as a social principle. Attempts to turn the poor nomad against the relatively well-to-do members of his clan ran up against long-institutionalized patterns of authority. This deeply complicated efforts to redefine Kazakhs in class, rather than segmentary, terms.[71]

In fact, blackbone elites, defined in clan terms, still enjoyed paramount authority over most everyday political matters. Olcott argues that the members of this local elite

> emerged from the Civil War period with their authority enhanced. Ten years previously, on the eve of World War I, Kazakh intellectuals and even relatively uneducated youth had distrusted their elders because traditional society appeared unequal to the challenges presented by the colonial power. Now . . . most Kazakhs . . . saw the old clan system and the traditional leaders as offering at least the hope of stability through the continuation and strengthening of a subsistence-based, livestock-breeding economy. . . . Clan, village, and *aul* authorities simply reconstituted themselves as soviets and governed their populations much as before.[72]

Clan-based competition overshadowed any class-based competition during the elections for cadre replacement. Blackbone elites used informal institutions to galvanize support for their candidacies to local councils. Mobilizing dense networks often based on kin ties, elites offered "hospitality" to visiting Soviet officials, who, in turn, instructed locals for whom to vote.[73] Also common was the convening of secret meetings of the local elites to decide on various candidacies, as occurred among the Adai segment in western Kazakhstan in 1927.[74]

In certain cases where clans of approximately equal size occupied a given territory, elites developed informal compromises, divvying up posts *before* the elections.[75] On the whole, blackbone elites largely controlled who would become representatives to the local councils, making this more a process of selection than election. As the Kazakh Central Election Commission remarked in 1926, "The Kazakh clans war [*vrazhduiut*] among themselves on grounds of land tenure issues, the use of pastures, livestock breeding, etc. This clan enmity becomes especially acute during the electoral campaigns, when it becomes an all-absorbing struggle for power."[76] It is worth highlighting that most competition centered on local clan, rather than umbrella clan, divisions. Umbrella clans had no arena for political expression. They were too high-level for most cadre-selection decisions. As Kuchkin notes, "[T]he arena for segmentary enmity is the *volost*-level congress, where the interests of several clans (4–7) located on the territory of the *volost* collide."[77]

Soviet officials were not ignorant of the need to bolster the legitimacy of new Soviet institutions. Accordingly, authorities created the Koshchi Union in 1921 to Sovietize the Kazakh countryside through propaganda and education that would render segmentary links inoperative. It considered among its own tasks "to conduct a decisive battle against all forms and means of serf-like [*kabal'no-krepostnicheskaia*] dependence of the poor on the well-to-do [*imushchie*] elements, forms and means that are connected both with the manifestations of power and authority of the patriarchal-feudal leadership and with their legal capitalistic exploitation in the *aul, kishlak*, and village. . . ."[78]

In spite of this official mandate, clan elites managed to co-opt local cells of Koshchi, in part because Koshchi lacked the financial and human resources to be effective. "We have instances when the poor peasants [*bedniaki*] announce that they will not join the [Koshchi] union if the rich one does not join, since they are connected to him by kin bonds," lamented one official.[79] In the northern region of Qostanai, a local leader chided poor nomads for seeking to join

Koshchi without consulting him first. In another instance from the same region, an elder warned, "If you join the Koshchi Union, then do not count on my *qumys* [fermented mare's milk] in the summertime."[80]

Nor did periodic purges of Koshchi meet with intended success. In one example from the Shymkent *uezd*, almost 40 percent of the Koshchi members were removed and declared to be *bais* or their co-conspirators. In the end, however, Soviet officialdom found it difficult to identify who enjoyed real, informal local authority because most Kazakhs preferred to conceal their kin bonds — itself a form of silent resistance.[81]

Decrying the "insufficiency of purges of the Koshchi Union from the *bai-atqamner* (local political authority) element and the presence of clan influence in the primary cells in nomadic regions,"[82] officials attempted to purge this institution further, but the attempts *themselves* seem to have exacerbated interclan rivalries. For example, in the Aqtobe region in 1926 the reorganization of Koshchi caused the "inflammation of clan enmity."[83] Thus, if the intention of Soviet state-construction efforts was to provide an institutional order that would marginalize subethnic divisions as politically unimportant, in fact they made them more politically salient by increasing the stakes involved in competition.

Changing Land Tenure Patterns

Similar politicizing processes occurred with questions of land use. As described above, Russian colonial expansion deprived the steppe nomads of land for extensive pastoralism. Soviet rule politicized the question further. The Bolsheviks had built much of their popular support in the Slavic regions on promises to solve the land problem; doing so became a central priority of Soviet governance. Thus, whereas under the tsar, land-use issues had garnered attention only to secure caravan routes or prevent anticolonial uprisings, now they were at the center of the political map. Moreover, like other expanding states, the Soviet state viewed nomads and seminomads as inherently resistant to the state's control and administration of territory.

Soviet authorities were thus determined to address the land question, and their efforts gradually became more radical as Stalin consolidated his power. As with cadre replacement, initial efforts in this area served to stimulate interclan competition. Using the language of class warfare to describe such competition, Kuchkin claims, "The *bai* of one clan organized a battle against the *bai* of another clan that had more arable land, [a battle that was supposedly] for the portion of land in favor of the 'poor' clan, but [was] in actuality in favor of the *bai* himself."[84]

One report on land reform from 1926 showed how in the Qostanai region, the blackbone elite had "stood to defend not only their rights and privileges passed down to them from their fathers and great-grandfathers, but also used in their own interests the tensions [*talas*], group and kin-based disputes that had emerged in the *auls* on the grounds of elections and traditions, taking under their influence and exploiting not only the poor [nomads] and customs, but also the *aul* councils, the Koshchi Union and even the *volost* executive committee."[85]

This politicization of land finds imperfect reflection in the archival record. Some documents describe these disputes as being between specific *auls*. Since neighboring *auls* were often from different local clans, inter-*aul* disputes were often interclan. Thus, in 1920 the People's Commissariat on Land (of the Kyrgyz Autonomous Soviet Socialist Republic) documented a dispute in the Torghai region between a certain V. Kornebaev from the Aidapsal segment and a certain A. Dzhanbusov "and his relatives" over the "seizure and illegal use" of land.[86] In the Turkestan autonomous republic in 1924, a similar dispute erupted between the *auls* Kesh-Mulla and Sary-Aghach.[87] The rich record on land disputes becomes spotty by the mid-1920s, as an idiom of class warfare was carefully cultivated to replace the vocabulary of clan divisions. Land disputes continued to be recorded, but the actors of record changed. That is, claimants were no longer recorded as clans but rather as members of socioeconomic classes or ethnic groups.

Given the prominent role of Slavs in the Soviet administration and the ongoing influx of ordinary migrants from Russia, many of the disputes in the 1920s took on an interethnic coloration. Most of those disputes recorded by the People's Commissariat on Land were between Kazakhs and Russians, and most were likewise from the northern regions, where these groups competed most aggressively for land resources. One report claimed that such interethnic land conflicts "threatened to spill over as mass phenomena [*v massovyi kharakter*]."[88] Here, too, we might reasonably ask whether conflict tended to be interethnic or whether the disputants were more likely to use ethnic categories in their appeals to officialdom. Since ethnicity was already considered a legitimate way to organize social life while subethnicity was not, it is entirely possible that land disputes among Kazakh clans continued but the parties seldom approached Soviet officials to assist.

Among the pressures on land use was the immigration of an ethnic "other"—Russian settlers. In spite of several attempts at land reform, early Soviet efforts could not accommodate the needs of a multi-ethnic population. In some cases, land reform had the opposite effect of exacerbating long-standing problems. For example, Soviet authorities decried how the tsar had sanctioned the illegal seizing of Kazakh land by Russian settlers. But unauthorized settlers (*samovol'tsy*) continued such practices well into the 1920s, and this became the source of a number of ethnically marked disputes.[89]

At the root of this challenge was Moscow's reliance on its Slavic migrants for support in the region; it could not afford to abandon this population, even if doing so would stem the land crisis. The reasons given were rational-technical in nature: migration was considered to be needed, since vast portions of Central Asia lacked the skilled labor force necessary both for the construction of a Soviet economy and for the creation of a proletarian class.[90] Naturally, by encouraging migration, Moscow only exacerbated the land shortfall. Official priorities came into tension with one another. On the one hand were those—represented by the People's Commissariat on Land—who in apparent earnest sought to solve land disputes by addressing the demographic pressures on land use; and on the other hand were those—represented by the All-Union Resettlement Committee—who sought to rationalize governance and economic performance through the physical movement of people.[91] Through the 1920s, solving the land question was ultimately less important than maintaining Slavic support.

The essential tension between the traditional livelihood of nomads and the regime's state-building efforts continued to the end of the 1920s, when the regime abandoned its piecemeal efforts to address the land question. The route to reconciling the growing population with the perceived imperatives of socialist construction was now to be more radical: the full sedentarization of nomads. This would establish clear practices of land tenure based on state-enforced legal boundaries. It would further economize on land, since it would turn land use from extensive to intensive practices.[92] Moreover, it would deal a frontal blow to traditional authority patterns that were intimately intertwined with extensive pastoralism as a mode of economy. One official report on the sedentarization process issued in 1931 captured this logic, claiming, "In the conditions of Kazakhstan, one of the most important factors of social reconstruction of agriculture is sedentarization that liquidates nomadic life [*kochevoi byt*], the extensive, rapacious economic conduct, the whole backwardness and stagnation of social and economic life of the nomadic *aul* of the backward national republic. . . . [O]nly sedentarization guarantees the unfolding of *sovkhoz* [Soviet agriculture] construction and the development of large-scale heavy industry."[93]

These measures had tremendous human and economic consequences. Initially, resistance to collectivization was widespread and overt, with many Kazakhs preferring to slaughter their stock en masse rather than cede it to Soviet authorities; an estimated 75 percent of the Kazakh herd was lost.[94] Famine led to mass migration, with an estimated 15 to 20 percent of the population leaving the republic for western China, Turkey, Iran, as well as other parts of Soviet Central Asia. Dramatic migration within the Kazakh steppe also occurred; the search for grain and livestock shifted entire populations.[95]

By 1933, 95 percent of the population was both sedentarized and had become a part of collective farms; by contrast, in 1929 the number had stood at 7.4 percent.[96] Extensive pastoralism gave way to Soviet forms of pastoralism, which involved the erection of permanent structures, the seasonal use of more limited pasturelands, and the elimination of long-distance migration. From the Leninist perspective, the state had fundamentally changed material conditions for the former nomad, and manifestations of subethnic identities (including their political manifestations) were thus expected to disappear. Forced collectivization and sedentarization of nomads and seminomads did, indeed, end land disputes as an overt expression of subethnic politics, until the late Soviet period.[97]

Criminalizing Clans

A third aspect to Sovietization deserves attention. State-led change involved more than the attempts to eliminate traditional patterns of authority and economy—attempts that reached their radical apex in the early 1930s. It also involved the criminalization of behaviors connected with subethnic identity. Among practices identified as crimes were bride-price (*qalym*), the punitive raid on neighboring nomadic encampments, blood revenge (*qun*), polygamy, premature marriage, forced marriage, and levirate. Collectively called "everyday crimes" (*bytovye prestupleniia*), these were the vestiges of traditional practices that the regime sought to root out.

Table 2.1 summarizes official statistics on state prosecution of these crimes in early Soviet Kazakhstan. As the table illustrates, over the latter half of the 1920s, the regime prosecuted such practices with increasing zeal.[98] Both the total number of cases and the percentage of those that resulted in a conviction rose steadily over these years. The percentage of convictions that resulted in severe punishments (prison time or hard labor), however, remained relatively uniform, hovering near 80 percent.

Table 2.1
Prosecution of "Everyday Crimes" in Early Soviet Kazakhstan

Year	Total Cases	% Convicted	Severe Sentences, as % of Convictions
1924–5	670	17.6	77.1
1925–6	891	21.1	84.6
1926–7	1,573	36.1	79.2
1927–8	1,707	41.2	82.6

Source: Central State Archives of the Republic of Kazakhstan, f. 1380, o. 2, d. 242, l. 58.

Note: The data included in this table include the following crimes: bride-price, underage marriage, premature marriage, and polygamy. The percentage of severe sentences (prison time or hard labor) stands in contrast to cases that resulted in probation or other milder sentences.

But, while the regime displayed an increasing commitment to rooting out these manifestations of subethnic behavior, enforcement was a perennial problem. The pages of the newspaper *Engbeqshy-Qazaq* (The Kazakh Worker) carried many stories of those guilty of such everyday crimes being sheltered by the members of the *aul*.[99] Even if punishments remained severe on paper, some archival documents indicate that they were more laxly implemented in later years, suggesting that the process had been co-opted by local elites.[100]

Proactive efforts at positive change, as those to change social relationships by recruiting women into Soviet structures, such as *oblast* courts, ran up against local resistance.[101] As in Uzbekistan, where Muslim women who removed the veil in the 1920s were subject to public humiliation,[102] Soviet efforts to criminalize traditional practices encountered long-standing patterns of behavior. There is a bit of truth in what Olcott suggests: "Laws against customary practices were simply not enforced, since the Kazakh officials themselves observed them."[103] Indeed, these practices continued well past collectivization, if in altered form.[104]

The criminalization of these behaviors did not have the intended effect, but the consequences of state policies should not be reduced to the intentions of state actors. However insufficient from the regime's perspective, this criminalization was vitally important to what clan identities would become. Chapter 3 details how the proscription on certain clan-related behaviors was related to a larger modernization project that lent these identities a public stigma.

NOMADIC PASTORALISM AND ITS IMPRINT

This chapter has detailed the close relationship between the clan system and the political economy of nomadic pastoralism. Nomadic pastoralism was the mechanism that sustained identity relations, dictating a particular relationship between social organization and land. Moreover, these traditional patterns of authority and social organization persisted through the 1920s, if in newly politicized form.

As a mechanism of identity reproduction, nomadic pastoralism left an imprint on the identity dynamic. Specifically, because nomadism fostered a particular relationship to land, it created group boundaries that coalesced around the predictability of seasonal migration. Thus, in the pre-Soviet and early Soviet periods, clan politics was a politics of clearly demarcated, nested group boundaries. Group interest, group obligations, and group resentments were central to the way that it operated. This stands in contrast to the political dynamic of clans in the post-Soviet period, as chapters 5 and 6 detail. By the 1990s, clan politics was no longer about relatively coherent groups that made demands on everyday behavior and political expression; rather, it was about flexible kin-based networks that were a resource for individuals in their political and economic affairs.

How this occurred is the story of chapter 3.

3

Two Faces of Soviet Power

Far more than in the premodern era, states have gone beyond
defense of the realm to offer a large chunk of the *strategies of
survival* that people construct for themselves. — *Joel Migdal*

Illnesses pass, but habits remain. — *Kazakh proverb*

A MONG THE CRITICAL IRONIES OF SOVIET RULE WAS THAT A
modernization project designed in part to eradicate clan divisions helped
to contribute to their ongoing importance. As we will see, by creating
a political economy based on endemic shortages, the Soviet state generally promoted tight-knit access networks—whether in Estonia or
Moldova or Russia. In Central Asia and the Caucasus, it particularly
promoted subethnic access networks by tapping the concealability of
clan divisions (introduced in chapter 1). What had previously sustained
clan-identity relations—nomadic pastoralism—was now gone, but in
the Soviet period, state-generated shortage performed a similar function. In replacing pastoralism, this political economy left a profound
imprint on how clan relationships were instantiated and how clan politics operated.

Soviet rule deeply transformed subethnic affiliations in Central
Asia. On the face of it, this point is as obvious as Soviet institutions
were coercive, but it bears emphasizing. The collapse of state socialism did not impel a wholesale return to pre-Soviet political or social
institutions; the Soviet collapse did not erase the Soviet experience.
To the contrary, state socialism left a deep mark on Central Asia in
ways that were only starting to become clear a decade after its conclusion.[1] This chapter shows that while Soviet authorities may have
preferred to eliminate clan identities, Soviet modernization repro-

duced them, in altered form. In this particular sense, clan divisions are resonant in post-Soviet Kazakhstan not *in spite of* the Soviet project, but rather *because of* the particular ways in which it was executed.[2]

Given the social transformations of the Soviet period, should we draw a terminological distinction between pre-Soviet and post-Soviet subethnic identities? This is a question worth considering. The philosophers ask, "When does a red sock continually darned with green yarn become a green sock?" For research on group identities with its emphasis on subjective self-definitions, the issue lies centrally with how the sock-wearer views the item in question. Were he to acquire a red sock and keep it (repairing it periodically with green yarn) over the years, it would likely remain *the* "red sock" in his imagination, a high percentage of green yarn notwithstanding. An outsider might disagree, measuring carefully the green surface area against the red surface area, but for the sock-wearer, the threshold to reimagine it as fundamentally different (as having become green) is much higher.

Likewise with group identities: most members imagine groups as substantively continuous, as exhibiting a core sameness across time and space—notwithstanding changes that they might identify. The use of the term "clan" to describe subethnic identities before and after Soviet rule is thus not merely a step taken for analytic convenience; it represents the subjectively imagined continuity of groupness over time.

To reiterate: the argument is not that clans—substantively unchanged from the pre-Soviet era—survived Soviet rule to manifest themselves in political and social life in the post-Soviet period. Nor is the argument that Soviet rule created clans (unless one defines "clan" as simply a tight-knit network that is not necessarily based on claims of kinship). Rather, because of Soviet rule, clans—imagined as substantively continuous—persisted in particular social niches into the post-Soviet years. Their function and meaning had been altered in particular ways by state socialism.

TOWARD THE ERADICATION OF CLAN AUTHORITY?

The efforts of states to transform subject populations lie at the heart of the modern condition. Demonstrating the "ecumenical character of high-modernist faiths," Scott shows that attempts at human engineering were most destructive in the former socialist bloc, but these cases were in no sense unique. Across the globe, radical schemes designed to "improve the human condition" by reconstructing social and political interactions have multiplied and resoundingly failed.[3] The Soviet state's extraordinary penetration into civil society is an extreme value on a more general trend.

This penetration into society had enormous consequences for clan relationships. First, the regime deliberately targeted kin-based divisions for eradication, as chapter two introduced. The intention was to eliminate traditional authority patterns and undermine the bases for behavior considered to be anti-Soviet, thereby facilitating the construction of the new social order. Second, many general practices of socioeconomic transformation could have been expected to diminish the importance of clan divisions. Among these were state policies that promoted urbanization, universal literacy and education—in short, a project of modernization. This modernization project, combined with a more general climate of terror and oppression that atomized the population, did notably diminish the role that clan relationships played under Soviet rule in public.

Coercion, modernization, and anti-clan campaigns removed clan identity from the public sphere. A leading Western scholar of Kazakhstan claimed in 1981 that "Kazakh clan identification is of no more than symbolic importance."[4] This was clearly the intention of Soviet policy makers vis-à-vis traditional authority in Central Asia, and it underscores that important transformations had occurred. I will suggest, however, that it does not do justice to the empirical picture. We should not conflate the lack of a public presence with the lack of importance. Too many forces moved in the opposite direction, reinforcing the import of clan divisions even as their role shifted out of the public domain.

There are a number of reasons why one might have expected Soviet rule to undermine traditional forms of authority and social bonds. Here, I have in mind the use of terror to atomize the population, the deep penetration of the Soviet state into society, and enormous demographic transformations. Arendt, focusing on the role of the purge, highlights the consequences of terror:

> In order to destroy all social and family ties, the purges are conducted in such a way as to threaten with the same fate the defendant and all his ordinary relations, from mere acquaintances up to his closest friends

and relatives. The consequence of the simple and ingenious device of "guilt by association" is that as soon as a man is accused, his former friends are transformed immediately into his bitterest enemies. . . . It has been through the development of this devise to its farthest and most fantastic extremes that Bolshevik rulers have succeeded in creating an atomized and individualized society the like of which we have never seen before and which events or catastrophes alone would hardly have brought.[5]

Even if one modifies Arendt's perspective to recognize horizontal surveillance by peers, the curious thing is that social bonds did not tear under the pressure as often as one might expect. Why? Did ordinary people encounter enormous pressure to sever their social and familial bonds, as Arendt theorizes; or, did they come into contact with a different face of the state? The reality of Soviet-era life was much more mundane than Arendt depicts. Even this state could not rule by terror alone.

Terror and the purge, however central to the Western image of the USSR, did not exhaust the tools of Soviet statehood. Among its additional tools was a heavy reliance on local and regional administration. Like the prefects in the French republics, regional administrators were given significant leeway to execute directives from the center as they saw fit.[6] The result was the entrenchment of existing patterns of authority, not their replacement with an undifferentiated mass of atomized individuals. A particularly common practice was forcible resettlement, a sort of "demographic engineering."[7] Indeed, in the 1920s, Moscow relocated the Kazakh population, en masse, both within Central Asia and beyond. Detached from their ancestral lands, many Kazakhs lost ties to their extended-kin communities and were forced to resettle in unfamiliar territory.

Policies of deportation and relocation were important, but their impact on kin ties should not be assumed. There are indications that population movements occurred in large groups; that is, large numbers of kin-related individuals found themselves forcibly resettled to new locations.[8] Second, ethnic Kazakhs remained disproportionately rural. They therefore generally stayed put in a given locale once the tumults of Stalinism were over. In fact, urban migration was more limited by the Soviet state than one might expect—a point sorely neglected in most accounts.[9]

Urbanization—along with education and economic development—was part and parcel of the Soviet modernization project. This project could be expected, all else equal, to diminish the importance of kinship. Literacy, the logic goes, produces social mobility by qualified individuals for increasingly specialized work. It severs traditional ties to place and kin by generating new social opportunities and relationships that edge kinship from the social scene. Education, especially exosocialization that physically removes individuals from tradition-bound locales, accelerates this process dramatically. Urbanization finally strains familial bonds and reduces the density of contact within kin. As a result, clan relationships suffer.

Although the outcome was not what modernization theorists would expect, these processes were operative under Soviet rule. Literacy became almost universal. Education levels rose dramatically, as Kazakhstan's levels approximated those for the USSR (table 3.1).

Table 3.1
Percent Population (over age 10)
with Higher or Secondary Education

	1959	1970	1979
Kazakhstan	34.7	46.8	63.3
USSR, total	35.4	45.8	63.9

Source: O. K. Makarova, M. P. Zhdanova, and E. A. Timofeeva, *Chislennost' i sostav naseleniia SSSR po dannym vsesoiuznoi perepisi naseleniia 1979 goda* (Moscow: Finansy i statistika, 1984), 30–31.

Note: There exist more recent data from the 1989 census concerning education levels, but the data are not comparable with that of earlier years because the former calculate percentages from age 15. See Gosudarstvennyi komitet SSSR po statistike, *Uroven' obrazovaniia naseleniia SSSR: po dannym vsesoiuznoi perepisi naseleniia 1989 g.* (Moscow: Finansy i statistika, 1990), 8.

Aggregate data on Kazakhstan do not speak directly to education levels among ethnic Kazakhs in particular. We have some data broken down by ethnic categories across the USSR. Table 3.2 shows that education levels for ethnic Kazakh specialists were the highest among Central Asian groups, although slightly lower than those for ethnic Russians. If education, *ceteris paribus*, undermines kinship, then Kazakh clans in particular should have been dealt a serious blow under Soviet rule.

Table 3.2

Specialists with Higher and Secondary Education
per 1,000 Population

	1959	*1970*	*change, 1959–1970*
Russians	72.8	134.9	62.1
Kazakhs	41.5	94.0	52.5
Kyrgyz	38.5	84.0	45.5
Uzbeks	30.3	75.7	45.4
Turkmen	39.8	79.9	40.1
Tajiks	32.7	67.5	34.8

Source: Robert A. Lewis, Richard H. Rowland, and Ralph C. Clem, *Nationality and Population Change in Russia and the USSR: An Evaluation of Census Data, 1897–1970* (New York: Praeger, 1976), 337.

Note: Data are restricted to the population aged 16 to 59. The authors indicate on page 336 that the "specialist" category is "composed mainly of technicians, agronomists, and the like."

Urbanization is a more complicated issue; while urban areas grew dramatically across Central Asia, titular Central Asians remained largely rural, and ethnic Slavs formed the bulk of the region's urban residents. From the aggregate data, the decline of rural population is clear (table 3.3). The more complete (although still aggregate) data available only for Kazakhstan present an even more dramatic change in that republic, from 93 percent rural in 1920 to 43 percent rural in 1989 (table 3.4).

Again, the territory-based data do not tell us about ethnic groups residing in that territory. Using ethnic categories, dramatic urbanization occurred for Kazakhs across the USSR, most of which occurred in the period from 1926 to 1959 (table 3.5). Thus, although more Kazakhs lived in rural than in urban areas, painting a more moderate picture of Kazakh urban migration, the process of urbanization in Kazakhstan, and the other Muslim areas of the USSR, was nonetheless dramatic.[10] Indeed, Soviet authorities, fearing that migration processes might prove ungovernable, limited the flow of migrants to the cities of Central Asia.[11] In any case, rural overpopulation was less the story of Kazakhstan, which, in contrast to the other Central Asian republics that relied heavily on manual labor in cotton fields, came to enjoy largely mechanized agriculture.

Table 3.3

Percent Rural Population by Republic

	1939	1959	1970	1979
Kazakhstan	72	56	50	46
Uzbekistan	77	66	63	58
Tajikistan	83	67	63	65
Kyrgyzstan	81	66	63	61
Turkmenistan	67	54	52	52
USSR, total	68	52	44	38

Source: O. K. Makarova, M. P. Zhdanova, and E. A. Timofeeva, *Chislennost' i sostav naseleniia SSSR po dannym vsesoiuznoi perepisi naseleniia 1979 goda* (Moscow: Finansy i statistika, 1984), 9.

Table 3.4

Percent Rural Population in Kazakhstan

1913	1920	1926	1939	1959	1970	1979	1989
90	93	91	72	56	49	46	43

Source: Gosudarstvennyi komitet Kazakhskoi SSR po statistike, *Narodnoe khoziaistvo Kazakhstana za 70 let: statisticheskii sbornik* (Alma-Ata: Izdatel'stvo "Kazakhstan," 1990), 9.

Table 3.5

Percent Urban Population by Ethnic Category

	1926	1959	1970	1979
Kazakhs	2.1	24.3	26.3	30.9
Russians	22.1	59.0	69.1	73.9
Total	8.3	43.8	50.3	53.5

Source: M. Kh. Asylbekov and A. B. Galiev, *Sotsial'no-demograficheskie protsessy v Kazakhstane (1917–1980)* (Alma-Ata: Ghylym, 1991), 137.

As with education and urbanization, other measures of economic and social development paint a clear picture: Kazakhstan was dramatically transformed under seventy years of Soviet rule. Healthcare provision became almost universal. If in 1920 there were 0.8 physicians per 10,000 people, by 1989 there were 41.0.[12] Even if we are wise not to put too much stock in Soviet economic data, growth rates for industrial production rose exponentially during the Soviet period.[13]

Dramatic pressures for socioeconomic change aside, we do not see from the above indicators any effect that they might have had on clan identities. Even in the midst of Soviet modernization practices—long after collectivization and sedentarization had been executed to ensure fealty to the Soviet party-state—subethnic networks were evident in patterns of political patronage. Kuchkin quotes the First Secretary of the republican Party Central Committee of Kazakhstan from a 1947 article, who reported,

> We have cases of the selection of workers by their kin and familial marker, which leads to the obstruction of the party and state apparatus with random and alien people, creates an atmosphere of nepotism [*semeistvennost'*] and groupism [*gruppovshchina*], slows the growth and education of Bolshevik cadres from the local population . . . [For example,] the First Secretary of the Karynkol Party district committee of Alma-Ata region Beisembaev puts in leadership positions people close to him who are from the same Alban clan as he, without consideration of their political or business qualities. Nine workers from the Alban clan were chosen for the apparatus of the party district committee (*raikom*).[14]

The reason, I suggest, is that key processes moved in precisely the opposite direction, reinforcing the importance of clan ties as a resource for ordinary people.

PRIVATIZING CLAN DIVISIONS

Moscow took two complementary steps that promoted subethnicity. First, it removed kinship from the public domain. Second, it lent clans import in private spheres. I take each step in turn.

Nationalities Policy and Cultural Modernization

Soviet nationalities policy—an evolving set of state actions vis-à-vis cultural minorities—served to remove clan divisions from public life, relegating them to private spheres. This occurred principally through deliberate state-led campaigns to root out manifestations of clan relationships.

On its face, Soviet nationalities policy was a creative policy designed first to accommodate preexisting cultural divisions, in order to transform them into something qualitatively new.[15] Early policy involved attempts at the republican level to consolidate "national" communities from preexisting cultural divisions. As a drive for modernization, Soviet policy was like other such nation-building efforts, except in one critical respect: it attempted to consolidate national communities at a level that was *not* coterminous with the territorial frontiers of the state. Thus, early efforts involved what Martin terms "affirmative action" policies to promote indigenous cadres and the broad use of republican languages—all within clearly demarcated administrative subunits.[16]

Once thus consolidated, the thinking went, these communities would in turn become part of a larger community represented not by ethnocultural frontiers, but by the new *Homo sovieticus*. Martin captures this awkward logic: "[T]he Communist Party assumed leadership over the usual process of national formation, and took positive action to construct Soviet international nations (nations in form not content) that would be content to be part of a unitary Soviet state."[17] Thus, Moscow institutionalized ethnoterritorial administration as part of a project of positive cultural transformation. The central notion was that by accommodating ethnic "needs," "the Soviet state had not only facilitated the achievement of stateness, but in many cases the consolidation of nationhood as well."[18]

Such practices inscribed ethnicity as a central principle of daily social and political life in the Soviet period.[19] As the Soviet experiment deepened, even in areas such as Central Asia, where ethnic distinctions had previously carried far less meaning than did other divisions, the outcome was to make ethnicity the vehicle for political competition and agendas. Many practices that at first blush de-emphasized ethnicity often had the opposite effect. Soviet internationalism came to involve a significant degree of linguistic, cultural, and demographic Russification. *Homo sovieticus* only *seemed* to be unmarked ethnically; in fact, Sovietization brought a significant degree of assimilation to the dominant Russian patterns.[20] In Kazakhstan in particular, a massive influx of Russians and a decimation of the Kazakh population rendered Kazakhs a minority in their "own" republic, at 39 percent of the population in 1989. Kazakhs who sought professional advancement gained their literacy and education through

Russian, which dominated all aspects of public life. This internationalism had a distinctively ethnic Russian face.

The Destructive Side of Modernization

Moscow thus promoted ethnic categories, elevating them as the legitimate vehicle for group identity. But Soviet policies of cultural modernization were Janus-faced. On the one hand, they involved the positive transformation of peoples into something new—something ethnic and, eventually, "international." On the other, they involved attempts to move peoples away from tradition. While the creative side of this policy privileged ethnicity, its destructive side set out to eliminate subethnic divisions.

A central teleology remained constant in the cultural modernization project, notwithstanding debates about specifics: populations were understood to advance along clearly demarcated historico-evolutionary stages, prodded along by various forces for social integration that consolidated identities at ever-higher taxonomic levels.[21] Deemed ill suited to the objective of socialist construction, identity groups that were "earlier" in their development were considered "culturally backward."[22] Marx-inspired in its particulars, this teleology also informed the efforts of European colonial powers to administer the populations of sub-Saharan Africa.[23]

Branded as primitive, the nomads and seminomads in Soviet territory were viewed as little different from sedentary groups.[24] Instead, beginning with a central normative and taxonomic principle—that class stratification propelled historico-evolutionary stages—the emerging regime classified such societies as a variation on the theme of feudalism.[25] From this perspective, clan identities that persisted into the period of socialist construction were considered the vestiges (*perezhitki*) of feudalism. The implication was clear: nomads and seminomads were subject to the same laws of historical development (and, what is more important, to the same rules of Soviet governance) as their sedentary counterparts.

Given backwardness, some populations had further to travel en route to socialist construction than others. Those so designated had to pass several stages of development in short order. As one official remarked about indigenous groups (*malye narody*) in Siberia at a 1931 meeting of the All-Union Central Executive Committee, the national republics saw "the creation of new nationalities out of tribes which had earlier never dreamed of national existence . . . [and] their transition in just six years through all the stages of development, which for other peoples required thousands of years."[26] The chairman of Kazakhstan's Sovnarkom wrote in 1937 that "the Kazakh people had evolved from backward and feudal tribes into a socialist nation and a socialist national state."[27] By 1967, one Kazakh scholar would claim that

> the Kazakh people [narod] achieved enormous successes in all spheres of life: in the shortest historical time-span, it liquidated its former economic and cultural backwardness, created modern industry [and] socialist high-mechanized agriculture, put into practice a cultural revolution, lifting itself from the middle ages to the heights of modern progress. Now the toilers of the Kazakh aul, in the great family of peoples of the Soviet Union, are constructing the bright building [sic] of communism."[28]

The modernization project discursively targeted clans. Every reference to them underscored their anachronistic nature, implying that it was merely a matter of time before the new state would eliminate the material bases for, and therefore any expression of, these subethnic behaviors. As if to underscore clans' incompatibility with Soviet institutions, many practices deemed ill-suited to the new order—even if their connection to the old one was tenuous—were considered vestiges of the past. Misdemeanor crimes as unspecific to the old order as theft, domestic abuse, or drunkenness, for example, were thus distanced from the new, socialist ones as anachronistic.[29]

By depicting kin-related practices as obsolescent and confined to generations that were literally passing away, the regime explained their persistence in ways that were consistent with socialist construction.[30] Officially, these were practices that were fated to disappear as the material conditions for their perpetuation changed, although it was not clear when this would occur. As one scholar put it several years after Stalin's death, "These and other phenomena that are alien to communist ideology have disappeared, or are almost disappearing. Only their vestiges remain, which are doomed to a final ruin in the nearest future."[31]

This prosecution of "everyday crimes" remained a centerpiece of the state's transformative agenda throughout the Soviet period. The bride-price, for example, earned the designation "socially dangerous" in the criminal codes of the Russian Soviet Federated Socialist Republic (RSFSR), Turkmenistan, Tajikistan, Kyrgyzstan, Georgia, and Armenia.[32] Ethnographic expeditions dispatched by the Academy of Sciences to Central Asia and the Caucasus focused specifically on these everyday crimes. Motivated in part by the imperative to root them out, they found many such practices. Many more may have been missed, as the practices often assumed covert forms that were less likely to be detected, let alone prosecuted.[33]

If the effort to prosecute was constant, its character changed after Stalin. As state strategy shifted from "terror plus ideology" to a greater emphasis on ideology and propaganda efforts in the post-Stalin years, some Soviet policy makers began to advocate cultural initiatives to combat subethnic behaviors.[34] As one Kyrgyz scholar emphasized, since the "objective" material bases for these behaviors had disappeared with the demise of nomadic pastoralism, any vestige thereof had to be "ideological."[35] And ideological ills demanded educational remedies: "[T]he carriers of vestiges of the past in general are not anti-socialist elements, but ordinary toilers, who, by virtue of an insufficient level of consciousness, become the custodians of vestiges. These people can be freed of vestiges only by way of education and re-education with the help of the means of Soviet culture."[36]

The public stigma that clan behaviors entailed was profound. Authors and scholars faced a difficult reception when their works touched on subethnic divisions. State censors would only allow publication on themes of subethnicity that either depicted these divisions as disappearing from the new socialist order, or treated them historically.

But even the historical treatment of these divisions entailed risks. Ilias Esenberlin's historical novels, beginning with *Khan Kene* in 1970, faced publication delays and the watchful eyes of censors; their publication generated a strong reaction in the republican press. He was accused of having "abandoned the real principles of literature, and giving birth to protection[ism], familial ties, localism, and clannishness [*rushyldyq*]."[37] By recounting the role of kinship groups in certain historical developments, the author had—as far as officialdom was concerned—implied the superiority of those groups over others. The mere mention of clan divisions among Kazakhs, even in their historical contexts, entailed risks. His work was "dangerous" and "yearned for the past."[38] It thus generated polemical public responses on the pages of the official newspapers such as *Sotsialistik Qazaqs-tan*. His work received the positive recognition that many felt it deserved only in the post-Soviet period.[39]

The stigma held for the work of historians and other academics as well. One prominent ethnographer, who wrote a book categorizing subethnic divisions of the Middle Umbrella Clan, described in an interview how his work was viewed as a form of "national deviation."[40] Critics contended that it heightened ethnonational sentiment.[41] Such a perspective had vitality; one such critic continued to view kinship divisions as dangerous well into the 1990s.[42]

This public stigma had consequences. If in the pre-Soviet era, subethnic difference had been established through the dense exchange of genealogical knowledge (recall from chapter 1 that Kazakhs held knowledge of at least seven generations of common ancestry as axiomatic), now such information was not exchanged publicly. In the absence of obvious visible markers that provided subethnic differentiation, place of residence began to play a more important role. In fact, especially for rural Kazakhs, the name of the collective farm on which one resided became an indicator of subethnic background. In this sense, collective-farm (*kolkhoz*) identity was not a novel identification, as one Soviet ethnographer implies: "In the contemporary *aul* the division of Kazakhs into clans and tribes has also disappeared. Their union into collective farms—*kolkhozes* created by the territorial marker . . . facilitated this. Upon meeting, Kazakh farmers ask now, not to which clan does one or another person belong, but from what *kolkhoz* is he: the consciousness of clan belonging has been replaced now by a consciousness of belonging to a productive collective."[43]

Collective farm identity was often not separable from subethnic belonging. Frequently, the *kolkhoz* itself contained the members of only one or very few clans. *Kolkhoz* was a marker that literally coincided with subethnic divisions.[44] The Korbe expedition report concluded that

in 1949 the collective farms that we visited [in southeastern Kazakhstan] consisted basically of the members of one ruu [*ru*, clan] with the exception of those sent by *raion* organizations or occupying paid positions (bookkeepers, accountants, drivers, carpenters, etc.). So, the population of the "Stalin" *kolkhoz* belongs to the Taz subdivision of the Alban clan, that of "Bel'basar" *kolkhoz* belongs to the Akhsha subdivision of the Dulat clan, that of "Engbekshy" and "Aral" *kolkhozes* which neighbor "Bel'basar" belong to the Khozhai subdivision of the same clan, that of the "Yntaly," "Zhanga Tyrmys," and "Tel'man" *kolkhozes* belong to the Shymyr subdivision.[45]

With the traditional means of establishing subethnic difference thus disrupted, *kolkhoz* residence was the only possible public marker of identity and difference. In private, however, the lines of clan identity and difference continued to pervade everyday life—in large part because of the critical advantages that they offered in navigating the Soviet political economy. In short, the net consequence of the Soviet project of cultural modernization was not to eliminate clans, but rather to critically diminish their public expression.

Shortage and Subethnicity:
Really-Existing Socialism for Ordinary People

Clan identities were driven from legitimate public space, but it was not inevitable that they would remain important in private affairs. Ultimately, they became salient outside of the public domain because the Soviet command system made it advantageous to employ them. The regime had undermined nomadic pastoralism, had conducted coercive practices that disrupted traditional social relations, and had embarked on ambitious projects of socioeconomic and cultural modernization. But it gave other, different impetus to subethnic clan relationships.

The idea that Soviet practices produced unintended outcomes is becoming clearer more than a decade after the Soviet collapse. We have noted that policies designed to contain, and eventually to eliminate, ethnic identifications willy-nilly encouraged expressions thereof. This much is now evident, even from a bird's-eye view.[46] A closer, ethnographic look at state socialism shows an important role for the shortages that plagued the system. Shortages fueled outbidding by ethnonationalist actors eager to rise to prominence, as Verdery has illustrated for the Romanian case.[47]

In Central Asia, the consequences of the shortage political economy were similarly unintended. The architects of central planning were not concerned with clans per se. Their main goal was to reach the pinnacle of economic modernism: to ensure the rational allocation and use of human and material resources, striving to perfect economic relationships by ensuring fairness for individual actors and unprecedented efficiency for the system as a whole.

The result—we now know—was quite different. In contrast to demand-driven systems, the state socialist political economy was particularly susceptible to supply fluctuations. Facing little in the way of a profit motive, producers were understandably preoccupied with lowering their costs by securing cheaper inputs; the quality of their outputs declined. Gaining access to these cheaper inputs became a central mode of operation.[48]

For their part, consumers, faced with the inferior quality and poor availability of goods, encountered escalating costs in the form of lengthy queues. They either chose to wait for goods to be provided through official channels or developed informal strategies to procure them. Thus, a gray market economy based on circumventing formal mechanisms emerged to shadow the official one and became all-pervasive under state socialism.[49] All along the chain of production, goods were scarce, giving rise to alternative means of acquisition. This second economy became especially institutionalized and routine in the 1960s through the 1980s, but historians have noted its operation even under the tumults of Stalinism.[50] Nor were these processes limited to economic goods; they touched on political goods (information, access to power) as well.

The networks under state socialism were unusual in scope, not in kind. Such networks play a role in all political economies, even laissez-faire ones, although the myth of the free market is that it involves individuals with full information and full access to all possible goods making choices that put pressures on prices and supplies. Real-world transactions rarely work this way. As Granovetter famously points out, networks of individuals are in one way or another necessary to any large-scale political economy.[51] Even producers in today's electronic commerce, who may enjoy a manyfold reduction in information deficits and access problems, bundle goods and services together in ways that belie the mythical functioning of a "free market."

Nonetheless, in the socialist political economy, access networks multiplied. Networks that in Russian are called *blat* and in Mandarin *guanxi* are examples of the same phenomenon—alternative means of access to scarce goods.[52] As Kornai models, the mechanisms for gaining access to goods through official channels were often inefficient and slow moving;[53] an urban resident could buy an apartment as authorized, but this might take years to accomplish. Alternatively, ties to those with privileged access to power, goods, or services could supply such goods in much shorter order.[54] The reciprocal granting of favors resulted in the proliferation of such networks of access.

Some of these modes of access were based on ties created during the Soviet period; others were based on pre-Soviet social relationships. Professional or educational background, ethnic affiliation, and ideological predisposition all could animate networks. Ledeneva illustrates the myriad ways in which such networks operated in the Russian context, where the word *blat* became a catch-all term.[55] Thus, even in those republics where kinship structures had not previously existed, the command economy produced access networks, what some mistakenly refer to as "clans." In the ex-Soviet south, where preexisting kin-identity divisions provided a ready cultural connection, the result was to shore up subethnic networks of access. In Central Asia and the Caucasus, networks coalesced around genuine kin connections, since subethnic background was considered axiomatic. Thus, across a vast region, the command political economy promoted access networks of many sorts, but it especially served to perpetuate preexisting subethnic ties.

In in-depth interviews from the late 1990s through 2002, ordinary Kazakhs who had been adults during the Soviet period found nothing extraordinary about using kin connections to secure access to economic, social, or political goods. Housing, healthcare, or consumer durables were the usual targets of their efforts, but some used their connections to gain some influence over local political decisions. Of course, the extent and depth of such networks were variables, not constants.[56] Some subethnic divisions were not preserved in this form, having instead been disrupted by terror, collectivization, famine, population movements, and other social cataclysms. But many such networks emerged as useful mechanisms by which individuals could survive the daily exigencies of state socialism. Figure 3.1 provides a model of how ordinary people were able to access goods through different networks.

The figure simplifies the choices that ordinary Soviet citizens faced. First, they could choose the formal sector (authorized channels, shopping in stores) or the informal sector (unofficial transactions, trading

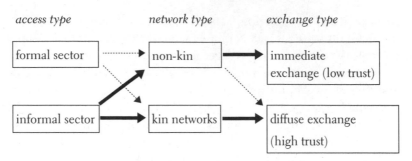

access type　　　　　network type　　　　　exchange type

Figure 3.1. Model of Options for Goods Procurement

goods through connections). While networks were never entirely absent even in the formal sector (suggested by the dotted lines), they were much stronger (suggested by the solid lines) in the informal sector. Networks were based on non-kin and/or kin-based connections. Either could provide access to goods. Kin-based networks, however, generated the high trust that allowed for diffuse exchange of goods, while many non-kin based networks required immediate exchange of goods (often, bribes), because they were not based on high levels of trust.

The model describes the everyday experiences of ordinary Kazakhs under state socialism. These patterns emerge from in-depth interviews for which ten interviewees were selected along a number of critical criteria. The average duration of these conversations was five to six hours. Because underground access networks are a sensitive topic, intensive interviewing was necessary to elicit internally valid responses. (See the appendix for details.)

All interviewees used access networks—some more frequently than others. As one woman reported, "If you do something good for someone, it will come back to you eventually." When she and her husband first moved to Kazakhstan from Soviet Russia, he received his position at a local prison not through normal job-allocation channels (Russian: *raspredelenie*), but rather "through an acquaintance" (*tanys arqyly*). In turn she, a nurse by profession, would return the favor by offering false documentation of a fictional medical diagnosis (*spravka*) that allowed the recipient to avoid service in the armed forces.[57]

Certain professions allowed the employee to navigate shortages with particular success. Accordingly, these jobs were considered more valuable than others. On collective and state farms, livestock experts (*zootekhnikter*) were responsible for overseeing the herd and could file official paperwork claiming that an animal had died a natural death, while in fact slaughtering it for private use. This accounting maneuver made the position particularly attractive. In a similar way, agronomists (*agronomdar*) were responsible for cultivation and informally set aside produce for private use. Mechanics enjoyed particularly good access to spare parts for tractors, combines, and other farm machinery, which was in perpetually short supply. They thus could generate additional income or acquire additional goods through barter.[58] Another respondent added to this list of valuable professions that of bookkeeper, since those who presented the formal accounting of enterprises to the authorities were prone to malfeasance.[59]

Those who worked in commerce, even as salespeople in small rural townships, also enjoyed a privileged position. They were the first to access hard-to-get goods that made it to the storefront, which they reserved either for personal use or for the granting of favors.[60] In a similar vein, an interviewee who had a career in education claimed that it made no sense to compare teachers with a warehouse manager (Russian: *zaveduiushchii sklada*), for the latter enjoyed excellent access to scarce goods.[61]

This mutual granting of favors was pervasive across the Soviet expanse; it often worked along kinship lines in Central Asia. Many interviewees explained their use of kin connections as something inherent to Kazakh hospitality.[62] "There was *Kazakhness* [*qazaqshylyq*] then," reminisced one respondent, contrasting the widespread granting of hospitality in the Soviet period to the lack thereof in the post-Soviet period. When she moved as a youngster from Russia, her relatives helped her family to resettle smoothly in Kazakhstan. The broad use of connections, bordering on nepotism (*sybailastyq*), is something that Kazakhs cannot avoid, she added. If someone from the kin group commits a crime, relatives do everything possible to free that person and set him or her straight.[63]

Mutual assistance among kin was what distinguished Kazakhs from other ethnic groups, especially Russians. Kazakhs "do not abandon their kin," the same respondent offered.[64] Even an interviewee who denied ever using kin connections (claiming instead that everyone in his extended family achieved success based on merit alone) admitted that it was a "habit" for Kazakhs to help each other during weddings, funerals, and the like. The sentiment was echoed by most other respondents.[65] One interviewee suggested that such mutual assistance was necessary only because, unlike native speakers of Russian, they did not enjoy significant social mobility because of weaker facility with the language. Kazakhs simply had to use their kin ties to get good jobs.[66] Another respondent lambasted a brother who had the wherewithal to help his kin but did not do so, saying that he was "like a Russian," and exhibited "Russian behavior."[67] An ethnically Russian interviewee offered a similar picture, characterizing Kazakhs' assistance to kin as "normal."[68]

Many critical goods—economic, social, or political—could be obtained through kinship. When children were sent away to study at institutes, they typically lived with distant relatives in the destination city. Even abundant cash sometimes could not make scarce goods become available; reliance on relatives was commonplace in such circumstances.[69] Using more distant clan connections, rather than close ties of extended family, also helped to avoid the appearance of nepotism—a prosecutable crime. In one case, an interviewee who categorically denied ever using kin ties in fact had his clanmates in the military committee (*voenkom*) get a job for one of his sons. Returning the favor years later, the interviewee held a position open for a relation of the clanmate in the school where the interviewee worked.[70] Such diffuse exchanges of favors characterized the moral economy of kinship relations.

Those who claimed early in interviews never to have used kin connections in fact had done so. Respondents were acutely aware that using clan networks was publicly frowned upon. Many were initially reticent to discuss the subject. Some romanticized Soviet governance as having provided such material plenty that no one *needed* to resort to kinship.[71] By the second or third hour of each interview, the respondents began to reveal kin connections that they had initially denied.[72] Typical was a teacher who insisted that he and his children relied only on their own merits and their own labor. Examples to the contrary eventually emerged: his younger cousin helped him to procure an apartment (a scarce commodity); relatives occasionally lent each other cash; and he used influence at the local school to secure work for acquaintances.[73] Another interviewee who claimed not to need kin assistance eventually admitted to benefiting deeply from relatives in the tax police, the internal affairs department, the local police, the local traffic police, institutions of higher education, and the like.[74]

With regard to higher education, kin relatives could provide anything from room, board, and study advice to direct connections to acquaintances on the admissions committees.[75]

One way to avoid public or state scrutiny with regard to clan connections was to rely on in-laws and their kin connections. Kazakhs traditionally elevated patrilineage as the central organizing principle of clan identity. Maternal background mattered relatively little in this regard. Naturally, this changed under the shortage economy, since maternal background was as useful for goods acquisition as paternal background was. Thus, one informant stressed how important in-laws were in making acquaintances (*quda zhek-zhat bolu*), who could prove useful in the future. Citing a Kazakh proverb traditionally used to describe the way a man chooses a wife, he infused it with instrumental content: "Choose the girl by looking at the mother" (*sheshesine qarap, qyz qylyp*).[76]

Clans were effective tools to navigate the shortages of state socialism, but most had lost touch with clans as a cultural phenomenon. Several interviewees made simple mistakes about the umbrella clan background of key historical figures. For example, one who recounted the umbrella clan background mistakenly claimed that Abai Qunanbai was from the same umbrella clan as Syrym *batyr*.[77] Another claimed that the Qypshaq subdivision was from the Younger Umbrella Clan, which is incorrect.[78] Few respondents used the corporate names of clans in the course of conversation; while they relied heavily on clan relations, they ceased to refer to them as collectivities. In one unusual case, a respondent referred to a relative by marriage as "the Qongyrat" (a prominent subdivision of the Middle Umbrella Clan)—an appellation used in lieu of the person's given name.[79] Another recounted in detail the history of her Zhangalbaily clan, from the Younger Umbrella Clan.[80] The remainder of respondents rarely used collective terms of reference.

What were the limits of the use of kin ties?[81] Cash could temper the salience of kin ties in everyday life. As one interviewee put it, "Those who have money forget their relatives and their enemies."[82] The logic was that money-based exchange allowed people to rely less on relatives and even engage on an equal footing with their (former) enemies. One interviewee was particularly forthright about his willingness to offer and receive side payments. He bribed an army official *not* to draft him in 1939 and offered a series of such payments to help his children with access to higher education. This need to offer bribes arose from the lack of personal connections.[83]

But the relationship between economic status and use of kin ties was a complicated one. Interviewees who were poor throughout the Soviet period often claimed not to have used kin connections.[84] One insisted that she could not get her daughter into an institute of higher education for lack of ties. On the other hand, this respondent admitted to being unusual in this regard, since she saw what she regarded as corruption and nepotism all around her.[85] One respondent from the Younger Umbrella Clan claimed that "Soviet power gave me nothing." Widowed early and the mother of ten children, she worked manual labor throughout much of her life and claimed that no kin ties helped her to overcome her difficulties. Her umbrella clan was ill-represented in the Shymkent region where she lived, her network of kin ties less extensive. But even she, when pressed, recounted an example of using kin networks when she described relying on a clan tie to get building materials for her rural home.[86] The geographic concentration of umbrella clans assisted people in using clan networks. Thus, a respondent who had grown up in Uzbekistan as a part of the Kazakh minority there professed never to have encountered "tribalism" (*traibalizm*) there, but when he moved to southern Kazakhstan (the native land of his ancestors), he encountered clan connections in full force.[87]

In a supply-driven economy without freed prices, money did not always win the day. An interviewee gave a bribe for his daughter's admission to an institute; she was denied entry, while the bribe was pocketed nevertheless.[88] Exactly the same thing occurred with another interviewee.[89] As chapter 7 illustrates, in the 1990s the introduction of a monetarized economy with largely free prices made money more valuable relative to kin connections.

The reciprocal granting of favors sometimes took on a locale-based, rather than kin-based, flavor. For example, one interviewee described the frequency of the practice of *asar*, in which the members of the community put aside time to offer their labor to other members of the community. The expectation of the helpers is that they will one day require such labor in return. This informal, rotating labor pool continued to operate in the 1990s.[90]

In some cases, kinship was circumscribed or overshadowed by other types of networks. For example, one interviewee who was a local union leader (a government post with considerable local authority) described in great depth the extent of his personal connections in the region. He claimed, with some plausibility, not to rely on kin; by virtue of his profession, he enjoyed the fruits of relationships with many non-kin as well. For him, it was the source of some pride that he could claim not to enjoy privileged insider relationships. His wife was even given an award (*mat'-geroina*) for having a large family that carried privileged access to consumer goods. Yet she did not avail herself of this privileged access. Because his above-ground, professional position accorded him a wide array of contacts, he did not need this additional benefit.[91]

Often, however, what at first glance appeared not to involve kin in fact involved them deeply. One informant described in great detail the members of his high-school class with whom he retained close ties over the decades. Upon further probing, it became clear that he remained closest to those with whom he was closest genealogically. Whether this was intended or not, he mapped kin relations onto his network of friends.[92] Along these lines, a case described above is particularly illustrative: the respondent had his clanmates in the military get a job for one of his sons in return for his holding open a position for a relation of that clanmate in the school where he worked. Both avoided the impression of nepotism by exercising favoritism not directly to relatives, but through an indirect exchange that only on its surface appeared to have nothing to do with kin relations.[93]

Ultimately, while non-kin networks were an alternative to kin-based ones, the former had a noteworthy disadvantage: they did not necessarily tap into the deep-seated trust that clan ties invoked. For this reason, transactions among non-kin were typically more immediate, more likely to be cash based, and more likely to be a tangible exchange than those involving kin (illustrated in figure 3.1). Transactions with non-kin involved a better chance of being deceived.

Non-Kazakh interviewees had a different perspective on the utility of kinship. The Russian community in southern Kazakhstan was relatively small, urban, professional, and they were the beneficiaries of many Soviet privileges. Moreover, their tradition of assisting kin was weaker than among Kazakhs.[94] As a result, the Russian respondent, who had moved to Kazakhstan from Leningrad (Russia) in 1973, detailed the frequent use of *blat* in the Soviet period:

In certain circles of the population, the word *blat* was used quite often. And some pronounced it with a sense of pride: "I got [it] through *blat*," or jokingly, or sometimes with a sense of envy: "He's got it good; he has *blat*." There was a saying of sorts that "*blat* is higher than the People's Committee [*narkom*]," since a person who had *blat* was considered all-powerful. *Blat* was necessary to get a better job and this did not mean a higher-paying one, but meant access to goods that were in deficit. Consultations with specialists, clothing, footwear—all of this was accessed through *blat*.[95]

All the same, she made clear the difference between Russian *blat* and Kazakh kin-based assistance:

Russian *blat* . . . pursued the goal of prestige, influence, and some sort of distinctiveness from other people. But the Kazakh [version] took root on the desire to have additional means, additional produce [*produkty*], because, as you know, the Kazakh family as a rule is large and therefore to have a little bit more was desirable. But they, of course, engaged in commerce [*pritorgovyvali*], since they did not have [a professional] specialization and lacked other options. So, they worked to supplement their income, procured produce, resold them at a higher price. They lived on this.[96]

Access to Political Goods

Access to economic goods is easier to document, but we know that kin networks pervaded the political sphere as well. With *glasnost'* and *perestroika*, close circles of patronage brought regular allegations of Central Asian "corruption," especially on the pages of Moscow newspapers.[97] An article in *Izvestiia* described "those clan and family ties that harmed south Kazakhstan's economy and produced fertile soil for the corruption of a great many people," and how "patronage was bestowed increasingly openly and brazenly. More and more people with family, or at least 'hometown,' ties gathered in the republic capital. And there was nothing the stringpullers would not do for their own people. They provided them with titles, distinctions, and jobs."[98] *Pravda* took a more didactic tone, instructing its readership that "relationships between friends or relatives must not be allowed to influence the work sphere . . . Strict action must be taken against those who use their official positions to promote unsuitable working people and protect them from just punishment."[99] An investigator sent by Moscow to examine abuses of power in Kazakhstan lamented that "if we took the path of instituting criminal proceedings against everyone involved in bribery, we could paralyze the work of a whole series of enterprises and organizations."[100]

These patterns reached the highest echelons of republican power. According to Nursultan Nazarbaev, the first president of independent Kazakhstan, "A narrow circle of those who had become close to the first person [Kunaev, First Party Secretary] settled practically all matters. . . . A person who was a part of the family of D. A. Kunaev could decide the fate of another person: give him a promotion or an award, fire him, or give him an apartment."[101] This pattern would replicate itself in the mid and late 1990s under Nazarbaev, as chapter four illustrates.

Were these ethnic networks, subethnic networks, or something else? Most analysts gloss the question, assimilating family and subethnic ties to higher-aggregate ethnic affiliations. They appear to assume that ethnicity was the most politically significant category in the Soviet period.[102] While there may be no analytic strategy that could adequately distinguish between subethnic and ethnic networks, especially decades after the fact, there is likewise no reason to assume that access networks were *solely* ethnic. To the contrary, as the patronage system became more entrenched after Stalin's death, both ethnic and subethnic identifications proved instrumental as means of access to scarce goods.

By way of illustration: under Kunaev a slow Kazakhification of positions of power, influence, and prominence in political and social life occurred. This was not solely ethnification. Kunaev himself makes clear that to be a Kazakh implies a subethnic belonging: "Each person should know his pedigree [*rodoslovnaia*] . . . [M]y predecessors were descended from Baidybek, a warrior [*djigit*] of the Elder Umbrella Clan. My closest genealogical tree looks as follows. . . ."[103] The selection of Kazakhs for positions of power and influence occurred along subethnic lines. He denies this fact, claiming that "it is sufficient to look at a list of officially selected [*nomenklatura*] workers to be convinced that not even the mention of a privileging [*vypiachivanie*] on the basis of national, let along kin-tribal, principle existed."[104] The public denial itself suggests a popular perception that clan patronage accompanied ethnic patronage.

THE FUNCTIONAL ADVANTAGES OF KINSHIP

To understand an identity, we must learn what types of support undergird its reproduction. Doing so not only helps to explain why identities persist (if they do), but also how the *character* of an identity division changes over time. The mechanism of identity reproduction leaves an imprint on the identity itself. The Soviet political economy of shortage reduced clan identity to its bare, functional advantages. Kinship connections were beneficial because they offered a ready cultural connection between access seekers and access providers, assisting those many ordinary individuals involved in the informal political economy.

As detailed in chapter 1, kin-based clans are based not on visible markers that distinguish members from non-members, but rather on genealogical knowledge. Networks based on kinship are easier to conceal because such knowledge need not be made publicly known; these divisions are easily privatized. Most other types of attachment, by contrast, involve visible markers of identity and difference. More specifically, kinship is an advantage in situations where:

1. Access networks are illegal. The Soviet state sometimes tolerated underground networks, but they were always subject to prosecution. Because clan identities are *concealable*, participants in networks can more easily avoid surveillance from the state and from peers;

2. Barter is preferred to cash payment. Barter exchanges benefit from a high degree of trust between participants because it is not always possible to exchange physical goods in one immediate transaction. Clan networks thrive on high degrees of trust;

3. Exchanges are delayed, not immediate. Given a stability of prices, personnel, and predictability of transactions (which were all hallmarks of the state socialist political economy), reciprocation was often diffuse. Again, clan networks thrive on the high degree of trust required for such diffuse transactions;

4. Exchanges are not of physical goods, but rather of information. As the state socialist political economy deepened from the 1960s through the 1980s, information about *how* to access key goods was almost as scarce as many of the goods themselves. Clan networks played the additional function of providing information.

These were the conditions under state socialism that made kinship advantageous as the basis for networks. They are present in all contexts by degree.

By stigmatizing and criminalizing kinship, the Soviet state *activated* these functional advantages; it reduced clan relationships to them.[105] No longer the comprehensive wellspring of social and cultural identity that it had been in the past, it now served a narrower purpose as an underground means through which Central Asians navigated everyday life. And, since its advantages centered on the issue of goods distribution, it had become a centrally *political* phenomenon. Who gets what, when, and how—these were questions that critically involved clan networks.[106]

The shift from paramount social identity to narrow political identity necessitates a changed analytic strategy for those studying late Soviet and post-Soviet clans. If clans could reasonably be understood as corporate bodies in the pre-Soviet steppe, Soviet rule reduced clan identity to its instrumental aspect. This becomes clear as we examine post-Soviet clan politics.

4

Continuity and Change
after the Soviet Collapse

For all practical purposes Leninism is extinct as a teleological project, but its leftovers continue to affect the post-Leninist political cultures. — *Vladimir Tismaneanu*

THE DOMINANT PARADIGM FOR STUDYING THE TRANSFORMATION of state socialist space in the 1990s came to be known, rather awkwardly, as "transitology." The approach was hopeful and optimistic about the prospects for "transitions" from state socialism to free markets and democratic institutions. Not surprisingly, transitologists harbored strong normative commitments about the need for positive change.[1] Some of the more nuanced analyses recognized that transitions would not everywhere proceed with the same speed and assume the same forms, but all transitologists focused on the ability of individual agents to create their own futures.

If voluntarism was in the wind, it was welcomed. Sovietological studies had assumed quite the contrary: that Soviet political culture was inherently undemocratic and that perversions of the market and of representative government were inherent to the region. Transitology gave the impression that anything was possible, and, indeed, in some contexts the unexpected did occur. Mongolia established viable democratic institutions, Russia succeeded in institutionalizing major democratic change, and even Kyrgyzstan from Central Asia flirted with democratic institutions (before it "backslid" in the late 1990s), managing macroeconomic reform that launched it into the World Trade Organization.[2]

Ever forward-looking in orientation, transitology had a tremendous blind spot. The legacies of Soviet rule and their significance in shaping political outcomes remained in shadow. The very language of transitions presumed end points and implied teleologies; it could not give adequate expression to these legacies. It was a language that betrayed the assumption that old practices were being left behind, perhaps slowly, as elites went about the business of constructing free markets and democratic institutions. Such old practices and their effects on transition deserved examination only to the limited extent that they hindered preferred outcomes. Transitology routinely shunted such legacies to the margins of analysis.

Normative preferences for markets and democratic politics aside, continuity is important to consider because it is a sociological fact. Like the former colonies of the African continent, the ex-Soviet republics replicated many of the institutional practices of the pre-independence political order. As Beissinger and Young put it, "the texture of contemporary stateness in African and Eurasia today embodies the colonial/imperial cloth from which the successor states were tailored."[3] Throughout the former USSR, political practice bore striking resemblance to previous forms of behavior; relationships among political actors were perpetuated through *habitus*, even after the original bases for the relationships evaporated.[4] In Central Asia in particular, modern institutions were, and continue to be, a creation of the Soviet era, as statehood itself was introduced to the region in the twentieth century.[5] Thus, state institutions were unlikely to assume something other than a Soviet cast.

As Soviet rule receded, some successor states—notably the Baltic countries of Latvia, Lithuania, and Estonia—engineered dramatic breaks with the political practice of their Soviet past. In those contexts more than others, ethnic nationalists had already during the Soviet period mobilized broad public support for radical reforms and, eventually, independence. Post-Soviet practices in those contexts never left the Soviet legacy entirely behind, but they moved further and faster than did their counterparts in the remainder of ex-Soviet space.[6]

Central Asia experienced the lowest degree of popular mobilization of any region as the Soviet state began to unravel.[7] Perhaps not surprisingly, the Soviet collapse brought not radical rupture to the states of the Central Asian region, but rather an unusual identity with past practices. Elite choices in the construction of political institutions were heavily saddled with institutional baggage from the Soviet period. Post-Soviet leaders were hardly able to make entirely free decisions.[8]

The passage of time allows us to locate a striking degree of continuity with the Soviet past. Such continuity is multifaceted and broad.[9] This chapter focuses attention on two aspects of continuity that have particular consequences for clan politics: the shortage economy and the stigmatization of clan that drives kin networks underground. Even had there been a radical rupture with the Soviet period, the ways in which clan identities informed politics might have had some staying power. Social and political practices do not change immediately in the wake of institutional reform; one might expect clan politics in the 1990s to bear the imprint of Soviet mechanisms that sustained clan identities. Be that as it may, there was no such radical rupture with the Soviet past, so clan politics in the 1990s exhibited a core likeness with what we witnessed in the Soviet period itself.

CONTINUITY IN NATIONALITIES POLICY

In the previous chapter, I argued that Soviet nationalities policy succeeded in driving kin identities out of the public sphere, deeply stigmatizing clan belonging. Notwithstanding the neglect of legacies in the literature on market and democratic transitions, this stigma continued in the post-Soviet period. Continuity was notable in several important senses: (1) ethnic categories were assumed to be the legitimate form of social organization and nationalities policy centered on harmonizing relations among ethnic groups; (2) supra-ethnic categories with questionable popular resonance were deployed in the attempt to harmonize interethnic relations; and (3) subethnic categories and practices were routinely stigmatized in public discourse.

Like its Soviet-era predecessor, the post-Soviet Kazakhstani state framed debates about cultural pluralism around the interrelations among ethnic groups, or "nationalities." Westerners seized these categories, depicting post-Soviet states as "ethnocratic," or "nationalizing states."[10] Indeed, the patterns were clear. Elites routinely justified an array of practices as stability enhancing, including efforts to shape patterns of language use in favor of dominant cultural groups, to rewrite histories to emphasize cultural roots, to alter demographic balances to redress for Soviet-era migration, and to promote ethnic cadres.[11] They involved:

claims made in the name of a "core nation" or nationality, defined in ethnocultural terms, and sharply distinguished from the citizenry as a whole. The core nation is understood as the legitimate "owner" of the state, which is conceived as the state *of* and *for* the core nation. Despite having "its own" state, however, the core nation is conceived as being in a weak cultural, economic, or demographic position within the state. This weak position—seen as a legacy of discrimination against the nation before it attained independence—is held to justify the "remedial" or "compensatory" project of using state power to promote the specific (and previously inadequately served) interests of the core nation.[12]

This turn to ethnocracy began as an explicit rejection of Soviet-era promises about interethnic harmony and the supposed benefits of assimilation. By the late Soviet period, ethnically defined elites had taken relatively empty slogans about "self-determination" of ethnonational groups and given them substance. Republican elites made meaningful the passports that had categorized ethnic belonging, the system of ethnic federalism that suggested the congruence of cultural and political boundaries, and the symbolic attention paid to ethnic languages, folklores, and histories.[13]

But if this ethnocratic trend was clear, the Soviet legacy was more multifaceted than a focus on ethnicity would suggest. Soviet nationalities policy trod a fine line between the multi-ethnicity that defined society (and the concomitant ideology of "internationalism") and an emphasis on ethnic titularity (and its ideology of ethnopolitical entitlement and national self-determination). The tension between the two did not disappear with the Soviet collapse. The dilemma of how to reconcile ethnic diversity with particular privileges for the titular ethnic group was especially acute in Kazakhstan, where Kazakhs represented less than a majority in their "own" republic. The commingling of these theoretically irreconcilable principles—which I call "internationalism with an ethnic face"—persisted from the Soviet period. As it did, it continued to stigmatize clan belonging as backward, retrogressive, and something to avoid.

Eurasianism: Internationalism with an Ethnic Face

One face of post-Soviet state discourse emphasized a vision of multi-ethnic harmony that reiterated Soviet-era categories of internationalism and *Homo sovieticus*.[14] Its central organizing theme was Eurasianism.

President Nazarbaev's notion of Eurasianism was designed to show the geographic centrality of Kazakhstan and the multi-ethnic population that occupied its territory. Based loosely on the ideas of Soviet scholar Lev Gumiliev, this Eurasianism was a celebration of the continent's multicultural heritage and a vision that reserved a formative historical role for the Turkic peoples, of which ethnic Kazakhs are a part.[15] Nazarbaev viewed Eurasianism as an organic outgrowth of the territory, explaining that it was derived from

> our geographic position at the cross-roads in the Eurasian region. The process of globalization of world economic and political processes [*sic*] elevates this factor as a key one. Our ancestors as a part of a united family of Turkic peoples [*narody*] used this important strategic factor to their advantage: along the legendary Silk Road a wide trading corridor between European and Asiatic countries was organized. Today, we are beginning to restore it in cooperation with other countries of our region and with the support of the world community. Of course, in the future the trading system, financial currents and migrations of people between Europe and Asia will grow.
>
> For this very reason, to say nothing about the many politically stabilizing factors, I issued forth and will develop the idea of Eurasianism [*evraziistvo*], which has, I am convinced, a strategic future.[16]

While this Eurasianism came at some cost to both historical fact and the political and economic realities of post-Soviet Kazakhstan, Nazarbaev pressed onward. Central to its "strategic future" was the president's transfer of the capital from Almaty in the southeast to Astana (formerly Aqmola) in the north-central region. Official reasons for building a new capital included Almaty's proneness to seismic activity, its inauspicious location at the base of the Zailiiskii Alatau mountains that hampered urban growth, problems with air pollution, and proximity to China. In reality, the primary reason (until 1998 rarely recognized publicly by authorities) was the demographic predominance of ethnic Russians in the north and the possibility of separatism. A new capital represented an opportunity to create new loyal political elites and simultaneously keep tabs on the *oblasts* near the Russian border.[17]

Making his strategy visible, Nazarbaev orchestrated a televised spectacle of the official presentation of Astana to the world in June 1998 that exhibited central features of Eurasianism. Ethnic groups living in Kazakhstan performed short pieces of "traditional" dance, each in their own "national" costume. The grandstands that formed a backdrop were filled with participants (largely schoolchildren mobilized for the occasion) who, at the appointed moments, raised, turned, and shimmied appropriately colored square cards, in effect spelling out central terms in the internationalist discourse; "friendship" and "no nukes" were rendered in Kazakh, Russian, and English.

The performances projected the connection between the diaspora communities of Kazakhstan, the diaspora culture, and the external homeland to which the diaspora was understood to belong. As Ukrainian dancers performed, the grandstands displayed the word "Kiev," and the television cameras honed in on Ukrainian president Kuchma, who was in attendance. This hearked back to Soviet-era strategies for highlighting the links assumed inherent between the ethnic group, the ethnic culture, and the ethnic territory. The most important dance came last, when a troupe of ethnic Kazakhs many times the size of previous troupes offered an extended routine.

Modifying the homeland-based system of ethnic "representation" from the Soviet period, this new internationalism created "national-cultural centers," which were to be "the organizational mechanisms for supporting and developing national traditions, cultures, and the original spirituality of the nations and national groups."[18] In principle designed as the basic units of extraterritorial ethnic representation, they remained closely watched by a hypertrophic presidential apparatus. Proclaimed as evidence of state commitment to its minorities, in practice, ethnic representation reproduced the ambivalent relationship of minorities to the Kazakhstani state; as the leader of the Polish center in Almaty wrote in 1998, "Kazakhstan is my second fatherland,"[19] a statement designed to show the multi-ethnic nature of Kazakhstan but that implied that the primary loyalty of nontitulars lay elsewhere.

Visions of a unified *Homo eurasiaticus* could become reality only if the state attended to the "needs" of all its ethnic groups. Not unlike Soviet internationalism, which institutionalized ethnic attachments in an attempt to dissolve the boundaries between ethnic groups, the new internationalism vested ethnic representation (and the ostensible satisfaction of ethnic "needs") in these centers. In reality, only cultural and linguistic issues were raised. According to a member of the Ukrainian center, their mandate was to facilitate the development of Ukrainian language and culture. In return, they received meeting space, sponsorship of Ukrainian-language newspapers, funding for Sunday schools and performance ensembles, and exchange programs for select Ukrainian children to study in Ukraine. He added that funding— always in peril—was certain to be cut dramatically, if not entirely, in the near future.[20]

The actual operation of these centers belied notions of equal ethnic representation, instead varying by the nature of interstate ties. Those centers (the Kurdish and Uyghur) representing groups without an external homeland were subject to close state scrutiny, since the Kazakhstani elite sought to normalize interstate relations (with Turkey and China). For those centers that had a titular external homeland, the external state played a critical role. Thus, the Russian center's activities were strictly cultural, given that overtly political issues were potentially destabilizing. The German center, by contrast, was the focus of strong efforts by Germany to repatriate Kazakhstani Germans and grant them German citizenship.[21]

Finally, this Eurasianist vision of internationalism was directed to foreign audiences, as the elite deliberately cultivated an image of commitment to integration in international economic and political structures. On the economic front, Kazakhstan's orientation to market capitalism and foreign investment was trumpeted. Similarly, Nazarbaev's proposals for a "Eurasian Union" that would entail a unified customs zone and a single market for the Commonwealth of Independent States, or CIS, (ideals that were in some part recognition of what was de facto practice: states were at pains to control transborder flows of goods and capital) held international appeal. Likewise, Nazarbaev engaged international political structures through a flurry of high-profile diplomatic visits around the world. In such ways, the Eurasianist vision tapped Soviet-era notions of interethnic "harmony" and ascendant international norms about integrationist liberal markets and civic polities.

Ethnicity and Ethnic Redress

Just as Soviet-era internationalism ultimately had a Russian face (holding a privileged position for ethnic Russians in the evolutionary march toward the "bright future"), post-Soviet Kazakhstani state ideology had a Kazakh face, singling out Kazakhs for linguistic, political, demographic, and cultural redress.

One of the distinguishing patterns of redress in post-Soviet space was its widely recognized but extralegal nature. In Malaysia, the New Economic Policy instituted after the 1969 ethnic riots contained specific goals that found reflection in explicit preferences granted Bumiputras and Malays, a disproportionate number of whom lived in poverty. The intention was to improve the economic standing of these groups through affirmative-action policies in education, skills development, and the provision of credit.[22] By contrast, in Kazakhstan, policies of affirmative action remained ad hoc and outside the law. The state elite, calling these processes "national-cultural revival"—a turn of phrase with seemingly neutral connotations that could apply to any of the "national" groups residing in Kazakhstan—actually singled out Kazakhs for redress in critical areas.

Nazarbaev emphasized the importance of such a "revival" for social stability, stopping short of an explicit proclamation of affirmative-action policies, when he claimed that "the national revival of Kazakhs in concert with general democratic processes, observance of human rights, is an indispensable condition for the development of other nationalities on a basis of equal rights. Without meeting obstacles to its development, the Kazakh nation [*natsiia*], undoubtedly, will treat the interests and requests of other peoples with understanding and respect."[23]

Accordingly, the state elite strayed beyond the rhetoric of just and temporary compensation to hold a privileged and permanent, if still ambiguous, position for the titular group. Nazarbaev routinely pointed to the "integrating role" of the Kazakh people amidst the country's cultural diversity. One letter published in the official *Kazakhstanskaia pravda* in 1992 typified this outlook, asking rhetorically, "Is it necessary to say that Russia is the state for Russians, India for Indians [*sic*], France for the French, in the name of whom their countries were named?"[24] Although Kazakhs were sometimes elevated as Orwellian "more equal pigs," what this special position entailed was left unspecified.

Central to national-cultural revival was attention to matters of language.[25] Given the profound Soviet-era incentives to learn Russian for professional development, many Kazakhs lacked adequate knowledge of Kazakh. Promoting Kazakh was therefore a state effort both to reverse a linguistic tide of Russification and to compensate those Kazakhs previously locked out of professional spheres for lack of proficiency in Russian. After rancorous debates and heightened interethnic tensions in the early part of the decade, a compromise was hammered out in 1996. Kazakh was to be the "state" language, while Russian was an "official language on a par with Kazakh."[26]

The language law placated the sides for the moment, but several parts of the document added layers of ambiguity. Central among them was the depiction that it was the "duty of every citizen" to learn the state language, "which is a most important factor in the consolidation of the people [narod] of Kazakhstan."[27] The requirement that state officials learn Kazakh within a ten-year period was dropped,[28] but the ill-defined distinction between "state" and "official" languages was one that might acquire different juridical content under changed circumstances.

In addition to the declaration of Kazakh as the state language, Kazakh-language primary and secondary education was broadly promoted. According to official statistics, the number of monolingual Kazakh-medium secondary schools increased by about 28 percent in the period 1989–96, while the number of Russian-medium schools decreased by approximately 37 percent in the same period. A similar rise was witnessed in the rising proportion of Kazakh-medium secondary students, from 30.2 to 44.7 percent from 1986 to 1996, while the proportion of Russian-medium students declined from 67.3 to 52.2 percent.[29]

It became possible to get a university education in the Kazakh language—not only in the humanities, where it had previously been available, but also in the increasingly popular specializations of law, economics, and business. From 1989 to 1996 in polytechnical education, the proportion of Kazakh-medium students increased from 8.4 to 21.8 percent. Between 1992 and 1996 in institutes of higher learning, the proportion of Kazakh-medium students rose from 22.1 to 30.9 percent.

Kazakh-language media received consistent state subsidies, although data on their extent are not available. Erbol Shaimerdenov, director of the state Department for the Development of Languages, described the relative lack of demand for Kazakh-medium newspapers in an interview, saying "we still haven't created the need" for people to get their information in Kazakh. The task of his department was to have Kazakh fulfill the functions of the "state" language through encouraging its widened use.[30] In 1999 his department became centrally involved in the enforcement of the legal requirement that 50 percent of television broadcasts be conducted in Kazakh,[31] a provision that was flouted even in predominantly Kazakh South Kazakhstan *oblast*.[32]

There was a wide divergence between the design of state strategies on language-use and their actual implementation.[33] For example, while legal documents were required to be published in Kazakh and then translated into Russian, the usual sequence was the reverse, and the corps of translators was often inadequate for the job.[34] As a result, a perceptible shift in state strategy on language redress became evident in 1998 with a new focus on those Kazakhs with poor facility in the language.[35] Shaimerdenov suggested that the informal new department slogan would be "May a Kazakh speak the state language with other Kazakhs," intimating that no one could expect nontitular citizens of Kazakhstan to speak Kazakh if significant numbers of Kazakhs themselves refused to do so.[36]

Since non-Kazakhs were unlikely to be proficient in the Kazakh language, language preferences were a vehicle for the political promotion of ethnic Kazakhs — a second area for redress. By one account, during the period 1985 to 1994 (the years of the most marked change among ethnic groups in the governing apparatus), the percentage of non-Kazakhs in high-level state posts dropped from fifty to twenty-five.[37] In South Kazakhstan *oblast* in 1998, the only non-Kazakhs in high-level office were those extremely few with a working knowledge of the Kazakh language.[38] At the national level, the chair of both the lower (Mazhilis) and upper (Senat) houses of parliament, as well as the presidency, were open only to those with fluency in Kazakh (i.e., in practice, ethnic Kazakhs). As a result of these preferences, according to one study of the biographies of 320 political appointees and members of parliament, 70.9 percent were Kazakh, 23.4 percent were Slavic, and 5.6 percent were of other background.[39]

A third strategy for redress was demographic engineering. This was to be accomplished by encouraging immigration of ethnic Kazakhs from diaspora communities in Mongolia, Turkey, China, Iran, and Afghanistan. Designed as compensation for losses resulting from the

forced emigration and death from famine associated with collectivization and sedentarization of nomads in the 1920s and 1930s, the
intention was to grant immigrants the material resources for beginning anew in their "homeland," as well as an ongoing stipend.[40] These
state priorities were reflected in local scholarship. Historians took a
special interest in the "historical fates" of Kazakhs-in-exile and a prominent demographer wrote a widely promoted series of books projecting the "natural" growth of the Kazakh population as in part a result
of the massive repatriation campaign.[41]

Demographic redress was critically tied to notions of self-determination. Topping the 50-percent mark was widely seen as tantamount to property restitution; after a long hiatus, the territory of
Kazakhstan was being returned to ethnic Kazakhs.[42] While no visible figure took a position against guaranteeing the rights of minority
groups, many privately voiced satisfaction that "majority rule" (the
central tenet of a crude democratic vision) would finally have an ethnic logic.[43]

If the design of official policy was not necessarily to drive ethnic
Russians from Kazakhstan, that was the effect, and a steady outflow
that peaked in the mid-1990s continued into 2000. Although much
unofficial movement was not reflected in statistics, official figures show
that the net emigration of ethnic Russians was 123,777 in 1993; 251,934
in 1994; 157,462 in 1997; 124,494 in 1998; 73,289 in 1999; and 77,800
in 2000. A gap in the official record for 1995 and 1996 suggests that
figures remained quite high in those years and that authorities sought
to hide this embarrassing fact.[44]

Ethnicity-based redress was finally reflected in state-led efforts to
promote Kazakh culture in the official and semi-official press. This
trend was particularly marked in the first half of the 1990s, when newspapers routinely devoted ample space to explaining ethnic traditions
and covering Kazakh cultural events. In academia, virtually any topic
that covered pre-Soviet history, depicted anti-Soviet or anti-imperial
movements, or portrayed the massive suffering that Kazakhs historically endured, received blanket endorsement. According to several
informants in the Institute of History and Ethnography, the institute's director, a powerful ally of President Nazarbaev, issued an order
(*instruktazh*) to researchers to find the roots of Kazakh statehood in
the Sak period (the first millennium BCE). This was a clear departure from established historiography that located such statehood in

the mid-fifteenth century.[45] On occasion, the drive to establish ethnic autochthony generated profound historiographic absurdities.[46]

The state also spearheaded efforts to restore various architectural monuments deemed to be of historical value, projects for which it lacked funds. A Department of Historical-Cultural Legacy, created in 1993 and liquidated in 1995, led merely a formal existence, receiving almost nothing from central authorities to cover its mandate. When the building that housed it was privatized, the department ceased to exist.[47] Given funding limitations, the state effort was often confined to the pages of the press, where monuments of historical or religious significance were detailed and their tragic condition lamented. One regional paper demanded (to no apparent effect) that the Hermitage Museum in Saint Petersburg (Russia) return to the Kazakh steppe a monument erected by Tamerlane (Amur Timur) after his conquest of the Golden Horde.[48] Another described how a mausoleum of a certain Abylgazi had been completely dismantled in the mid-1990s, presumably by someone interested in reusing the materials for another construction project.[49] The enormously important Yassaui mausoleum in the city of Turkestan (South Kazakhstan region), even with massive financial assistance from Turkey, was not finished in time for the 1000th anniversary scheduled for 1998. The celebration was delayed until 2000.

Some cultural projects received generous state funding, like the "ethnocultural expeditions" carried out in 1998. Instructed to spotlight ethnic Kazakh cultural traditions, teams of scholars were dispatched to each of the fourteen *oblasts* to examine which sayings and proverbs, traditions, customs, and toponymns had persisted into the post-Soviet period. Funding issues aside, the effort was uneven, facing additional problems: a lack of Kazakh-language facility among researchers, a lack of experience conducting ethnographic fieldwork, and the "passive relations" of local authorities whose cooperation was necessary to identify sites and provide logistical support.[50]

The practice of these research expeditions was also profoundly shaped by political imperatives—to provide a model of "genuine" Kazakhness that best conformed to images of pre-Soviet traditions. Although the research carried the generic name "ethnocultural," the exclusive focus was on Kazakhs. Research teams relied heavily on regional and local administrators (*akims*), whose instructions were to find predominantly ethnic Kazakh regions that had a comparatively well-preserved mixture of traditional practices.[51] Thus, research ignored the many multi-ethnic regions in which the vast majority of Kazakhs resided.[52]

These expeditions were conducted as part of a grander state project celebrating the "Year of People's Unity and National History." Building on the imperatives of establishing a "historical consciousness" set forth in 1995,[53] the year's stated objective was to "systematize all historical events and phenomena, revive historical memory and provide a spiritual cleansing. This is necessary in order deeply to recognize and better understand the many-centuries aspiration of the people to state independence, unity, freedom of spirit and human dignity."[54] In practice, the project centered on the history of ethnic Kazakhs, with few efforts spared to demonstrate the validity of Kazakh claims to this territory. The exemplar was a prominent scholar and occasional speechwriter for Nazarbaev, Manash Qozybaev. An erstwhile expert on Communist Party history who effected a seamless transition to promoting ethnic Kazakh history, Qozybaev regularly attempted to assimilate to Kazakhs many of the military, political, and scholarly achievements of all Turkic peoples, as well as of Asia more generally.

Viewing Clans as Retrogressive

Internationalism with an ethnic face contained principles that were in tension with one another. To the extent that the polity was internationalist, it embraced what Western scholars label "civic" principles; that is, ethnicity and cultural background were de-emphasized and common residence in the territory of Kazakhstan was emphasized. To the extent that the state pursued its ethnic face, it promoted Kazakhs to compensate for their suffering during the Soviet period.

Both principles, however, privileged high-aggregate identity categories and propagated further the Soviet-era stigma about subethnic clan divisions. While the Soviet version of modernization was discredited with the collapse of the Soviet state, identity discourse in the post-Soviet period differed strikingly little from its Soviet-era predecessor. At its heart was a high modernism that held no legitimate place for subethnic identities, as I detail more fully in chapter 6.

CONTINUITY IN POLITICAL ECONOMY

The post-Soviet elite claimed to embark on massive economic and political reform, and change did come. Particularly in macroeconomic policy, there was a wholesale shift to a neoliberal market orientation. It is noteworthy, however, that there was substantial continuity in personnel from the Soviet period into the 1990s; these were the very same apparatchiks who had been socialized to demonstrate publicly their commitment to normatively appealing principles while privately manifesting dexterity in the informal mechanisms of a corrupt polity. Their modus operandi was a Soviet-era product.

As chapter 3 examined, the Soviet command system had created incentives for the maintenance of hierarchical networks of distribution. Since the system was largely based on endemic shortages, elaborate networks for ordinary people to gain access to scarce commodities (consumer goods, access to power, inputs for state enterprises) were the useful tools of the enterprising citizen-subject. Kinship-rich societies were thus the site of distribution networks with a distinctive genealogical outline.

In central ways, post-Soviet Kazakhstan in the 1990s reproduced these patterns, preserving hierarchies in political and economic life. Appearances, of course, were deliberately cultivated to the contrary. President Nazarbaev widely used the term "democratization," deploying it to cloak moves away from political openness. For example, in late 1998 the president moved to hold early presidential elections in January 1999 in a series of choreographed events in which the parliament "pressured" the president into "reluctantly" heeding the "democratic" call for the early vote. In fact, this was merely a drama designed to lend legitimacy to what was essentially an extraconstitutional decision, by suggesting that it had emerged from parliamentary "representatives," themselves ostensibly elected by a popular vote.[55]

Elections, both to parliament and the presidency, were marred by significant irregularities. Parliamentary candidates who supported the president and his program received the financial and political support of the state apparatus, while alternative candidates were routinely harassed. Those with emerging independent power bases became the particular targets of state-led campaigns. Thus, former prime minister Akezhan Kazhegel'din, whose personal wealth was estimated in the millions, was forced into exile in 1998 on charges of tax evasion that were clearly politically motivated. He had earlier been disqualified from competing in the 1999 presidential elections on a cleverly crafted technicality. Kazhegel'din's Republican People's Party, which was to field candidates for the fall 1999 parliamentary elections, was the object of intense state scrutiny, and its official registration was delayed. Ethnic Russian Piotr Svoik was beaten by unidentified assailants at the height of the political power of the alternative Citizen (Azamat) movement in December 1997. The pattern, which went far beyond these few examples, is that the regime periodically intimidated the members of a diverse opposition and systematically rewarded fealty to the current leadership. This prompted the Organization for Security Cooperation in Europe (OSCE) to urge authorities to scrap the 1999 presidential contest, a call that fell on deaf ears.[56]

The run-up to the parliamentary elections scheduled for September and October 1999 departed little from previous campaigns. According to 1998 amendments to the election laws, parliamentary seats would be allocated by a combination of proportional representation from party lists and single-member district plurality seats, but this did not affect the shape of prevote competition. Pro-Nazarbaev parties (Fatherland and the Civic Party) were easily registered and given strong state backing, while alternative parties (Republican People's Party, Citizen, Progress [Orleu], Republic, the Communist Party, and the Association of Slavic and Russian Organizations) encountered insufficient campaign time, difficulties with registration, more limited media access, as well as internal divisions. Given these conditions, in addition to anticipated problems with fraud and reporting at the polls, a pro-president parliament was the result, as usual.

Once elected, these bodies had little independent authority. By the 1995 Constitution, presidential decrees had the force of law. Impeaching the president required a three-fourths vote of both houses, and the president selected seven of the Senat's forty-seven members. There was no binding power to no-confidence votes, and while parliament had the right to disagree with any proposed decree or legislation, the president could dissolve the body if it voted no-confidence or twice refused the presidential recommendation for prime minister, as well as under conditions of any ill-defined "political crisis" between state organs.[57] Constitutional changes initiated with great fanfare under a banner of "democratization" in October 1998 had the central effect of lengthening the terms in office, from five to seven years for the president, from five to six for the Senat, and from four to five for the Mazhilis; they did not alter the concentration of power.

As highlighted above, an unelected, publicly unaccountable, and extraconstitutional People's Assembly was the occasional agent of

Nazarbaev-led initiatives. The Assembly was depicted as representing popular interests, defined ethnically through the national-cultural centers, but this was not its political role. In 1995, after a power struggle that led Nazarbaev to dissolve the parliament under the pretext of upholding constitutionality, the Assembly, a body of hand-picked supporters of the president, was the forum in which a new constitution was developed.[58] The Assembly's efforts reached ordinary people as well. For example, in June 1997 what initially seemed to be an open student discussion on interethnic relations at a prominent local institute in Almaty turned out to be a thinly veiled propaganda campaign organized by members of the Assembly.[59] The more attention the Assembly received in the official press, the more suspicions were heightened that some extraordinary presidential move was imminent, leading the political opposition to argue that the body was an "instrument" of the president.[60]

Thus, the general pattern since 1991 was the entrenchment of Nazarbaev's power. The downsizing of the state apparatus served as an opportunity for power consolidation.[61] Entire agencies and state committees were shifted to direct subordination to presidential authority.[62] The large public-sector employer Academy of Sciences was dissolved in 1999, its various institutes placed under the direct control of the Ministry of Science. The transfer of the capital from Almaty to Astana was a further chance to keep close tabs on those actors whose offices were moved and to shut down the operations of others.[63]

All major policies were created in top-down fashion, with the president centrally involved. Civil service reform went nowhere until the president clearly signaled his active support in 1998.[64] In 2002 a land-tenure reform effort stemmed directly from presidential initiatives. Moreover, the strategic vision for the prosperous resource-extraction industries (primarily oil and minerals) was centered on the preferences of the president.[65] While reserving decisive control over such decisions, the president insulated himself from eventual criticism by appearing to delegate responsibilities to others. An August 1999 scandal in which shipments of MIG fighters were stopped en route from Kazakhstan to their purchasers in North Korea was thus depicted as the independent initiative of a rogue group of state officials, about which the president knew nothing.[66] Similarly, the members of the presidential entourage opened Swiss bank accounts with enormous bribes from foreign investors; this created the impression that the president had himself not personally benefited, even if the indictment of American businessmen in U.S. federal courts in 2003 on charges of supplying the bribes created the opposite impression.

The president sat atop a relatively effective vertical structure, widely referred to as the *prezidentskaia vertikal'*. He appointed the governors (*akims*) to each of fourteen *oblasts*, as well as the cities of Astana and Almaty. Each governor was responsible for making a whole host of appointments at the regional level that mirrored the structure of republic-wide agencies. Beneath these regional governors were the city and district (*raion*) administrators (also called *akims*), who were in turn responsible to their superiors. Because of this essentially nested structure, frequent turnover of *akims* and their appointees served to prevent the emergence of alternative power bases. This was critically important, since the tendency was for local and regional authorities to consolidate authority through patron-client relations.

According to the 1995 Constitution, a degree of self-administration was reserved to the regional and local level in the form of an elected body (*maslikhat*). The reality was quite different, with local administrative authorities (*akimats*, administrations of the *akim*) given priority in all relations at the local level.[67] The *maslikhats* could make budget recommendations, but central authorities, through their *akimats*, were under no obligation to consider them. Moreover, local *akimats* had broad authority to issue charters to businesses and organizations under state auspices and to register private enterprises.[68] As the press focused on the local power of these administrators, members of the opposition voiced increasingly frequent calls, such as that by members of the Citizen movement, for the *akim* to become an elected post. The president made clear that he refused to do so.

If the consolidation of presidential power was clear on most counts, there was initially considerable liberalization in the area of press freedoms. Most notable were the relatively free information flows on economic trends and opportunities. Privately owned business-oriented newspapers enjoyed favorable relations with the regime. Exchange rates, investment forecasts, and the activities of a nascent stock exchange were widely publicized, and even the shock from the 1998 Russian financial collapse did not alter the regime's strategy in this regard.

Media with a political bent also enjoyed a modicum of editorial freedom, especially relative to those in neighboring Uzbekistan and Turkmenistan.[69] The extremely popular tabloid weekly *Karavan*, with an independent resource base, was especially bold in its criticisms of political developments, but even it came under state scrutiny in 1998 for articles that raised provocative questions about the shape of interethnic relations.[70] Papers such as *Vremia po Grinvichu*, *XXI vek*, and *Dat* were all the target of inquiries by the Tax Police, as well as the victims of more run-of-the-mill forms of physical intimidation. *Dat*, the only nationwide oppositionist Kazakh-language newspaper, published merely for a few months in 1998, an indication that the regime found the prospect of Kazakh speakers turning against the establishment an unacceptable political possibility that required immediate action.[71] In general, as long as the media did not implicate the president directly—as did Sergei Duvanov in 2002 when he reported on allegations of presidential corruption and subsequently was arrested and tried—critical stances were allowed. But periodic instances of state intimidation created the restraint of self-censorship.

Just as the post-Soviet polity (in spite of reforms) continued to limit public access to the policy-making process, the economy (in spite of notable changes) retained a vertical and hierarchical structure. To be sure, the economy *looked* much different with a virtual explosion of inexpensive consumer goods. Open-air markets—first in Almaty, then in other urban centers—were flooded with cheaply imported consumer wares, even if their poor quality was widely rued. Flea markets and swap meets (*barakholki*) in Almaty, in particular, sprawled for miles at the city limits, suggesting that they filled a genuine market need, and many residents reported spending countless hours on public transportation seeking the bargains these places offered. The chaotic scenes most of them produced were that of an unregulated market selling wares produced almost exclusively outside of Kazakhstan.

Poverty was widespread, and massive unemployment and underemployment, a downturn in industrial production, and high inflation kept much business in these informal *barakholki*, rather than in the formal storefronts. The jobless rate rose in the mid-1990s; although official statistics reported only a 5.6 percent rate for 1996, much unemployment was hidden, as registration of the jobless was quite uneven.[72] Industrial production fell to a low in 1995 as many factories stood idle, and a very slow recovery in export-oriented sectors ran up against low world prices in 1997–98. Inflation reached near-catastrophic levels in 1994–95, and after a relative stabilization of the new Kazakhstani currency, *tenge*, in 1997, the Russian financial collapse sent prices up again in 1998. The currency again stabilized in the late 1990s and into the first years of the following decade, as a result of fiscal austerity that undermined the population's social safety net. The consequence was that ordinary citizens lacked the resources to access many of the goods now theoretically available. As Werner has described and as chapter 7 highlights, many Kazakhstanis resorted to their subethnic connections for access to economic goods rather than engaging market mechanisms.[73]

Likewise, a weak banking system continued to limit the availability of credit.[74] While official statistics report that overall credit investments in Kazakhstan totaled almost $950 million in 1998,[75] the data do not discriminate between foreign-owned banks operating in the country and Kazakhstani banks, nor is there information on recipients. Indications are that credit was not extended to most ordinary Kazakhstanis. A loudly proclaimed effort to meet this need by extending microcredit of $400 encountered myriad problems of administration, coordination, and resources. Various informants in South Kazakhstan *oblast*, for example, laughed off the program as a conceptually attractive but practically stillborn project.[76]

Moreover, privatization ushered in a massive flow of foreign direct investment into extracting the vast oil and mineral resources of Kazakhstan that generated growth in these sectors, but most Kazakhstanis received little tangible benefit from these operations. As in the Russian Federation, there were many questions about the role of the former *nomenklatura* and the fairness of state-held auctions and competitions. Many of the jobs created by foreign multinational corporations were filled by contract workers from Russia or Turkey, who were declared more qualified. The city of Atyrau, for example, which is near Tengiz, the most productive of Kazakhstan's oil fields, continued to be mired in poverty; most local residents were not even allowed onto the premises that Chevron controlled, let alone employed there.[77] This limited access to generated wealth followed the pattern of other hydrocarbon-rich states.[78] Even assuming the monumental political will to change this equity problem, the higher exchange rate sustained by such operations made other forms of investment in Kazakhstan all the more expensive.

The continuity examined here is meant to highlight factors not normally illuminated through transitological approaches. It suggests that while the visual transformations of places like Almaty from a sleepy provincial town to a capital-rich financial center for all of Central Asia were real, the depth of the changes should not be assumed. Political and economic structures throughout the 1990s still rewarded those with privileged access and, in this sense, belied the public facade of open politics and markets that the regime attempted to propagate. As during the Soviet period, the result was that clan networks continued to be vibrant and important, well after the demise of the Soviet state itself.

PART TWO

The Political Dynamic
of Informal Ties

5

Clan Conflict

What we can understand of something depends on how we think
our way into it in the first place. —*Katherine Verdery*

IN THE 1990S THE STRUCTURE OF ACCESS TO POLITICAL AND
economic goods was strikingly similar to that of the Soviet period, and
this legacy continued to fuel clan politics. Unlike the Soviet period,
however, when clan politics remained subordinated to other high-
stakes struggles, in post-Soviet Central Asia clan conflict flourished.
The state-building and nation-building efforts of newly independent
Kazakhstan now included intense competition for control of the state,
and, consequently, for resources that were increasingly valuable on
international markets.

Jockeying among kinship-based groups was apparent, although its
specifics were often shrouded in secrecy. As one observer noted,
subethnic politics was like watching bulldogs fight under a carpet; the
outlines of this struggle became clear in the event that one combat-
ant emerged temporarily, only to return to the fight.[1] Given shifting
relationships and highly imperfect information, the contours of this
clan competition are not always easy to establish.[2] It is nonetheless
worth taking a look at the empirical record to discern patterns. This
chapter pays particular attention to the background of the political
and economic elite to evaluate the widespread assertion (by journalists both in Central Asia and abroad) that President Nursultan
Nazarbaev's clan-based network dominated political and economic
life in the 1990s. I will show that Nazarbaev privileged his umbrella
clan and extended family, but he also sought to avoid a fundamental
imbalance in the relative power of the three umbrella clans. Thus,
the politics of clan networks was deeply etched into post-Soviet real-

ity, but not in the ways that many analysts described them. Clan conflict was vibrant, but it stopped short of the "social closure" that Weber describes as typical of group relations. That is, one clan group did not seek total exclusion of other clan groupings.[3]

CLAN NETWORKS IN CONFLICT

Students of informal politics often find it useful to make a series of assumptions about their subject of study. Central among them is the notion that every informal relationship is dyadic in nature; that is, it involves relations between two (and only two) actors, and this relationship may be described for its durability, issue coverage, and exclusivity. A second central assumption is that such informal relationships involve an exchange of goods; that is, things of value move (often in both directions) between the two actors. A third premise is that this exchange between actors occurs according to some notion of what is considered "rational" for each actor; that is, each party is assumed to benefit from a relationship that otherwise has no reason to exist. The picture that these assumptions paint is that individuals ensnared in informal relationships are scarcely part of larger societal wholes. They are not the members of groups understood in some corporate sense; rather, they are individuals whose political interactions may be usefully reduced to the rational exchange of goods with one another.[4]

Though this tripartite premise is useful to tease out theoretical propositions based on the rationality assumption, do these assumptions make empirical sense with regard to the concrete contexts in which real-life political competition occurs? After all, there is no logical reason to assume a priori that individuals are parts of dyadic relationships (rather than N-sized groups of people with whom they have little face-to-face contact), exchange goods (rather than play social roles, for example), and exhibit goal-seeking, rational behavior (rather than behave in ways to which they are habituated).[5] To be most useful, our assumptions should line up neatly with the empirical contexts that we study.

This chapter suggests that, for contextual reasons rather than logically deduced ones, these three premises do make sense in the study of clan politics in post-Soviet Kazakhstan. Because of the Soviet experience, they are empirically defensible. First, Soviet rule deprived clan

groupings of their cultural content. Clans were no longer the corpo-
rately defined kin groups that dealt with a wide array of cultural, social,
and political matters. In the post-Soviet period, individuals used kin
networks often without imagining clan as a coherent group. I move
from a Durkheimian, group-centered perspective on clans to a Weberian, individual-based one for this reason. Second, the Soviet period
limited kinship to particular social niches associated with gaining access
to scarce goods. Thus, clan emerged as distinctly *political*, by becoming ensnared with questions of distribution and exchange. Third and
related, clan became associated with goal-seeking behavior. It was
increasingly invoked when one had a goal in mind.

The language of networks (rather than groups) is particularly
appropriate at this juncture. Individuals involved in goods acquisition
create networks, since individuals acting alone hardly reap great
rewards. Networks involve greater fluidity and less exclusivity of relationships than do groups. One network necessarily overlaps with others; competing networks may even occasionally have members in
common. Some networks operate actively for the acquisition or
exchange of a particular kind of good; other networks are activated to
procure or trade other types of good. Some networks lie dormant for
years, as if awaiting the circumstances in which their content proves
useful, while other networks remain actively useful. Still other networks may succumb to centrifugal pressures and dissolve.

The conflict of clan networks has distinguishing features. First, I
have suggested that the concealable nature of clan ties makes them
an asset under a shortage economy. Given shortage, clan ties are therefore more likely to survive to animate access networks. Concealability makes clan more likely to survive, but it is the multilevel nature
of clan divisions that lends them an unusual political dynamic.

Kinship is a unique basis for identity politics to the extent that it is
scaled at multiple levels simultaneously. This is clearest with the former nomads of Central Asia, among whom an individual could be
the member of a small kin-based aggregate of one hundred people,
which in turn was a subunit in a larger aggregate of one thousand
people. This larger aggregate could be a subunit in a still-larger aggregate of ten thousand members, and so on. With ethnicity, an individual often feels compelled to choose (if a choice is in the offing);
either she is a member of the in-group or a member of the out-group.
Gray areas are usually excluded from ethnic categories, perhaps in

the drive to preserve an elusive purity of in-group identity. This is where Barth's understanding of ethnicity as boundary-keeping and Douglas's notions of ritual purity coincide.[6]

Clan is different; any two human beings can be described as related to each other through kinship. On such a conceptual map, the degree of kin closeness varies, but a blood connection is always understood to be present. As a result, clan politics is always scaled at multiple levels and kinship networks are activated in differently scaled contexts at different contextual moments.

CLAN COMPETITION IN THE 1990S

Scaled at multiple levels, clan politics in the 1990s played itself out differently at different levels of analysis.[7] First, at the republic-wide level, the regime tolerated and itself used patron-client ties along subethnic lines, as patterns of political appointments suggest. While some effort was made to ensure a balance of umbrella clan interests, the presidential family nonetheless disproportionately benefited from umbrella clan politics. At the *oblast* level, the regime attempted to undermine the efforts of clan patronage networks to create regional power bases that might challenge the Elder Umbrella Clan's control of the state. At the district level, lower-aggregate clan divisions became relatively more important, as many locales were the site of umbrella clan homogeneity that rendered lower-aggregate differences all the more politically salient.

Republic-Wide Competition

As chapter 2 described, the Elder Umbrella Clan traditionally inhabited south and southeastern Kazakhstan, while the Middle Umbrella Clan dominated the north and northeast—areas that now largely abut the Russian Federation—and the Younger Umbrella Clan was most powerful in the western reaches, especially along the Caspian Sea. At the end of Soviet rule, Younger Clan Kazakhs were relatively marginalized from distant Almaty, the Middle Clan dominated technical professions with their higher degree of Russification, and the Elder Clan remained politically predominant, given its proximity to Almaty.

In the post-Soviet period Nazarbaev continued the general, republic-wide patronage practices of Dinmukhammed Kunaev, long-time

Soviet-era Communist Party First Secretary in Kazakhstan and mentor to Nazarbaev, by propelling members of the Elder Umbrella Clan
(to which Nazarbaev belongs) into the ruling elite. Nurtai Abykaev
(the president's closest advisor), Akhmetzhan Esimov (deputy prime
minister from 1996 to 1998, chair of the president's administration from
mid-1998), Al'nur Musaev (director of the Committee on National
Security, successor to the KGB), Kasymzhomart Tokaev (Minister of
Foreign Affairs), Mukhtar Abliazov (Minister of Energy, Industry, and
Trade), Omirbek Baigel'di (chair of the Senat), and Altynbek Sarsenbaev (director of the National Agency on Press Affairs and Mass Information) were some of the most prominent Elder Clan Kazakhs under
Nazarbaev in the late 1990s.

The dominance of the Elder Umbrella Clan among the top elite
helped to consolidate the power of Nazarbaev and his kin. From the
mid-1990s, especially with the introduction of mass privatization and
the opening of Kazakhstan to large-scale foreign direct investment,
the political reach of members of Nazarbaev's family was dramatically
enhanced. Most significant were the increasingly close ties between
Rakhat Aliev, the director of the Tax Police who also had an interest
in oil development in the Caspian area, and the president, whose
daughter Dariga was Aliev's wife. In 1998, private conversations and
the occasional bold publication drew parallels between the dominance
of the Suharto family in Indonesia and that of Nazarbaev and his kin
in Kazakhstan—an increasingly apt comparison.

If the Elder Umbrella Clan dominated at the top, patterns in the
broader state apparatus were more complex, as an examination of more
than 480 members of the political and economic elite reveals. A database was compiled from the leading reference guide to the elite.[8] Elite
birthplaces were taken as an indicator of umbrella clan background;
thus, this was a compendium of information on umbrella clan composition of the broader apparatus. Of the 481 republic-level appointments evaluated, 218 were rural-born Kazakhs, 141 were urban-born
Kazakhs, and 122 were non-Kazakhs (table 5.1). For rural-born Kazakhs, umbrella clan background was discerned by referencing rural birthplace to patterns of clan settlement. The umbrella clan of urban-born
Kazakhs could not be reliably discerned, given Soviet-era migration
to urban areas, as well as the practice of assigning young cadres to jobs
outside their birth areas. Non-Kazakhs have no clan background.[9]

Table 5.1

Composition of Elite (1997, 2001)

Background	Number	% of Total	% of Total Rural-Born Kazakhs
rural-born, Younger	25	5.2	11.5
rural-born, Middle	84	17.5	38.5
rural-born, Elder	83	17.3	38.1
rural-born Kazakh, clan background unclear	26	5.4	11.9
urban-born Kazakh	141	29.3	*
non-Kazakh	122	25.4	*
TOTAL	481	100	*

Table 5.2

Umbrella Clan Background of Rural-Born Elite (1997, 2001)

Background	% of Rural-Born Kazakh Elite	Estimated % of Population[a]
Younger	13.0	33.96
Middle	43.8	41.24
Elder	43.2	24.63

[a] Data on overall population are from estimates presented in Cynthia Werner, "The Significance of Tribal Identities in the Daily Life of Rural Kazaks in South Kazakhstan" (paper presented at the conference of the Association for the Study of Nationalities, Columbia University, New York, 24–26 April 1997).

Among rural Kazakhs in the elite, there was a numerical predominance of the Middle Umbrella Clan, with the Elder Umbrella Clan not far behind. This is not surprising, given that education levels correspond to more Russified milieus, from which Middle Clan Kazakhs generally come. The Elder Umbrella Clan dominance of power structures was less complete than often believed, perhaps for this reason. The Younger Umbrella Clan was the big loser in the area of cadre promotion. This, too, can be seen as a Soviet legacy, given the vast distances between Younger Umbrella Clan territory and Almaty and the fact that the extractive industries prominent in Younger Clan territory were structured by the Soviets to deal directly with Moscow, rather than through Almaty as an intermediary. The result was lesser representation for these Kazakhs.

The patterns are less striking, but still noteworthy, if one compares the umbrella clan breakdown in the elite to the estimated breakdown of umbrella clan in the population overall (table 5.2).[10] As with the raw numbers, there is an overrepresentation of the Elder and Middle Umbrella Clans, with a distinct underrepresentation of the Younger Umbrella Clan.

Because Middle Clan Kazakhs were disproportionately educated and linguistically Russified (compared to other Kazakhs), they enjoyed a prominent position in the political elite at the end of Soviet rule, notwithstanding Kunaev's attempts to weaken the clan's position.[11] This translated quickly into bargaining leverage vis-à-vis the emerging regime of Nazarbaev. Specifically, the threat of separatism in the northern *oblasts* worked to the Middle Clan's benefit. The regime feared an alliance between these more Russified Kazakhs and ethnic Russians who faced a choice of exit (separatism) or loyalty (political quiescence). Middle Clan Kazakhs were themselves not considering separatism, but the regime sought to retain the loyalty of Middle Clan Kazakhs as a hedge against separatism in the region.

Especially from 1993 to 1995, the northern *oblasts* were the sites of various attempts to question the integrity of the new state. In Russia, a widely respected author called for the incorporation of certain northern regions into the Russian Federation, dramatically heightening tensions along a vast borderland.[12] On the Kazakhstani side, Cossack groups whose political identification leaned toward Russia agitated for cultural and political autonomy. The country's cultural mix was widely viewed as an ethnic tinderbox.[13] By the late 1990s, this wave of escalated tensions had subsided through a combination of legal guarantees, state coercion, and symbolic politics.[14]

Securing the loyalty of Middle Clan Kazakhs was critical in this period. This is the best explanation for the selection as prime minister of, first, an ethnic Slav (Sergei Tereshchenko, 1992–94), then a Middle Clan Kazakh (Akezhan Kazhegel'din, 1994–97). Through such top elite appointments, patronage along umbrella clan lines was a strategic concession to forge loyalty to the new state structures in a period of high uncertainty.

Such an alliance is visible in the broader elite as well. This occurred, however, with some lag after the appointment of prominent

Middle Clan Kazakhs like Kazhegel'din. Patronage networks are not mobilized instantly when top-level appointments occur; new patterns in personnel appear only gradually, as positions open through retirements, firings, and political maneuverings. It takes some time for changes in the central elite to affect personnel appointments in the wider elite.

Table 5.3 takes a deeper look at the elite background and relates it to the president's estimated degree of influence. The table shows that there was no alliance yet visible between the Elder and Middle Umbrella Clans. In 1997 a member of the Younger Umbrella Clan was no less likely than a member of the other clans to be selected for a post over which the president had high influence. The Younger Umbrella Clan was underrepresented in general in the elite (table 5.2, above), but a Younger Clan Kazakh in the elite assumed the same access to power as did his other Kazakh counterparts.

Table 5.3
Absence of Elder-Middle Umbrella Clan Alliance (1997)

Estimated Degree of President's Influence on Post	% of Elder-Middle Elite Occupying . . .	% of Younger Elite Occupying . . .
low	18.1	24.0
medium	46.4	44.0
high	35.5	32.0

Note: A simple statistical test shows that there is little chance of a significant difference in the distribution of posts between the Younger and Elder-Middle Umbrella Clans. $X^2 = .510$ (d.f. = 2), p = 0.775, N = 191.

The situation had changed appreciably through patronage politics by 2001. An emerging source of Middle Umbrella Clan patronage was the relocation of the capital city from Almaty to Astana in late 1997, which accorded Middle Clan Kazakhs greater influence over personnel appointments. Table 5.4 shows that if one was from either the Middle or Elder Clans in 2001, she or he was much more likely to assume a post with high access to power than if one was from the Younger Clan. The alliance established between the Middle and Elder Clans in the middle 1990s had trickled down to the broader elite by 2001. Notably, the position of the Middle and Elder

Clans, taken individually, was weaker than when we consider it as an alliance.

Table 5.4
Presence of Elder-Middle Umbrella Clan Alliance, 2001

Estimated Degree of President's Influence on Post	% of Elder-Middle Elite Occupying...	% of Younger Elite Occupying...
low	8.4	24.0
medium	51.8	48.0
high	39.8	28.0

Note: A simple statistical test shows an extremely high probability of a significant difference in the distribution of posts between the Younger and Elder-Middle Umbrella Clans. $X^2 = 5.875$ (d.f. = 2), p = 0.053, N = 191.

By the late 1990s, the strategic situation for umbrella clan politics had changed. The Russian population dwindled due to out-migration; those who remained were disproportionately elderly and politically quiescent. Separatist sentiment was rarely palpable, notwithstanding an apparent attempt by Russian separatists to seize the regional governor's administrative buildings in Oskemen in 1999. The new challenge came from a source exogenous to clan politics. Gas and oil extraction in western Kazakhstan began to attract the attention of international actors, as well as that of the state elite. But the development of a resource base quite distant from Almaty, in the stronghold of the Younger Umbrella Clan, begged vigilance. The regime succeeded in steering all major investment deals through Almaty (and later, Astana), to prevent any end-around attempts by local Younger Umbrella Clan authorities. Moreover, Prime Minister Kazhegel'din was replaced in 1997 by Nurlan Balgimbaev, from the Younger Umbrella Clan and until then the president of the state oil company, Kazakhoil. One might expect the representation of the Younger Umbrella Clan to improve in the elite in subsequent years.

Regional and Local Competition

The politics of umbrella clan at the republican level ran up against the politics of regionalisms at the *oblast* level. Preventing regionalism was a central political concern of the 1990s, as the regime sought to preclude subethnic networks from finding explicit territorial expression. In 1997 a consolidation of administrative units reduced the number of *oblasts* from nineteen to fourteen. While this was officially described as an attempt to reduce redundancy in state services and to streamline their provision, the evidence suggests that the logic of the changes was in part to prevent umbrella clan–based regionalisms. Proposals for an administrative union of Younger Umbrella Clan–dominated *oblasts* (such as Atyrau and Mangystau, which had been often forwarded) were deemed too threatening, as such groupings would have created a bloc based on the Younger Clan. The Younger Clan enjoyed both a tradition of defying state authority and simultaneously a recent boost to its economic position. The ingredients for separatist sentiment appeared ripe.[15] Administrative units were combined only in those cases where doing so would not strengthen the Younger Clan.

If Nazarbaev had a particular fear of Younger Umbrella Clan regionalist movements, he appears to have feared regionalisms more generally. He rotated *oblast akims* frequently, rewarding those who were particularly loyal and relocating those who appeared to challenge his central control. From 1991 to 2000, the average tenure for these *akims* was 23.5 months, after which most were reassigned to high-level positions (other *akim* positions, ministry posts, seats in the legislature) or became successful in private business.[16] Thus, Nazarbaev created a core, circulating elite that benefited from his patronage. Moreover, turnover was largely the same across the whole country. The lowest turnover (three *akims* served during the period) occurred in West Kazakhstan *oblast*; the highest (six *akims* served) occurred in East Kazakhstan *oblast* and Mangystau. Through this rotation, Nazarbaev sought to undermine regionalisms that could compete with the power of the center, not to mention his personal power, appearances of decentralization notwithstanding.[17]

Those *akims* who enjoyed genuine regional popularity (and thereby were perceived as threatening) were dealt with harshly, as was Galimzhan Zhakiyanov of Pavlodar *oblast* in 2002. These potential political rivals were not angels, as many of them had personally benefited from their positions in the past. Thus, material that would compromise their reputations and justify their downfall was never hard to find. But even those who were relatively clean could be intimidated into submission by a legal system that took its orders from central authorities. Thus, a prominent opposition journalist in 2002 first was beaten by "unknown assailants" and several months later arrested (on the eve of a 2002 trip to the United States to speak with human rights groups) for ostensibly raping a fourteen-year-old girl.[18] Those who would not partake of Nazarbaev's system of spoils were dealt with harshly.

While rotating personnel was among Nazarbaev's political tools, clan was still operative. At the *oblast* level, lower-aggregate divisions became increasingly salient. In 1997–98, informants contended that *akims* tended to be from the clan dominant in the region. Most found it hard to imagine a situation in which, for example, the *akim* of South Kazakhstan region could be a non-Dulat, or the *akim* of Atyrau region could be a non-Zhetiru. When the *akim* of a region was not from the dominant clan, his legitimacy could be called into question. Much depended on his ability to procure goods from the center. However, his behavior was scrutinized thoroughly and any evidence that his performance lagged was immediately attributed to his being a clan outsider.[19]

Once appointed, *oblast* governors operated with a striking degree of autonomy, hiring and firing lower-level administrators in subordinate *akimats* often without legal justification.[20] In many instances, state administrators allocated resources to clients in open and brazen ways. One informant illustrated how the former *akim* of the city of Atyrau pressed the city to issue a hard-to-get license to a local entrepreneur to open a bazaar in a prominent and profitable location. Because of the *akim*'s intervention in the licensing process, this man became a quite successful entrepreneur at a time when poverty was widespread in Atyrau.[21] In the context of economic scarcity and privileged access to goods, goods were often distributed to clients as part of dense networks of exchange.

If clientelism in general was widespread, it often specifically followed clan or umbrella clan lines in the predominantly Kazakh regions. When Amalbek Tshanov became the governor of Zhambyl *oblast* in 1995, for example, he removed 140 employees, replacing 80 percent of them with members of the Zhanys subdivision of the Dulat division (Elder Umbrella Clan). Members of this clan, to which Tshanov himself belonged, occupied key posts in the region.[22] A similar situation occurred in Torghai region (now a part of Qostanai *oblast*), when the new governor broadly promoted the members of his clan Zhoghary-Shekty of the Arghyn division (Middle Umbrella Clan) at the expense of traditionally predominant Uzyn and Qulan-Qypshaq subdivisions (also Middle Umbrella Clan, but of the Qypshaq division). He offered a spirited defense of his actions, saying, "I will not deny these people, first, as Torghai residents and countrymen [*zemliaki*], as comrades at work, and as members of a single team."[23]

In South Kazakhstan region, the extent of clan clientelism was especially noteworthy, as a former member of the regional *maslikhat* documents. Local subethnic patronage networks reached national-level politics, ensnaring particular members of the lucrative extractive industries, who had a stake in Shymkent's local oil refinery.[24] There were other signs that South Kazakhstan region saw particularly active subethnic ties. Its Saizaq district was the first district in the country to create a local "council of elders" to adjudicate local disputes. These elders were the most prominent members of the clans that dominated in the area. In northern Kazakhstan, a similar proposal appears to have fallen on deaf ears.[25]

If in many cases, patronage led to abuses of power for the benefit of kin groups, these ties were not uniformly understood to be negative. According to one prominent informant, the regional governor of Atyrau in 1998, Ravil' Cherdabaev, had strong ties to the region's dominant subethnic division, and this was a positive; it meant that he understood local conditions and pursued the region's interests. His temporary replacement by a clan outsider was a detriment to the region, and his eventual return to the office a boon, as it brought enormous investment in the region's extractive industries.[26]

Whether one viewed such local, subethnic ties as a political asset or a liability depended in part on one's own clan background. An outsider was more likely to claim abuse of power and exclusive subethnic networks, while an insider was more likely to view the same patterns as evidence of political acumen and knowledge of local conditions. Perhaps for this reason, the most vocal critics of existing power relations in South Kazakhstan region were from the Middle Umbrella Clan, which resented domination by the Elder Umbrella Clan elite. Similarly, in Atyrau, where the Younger Umbrella Clan dominated, those who would take the risky step of criticizing existing power relations tended to be from the Middle Umbrella Clan.[27]

At the most local level (cities and districts), kin background was a primary consideration in political patronage. As one long-time employee of the Shymkent city *akimat* noted, when the new *akim* was appointed, he usually replaced about 50 percent of the office staff with his supporters. These people were usually from the same umbrella clan and frequently from the same subgroups.[28] Even where hiring did not occur along strictly subethnic lines, employers in state agencies often required job candidates to proffer their subethnic background, as a way to test their trustworthiness. Those few who refused to give their background could be eliminated for not cooperating or accused of not knowing their ethnic roots—that is, for being a Russified Kazakh.[29]

In everyday life, the conflation of kin ties with professional ties was strikingly normal outside of the major cities.[30] While living in the family of a highly placed police officer in a large town in South Kazakhstan region in 1997, I noted that the police force was staffed by a striking number of members of the same clan. Although the precise nature of such kin ties, not to mention their frequency, was difficult to gauge, there was no question that the average workday intertwined kin and professional obligations. This occurred, for example, when the leadership of the local police force attended—during work hours— the funeral of a prominent relative who had been a highly placed member on the force.[31]

Similar patterns emerged in higher education. In Shymkent, one ethnic Russian professor may have been exaggerating when he claimed that "kinship determines everything" in faculty appointments to local institutes,[32] but it is true that kin connections offered broad social utility. For example, it was common for an instructor to give preferential treatment to students from closely related kin background while requiring that poor performing non-kin students who desired to pass the course pay bribes. In such cases, the instructor would informally use kin-related students as his or her *uzyn qulaq* (long ear) to find out which non-kin students sought to offer such bribes.[33] The widespread practice by which students from rural, or otherwise remote, areas lived with extended families in the city while pursuing higher education also solidified kin-based attachments.

Clan played a still-greater role in rural locales. Given declining economic conditions (particularly for animal husbandry), access to scarce goods was established through subethnicity. Place of residence on a micro scale (e.g., who lives on the east side of the river, who lives on the west side) was understood to correspond with clan divisions. Thus, when massive agricultural privatization brought the dismantling of state and collective farms, it raised the stakes for clan politics. In the process, the members of one local clan often sought to privilege their kin. This could be accomplished through illegal means (by rigging the privatization process to favor kin), but it could also be achieved through legal means. Among them was the legal provision under privatization by which nonfarmers (generally professionals — schoolteachers, doctors, nurses — who had been assigned to work in rural areas during the Soviet period) were not entitled to receive privatized land and were therefore forced to migrate from the locale.[34]

Russians: The "Fourth Umbrella Clan"?

Competition among Kazakh clans was at the center of post-Soviet Kazakhstani politics, but it was dependent, in part, on the larger milieu of interethnic relations. As in any multi-ethnic state, patterns of politics within subpopulations depend on larger societal dynamics. Here, I stop to highlight ways in which changed interethnic relations intensified interclan competition in the late 1990s.

Metaphorically, ethnic Russians were occasionally referred to as a "fourth umbrella clan." The logic was that Russians, at approximately 30 percent of the population, could only compete with Kazakhs or individual clan networks if they adopted modes of behavior similar to that of titular Kazakhs; to survive, Russians had to become clannish, by systematically privileging their own kind through patronage. The depiction has a certain logic: the more non-Kazakhs were blocked from access to political and economic goods, the more attractive it became to replicate Kazakhs' access networks.

Demographic trends in the 1990s fueled the process. As the relative size of the ethnic Kazakh population increased, clan networks became more and more operative in political life. If, in the past, a powerful Kazakh with alternative networks at his disposal would have had to contend with networks that included any number of others (Russians, Ukrainians, Uzbeks, etc.), now such a powerful Kazakh would contend increasingly with other Kazakhs (among whom he distinguished through their clan background, among other factors). As the relative size of the ethnic Russian population dwindled through emigration, their political marginalization increased and the need to use networks became more apparent.

The problem with such a depiction is that it gets the Kazakh side of the story correct while mischaracterizing the Russian side. In the face of clan-based networks, Russians exhibited some degree of cohesion that on occasion resembled kinlike behavior. In this sense, clan may be used as a metaphor. But it is more difficult to generate the trust that is the glue of network behavior when identities are neither concealable nor multitiered in nature. The result at the republican level was that Nazarbaev found it relatively easy to reward individual Russians for their personal loyalty, undermining any fealty to a larger Russian community. If an ethnic Russian chose not to become ensnared in such patronage relationships, his or her opportunities for professional advancement were correspondingly more limited.

HOW IMPORTANT WERE CLAN NETWORKS?

In the foregoing, I paint a slightly misleading picture of clan politics. Although I have tried to count them, clans are among those political phenomena that are hard to quantify. They are concealable, often invisible, private, and (as the next chapter elaborates) hotly contested. They are not election results or interest rates; they lend themselves poorly to quantification. It is imperative to study their impact using qualitative methods.

Yet, ascendant modes of analysis focus on precisely what Kasza calls the "countables" (i.e., that which lends itself to quantification) to tease out the impact of various factors of political life.[35] Such analyses begin innocently enough, asking that we pose questions in causal terms. How does an array of factors (structural or agent-based; general or contextually specific; interactive or direct) influence a particular political outcome (such as an electoral result, a policy decision, or regime transformation)? These analyses ask that we pay close attention to scientific research design, arguing that successful design can isolate the extent of each factor's causal impact on the outcome in question.

The problem with such modes of analysis is not, as the cliché goes, that statistics "lie." Numbers, and the statistical manipulation thereof, are abstractions that may be more or less useful, depending on the subject under study. The problem is that much depends on how the factors and outcomes are conceptualized in the first place. And our initial conceptualizations are often created with an eye to their eventual quantification. Put simply: we focus on those aspects of a political life that are easily counted. This may have professional utility for the researcher, but if it drives our research agendas we should be suspicious of our own conclusions.

Above, I sought to use patterns of political appointments to discern the contours of clan conflict in post-Soviet Kazakhstan. Here is the crux of the problem: I conceptualized clans in a particular way. I painted a picture of clans as networks that allow individuals to access goods that they otherwise would find difficult to procure. Based on what I have observed and learned, I believe that this is much of what clans became in the Soviet period. Beginning with this conceptualization, a core expectation emerges: to the extent that clans "matter" in post-Soviet Central Asia, we will find a state in which the dominant clans systematically privilege their own. We will find that clans privatize the state and its associated resources. We will witness attempts at "social closure" that Weber describes.

When we discover that Nazarbaev privileged his own umbrella clan but not to the extent expected, we jump to the conclusion that clan indeed has an impact—but not an overwhelming one—on political life. In statistical language, it affects political life at the margins, and those margins are not enormous. But if we accept this interpretation, we have a pure example of how our conceptual categories (created in part for their "countability") generate our conclusions.

It would be a mistake to suggest that clan influences politics only in the sense conceptualized a priori. Take the following hypothetical outcome. In Ministry X, we find that the profile of the personnel mirrors that of the population at large. That is, we find roughly representative numbers of Younger, Middle, and Elder Clan Kazakhs. If clans are exclusive networks that systematically privilege their own kind, we conclude that clan plays little role in the ministry. No systematic exclusion of clans is visible. On the other hand, what alternatives are we missing? One invisible possibility is that the three clans are at a standoff; each seeks to gain exclusive control and systematically privilege its own kind, but none gains ascendancy. A second is that the three clans are not at a standoff but rather have compromised; each retains exclusive control over particular functions within the ministry. Neither of these two possibilities involves a fundamental reconceptualization of clan politics.

A third invisible possibility recommends that we rethink how clans behave. What if an act of clan balancing is occurring? That is, what if the clan that is dominant at the margins seeks to retain its marginal advantage *precisely by appeasing the other clans* on an at-least-minimal level? In short, what if a clan's strategy is not to exert its domi-. nance to the fullest extent possible but rather to retain its position by restraining itself from systematically privileging its own kind? In rational-choice language, it may not be a stable equilibrium for clan groups to systematically privilege their own to a degree that categorically excludes alternative clans from power. If dominant clans engage in such behavior, they will undermine the state itself, thus killing their ability to reap benefits. The rational, dominant clan would therefore seek to please its opponents at a minimal level, to avoid such a fate.

There is no way to know a priori if this third interpretation is more plausible. It creates an analytic challenge and an empirical one. The analytic challenge is that the *outcome* of such a situation looks strikingly like a situation in which clans fall by the political wayside. Without tracing the concrete process involved, we have no way of distinguishing among similar results. The empirical challenge is the Somalia case, in which the dominant kin groups simply privatized the state's resources, undermined alternative clans, and thereby fostered the unraveling of the state itself. Either Somali actors did not care whether or not their equilibria were stable, or they had very different goals than most rational-choice analysts would in their place.

Clan politics mattered in Central Asia, but in two ways that are theoretically in tension. These might be called "clan clientelism" and "clan balancing." In the Somalia case, clan clientelism contributed to the collapse of the state but little balancing occurred. In Morocco, something closer to clan balancing occurred, with the monarch lifting himself above the fray of clan competition to adjudicate fair solutions to clan conflict and ensure a relative stability of interclan relations.[36] In Kazakhstan, both occurred simultaneously. At the core of the regime were practices of clan clientelism, with Nazarbaev creating a pocket of privilege for his extended family and elite members of his umbrella clan. In the broader elite, such privilege was relatively diminished as Nazarbaev sought to foster a degree of clan balancing. Nazarbaev apparently calculated that, even as he sought to privilege his own kind and bring his family material benefit, he ought to avoid the most fundamentally destabilizing practices of clan-based patronage. Individual regions, cities, and districts saw contextually specific mixes of the two principles.

Why clan clientelism emerges in some cases while balancing occurs

in others is a subject that deserves further study. In either case, however, clan remains an operative political factor. Clan balancing is the
successful management of clan ties (as this book's conclusion explores);
it is not the absence of clan as a political factor. In the end, to distinguish between similar outcomes, there is no substitute for in-depth,
case-specific knowledge. Analysis that fails to conduct a Geertzian
"thick description" risks being correct in a logical-deductive or
statistical-mathematical sense but fundamentally at odds with the
empirical reality of context-specific politics. It risks ignoring, in
Geertz's terms, the difference between an involuntary twitch of the
eyelid and a wink that signals conspiracy.[37] Close familiarity with cases
enables such important distinctions.

6

Clan Metaconflict

How much effort and love for genealogies is necessary in order to verify and sort through the testimonies, in which one Kyrgyz [Kazakh] says that his clan [*rod*] divides into 5 or 6 parts, another from the very same clan assures that there are 12, a third confuses outside divisions with his own, and a fourth, and the most frank [informant], responds that he is completely ignorant. —*Aleksei Iraklievich Levshin*

CHAPTER 5 DESCRIBED THE CONTOURS OF KIN-BASED NET-works and their bearing on state-building outcomes, especially in personnel recruitment. The analysis was predicated on an assumption: that actors have good information about other actors' kin background and therefore may choose to privilege their kin at the expense of non-kin. In this chapter, I relax this assumption because, as a matter of everyday political life, actors often faced just the opposite in post-Soviet Kazakhstan: an information deficit.

This information deficit lent clan politics an additional dynamic that centered on discursive conflicts about clans. When information about kinship is widely available, political actors may use such information and may also scrutinize the behaviors of others for possible favoritism. But such information is not always available. Under such circumstances, a metaconflict over the contours of clan networks, the meanings attributed to clan divisions, and the character of insider politics ensues. This metaconflict—a discursive battle over the role that clans are understood factually to play in contemporary politics and over the role that clans *ought* normatively to play in political life—occurs because the ongoing stigma attributed to clan divisions removes them from legitimate public space and disrupts the free flow of information about kinship.

Because kin divisions continued to be driven from public space, political and social actors often possessed quite sketchy knowledge of the kin background of other actors. But this sketchiness of knowledge was an opportunity, since it allowed political entrepreneurs to speculate grandly, using the language of clans to discredit their political opponents. Thus, the modernist discourse that stigmatized clan divisions as "regressive" or "primitive" meant that political actors had to find ways to deny acting in a "clannish" fashion.

The shift in discussion that this chapter undertakes is represented in figures 6.1 and 6.2, below. It begins with the picture painted in the previous chapter: in recruitment to the state apparatus, kinship was clearly operative. But clan networks played one role when information on clan background was widely available (figure 6.1) and another when it was not (figure 6.2).

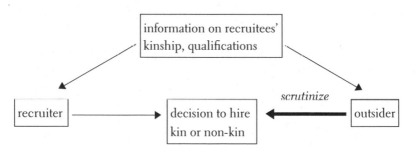

Figure 6.1. Role of Kinship in Information-Rich Environments

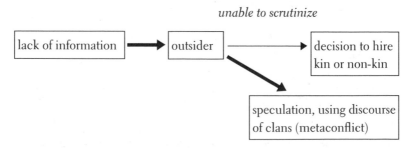

Figure 6.2. Clan Metaconflict in Information-Poor Environments

When information on clan background is available to insiders/ recruiters (figure 6.1), they use it in making decisions in personnel appointments. When the same information is available to outsiders, the latter may scrutinize hiring practices for possible biases. Outsiders and insiders thus engage in clan conflict, as they angle for access to goods and scrutinize each others' behavior.

At the same time, information on clan background is often unavailable to outsiders (figure 6.2). In information-poor environments, outsiders not privy to insider information cannot discern how important kinship considerations are in hiring practices. This presents for them an obstacle: they cannot closely scrutinize the behavior of insiders on the basis of high-quality information. On the other hand, it also creates for them an opportunity: they may use the language of clan divisions to paint insiders as behaving in regressive and evolutionarily primitive ways that undermine the effectiveness of state institutions.

This chapter discusses two clusters of actors ensnared in this metaconflict: quasi-state actors and members of the opposition. Each was deeply involved in shaping the discursive politics of clan divisions. Quasi-state actors (i.e., local agents occupying formal, state posts but who pursued their own political agendas) attempted to dismantle the anti-clan modernist discourse by depicting clans as the source of Kazakh ethnic pride. At the same time, the members of a broad opposition used the modernist discourse to criticize the Nazarbaev regime for its insularity, corruption, and familialism.

QUASI-STATE ACTORS

Quasi-state actors are those agents of state authority who manage to pursue their own political agendas while implementing official policy decisions. They find considerable room for maneuver even as they work on behalf of central authorities. In post-Soviet Kazakhstan, regional and local *akims* may safely be described using this language. Perhaps the single most important policy area for these quasi-state actors in the 1990s was ethnic redress (i.e., affirmative action). In this area their leeway to implement policy in ways that made local political sense deeply shaped clan metaconflict. Why this was the case requires some explanation.

Broadly speaking, state-led efforts of affirmative action provided material benefits to many Kazakhs. It is noteworthy, however, that the commitment of the state elite to Kazakhification was often more discursive than immediately material. If in Malaysia, preferences were explicit and given legal grounding (even if the implementation was uneven and the subject of ongoing political debate), in Kazakhstan these policies were ad hoc and extralegal from the start. Moreover, problems with funding, implementation, and logistics rendered this in no small part a multilayered campaign on paper. One state official admitted that Nazarbaev's widely promoted Strategy 2030, for example, did not affect ordinary people as intended, a fact he attributed to popular demobilization and widespread apathy towards anything political.[1]

By creating a diffuse, discourse-based campaign of Kazakhification, the state spawned a whole series of consequences, many of which were unintended. Unlike more focused state-led discursive efforts—such as, for example, televised anti-drug campaigns that target teenagers in advanced industrial countries—this campaign was diffuse. As such, its impact lay crucially in the hands of those state officials and quasi-state agents in individual locales who endeavored to translate state discourse on Kazakhness into political practice on the ground.

A few incidents illustrate the liberties taken at the local level. Article 19 of the Constitution unambiguously states, "Each person is permitted to define and indicate or not indicate his/her national, party, or religious affiliation,"[2] but local officials in South Kazakhstan *oblast* frustrated an ethnic Russian journalist's attempt to prevent his ethnicity from appearing in his new internal passport. After several months in national-level courts at considerable personal expense, he secured the right to withhold his ethnicity. He attributed his relative success to his being an exceptionally visible journalist.[3] While the republic's Constitution was widely available for sale and loudly trumpeted as a feature of modern statehood, these local officials had clearly taken their cues from other sources. In another case, a local state official in South Kazakhstan *oblast* in 1998 justified local initiatives to promote the Kazakh language with reference to a single aspect of state language law: that the language was considered a "consolidating factor" in a multi-ethnic Kazakhstan. Conceding that there were critics of local initiatives to promote Kazakh, he added, "We found a general consensus over all [of them]."[4]

The broad promotion of the markers of Kazakhness led to a reconstitution of politically salient subethnic identities, in large part by individual local initiative. In a state with a significant ethnic Slavic minority and that was popularly viewed as bi-ethnic, clan and umbrella clan genealogies experienced a revival as traits that distinguished ethnic Kazakhs from the nontitular citizens of independent Kazakhstan. An explosion of interest in genealogical knowledge, widespread celebrations of clan-based historical figures and monuments, and a dramatic increase in private and semipublic discussion of the subethnic backgrounds of others all testify to the mounting significance of these identities. In short, genealogical knowledge was understood to be axiomatic (even if it required reviving in the 1990s).

Many considered such knowledge to have a functional purpose as well. The contention was that genealogical knowledge enabled strong community relations among Kazakhs, which ultimately was a mechanism for the preservation of groups under severe ecological conditions.[5] The powerful governor of Almaty *oblast* described the close relations among relatives: "Concern of close relatives for the family of a brother who had passed away was, even in the postwar troubles, a distinguishing feature of the behavior of Kazakhs. Neither the change of regime, nor the relatively new code of ethnic establishment of powers, nor the little-allowed observance of traditions of the ancestors of the steppe generations [*kolen*] were capable of shaking the eternal, sacred duty of relatives to care for their close ones who had come upon misfortune."[6]

Of course, by the late Soviet and post-Soviet periods, there were too many competing allegiances—to Party, to internationalism, to nontitulars with privileged access to scarce goods, and so on—to accept these depictions as descriptively accurate. The argument here is not that genealogical knowledge was an inalienable, inherent, or primordial trait among Kazakhs, but rather that quasi-state actors held it up as such. Thus, the picture should be one of directionality, that is, that there was a movement to (re)discover genealogies. One young professional living in Almaty described how in the early 1990s she developed an interest in her genealogy, although in her urban childhood she had not been socialized to know much beyond her grandparents' generation. This revived interest appears typical for Kazakhs during the period.[7]

Unlike the genealogies (*shezhire*) of the pre-Soviet period, which were largely committed to memory and transmitted orally, the genealogies of the post-Soviet period were published for an almost universally literate Kazakh population. Some were reprints of classic authors' attempts at universal classification of Kazakhs' and related peoples' backgrounds.[8] Others were more contemporary versions thereof.[9] The vast majority, however, sought to catalogue ancestors among a more specifically defined subdivision. For example, one offered almost seventy-five pages of diagrams of interrelations among the politically important Qongyrats of the Middle Umbrella Clan.[10] These works offered the backdrop for more homespun, self-published or unpublished accounts of the genealogies of very specific segments that often included the author himself.[11] While no data are available on the number of written genealogies generated since the Soviet collapse, indications are clear that the practice was widespread, as informants described that even in urban areas these books were a popular gift in the early to mid-1990s.[12] In addition, the print runs in some cases ran as high as one hundred thousand, an enormous figure in a country with approximately eight million Kazakhs whose disposable income for nonessentials had plummeted since the Soviet collapse.

An emphasis on genealogical knowledge came from Kazakh-speaking milieus. Kazakh-language newspapers depicted the revival of genealogies as an imperative for all Kazakhs. "To know one's origins is a sign of a good upbringing," proclaimed one 1997 article in the culture-oriented *Qazaq adebieti*.[13] Discussing the Russian-style patronymic endings ethnic Kazakhs assumed in the Soviet period, it suggested, "In the period of the red empire, we were fearful and too intimidated to inquire about our family origins. These legacies of age-old customs were associated with nostalgia for the past. Was that right? Not only was the great national quality, our distinctiveness, cast off from our family origins, but were we not made to wear the yoke of Russian 'ov' and 'eva?'"[14] Thus, the broad rhetoric of a return to original markers of Kazakhness found reflection in a renewed interest in genealogies.

In addition to a revived interest in genealogies, individual locales and regions began to identify and glorify clan-based heroes, to rename streets, schools, and former state farms in their honor, and to emphasize the role of particular segments in Kazakh history. In short, regional and local elites sought to restore to clan identities the cultural content, of which the Soviet experience had deprived them. To what extent were these local initiatives manifestations of subethnic identities, and to what extent were they simply a return to important but forgotten aspects of an ethnic *Kazakh* history? For many cases, it makes little sense to disentangle whether what was being celebrated had an ethnic or a subethnic basis. The two categories are not mutually exclusive; moreover, they are *nested* in the sense that manifestations of the lower affiliation generally imply a simultaneous enactment of the higher-level one.[15] From this perspective, it is not surprising that a promotion of ethnicity would entail a simultaneous promotion of subethnic affiliations.

On the surface, many local efforts to celebrate the historical significance of local figures or places appear to have been ad hoc and idiosyncratic, but the sheer frequency of their occurrence across a broad territory was striking. For example: The authorities in Zhezqazghan *oblast* attempted to draw attention to Ulytau, the mythical place where Kazakh statehood is said to have begun.[16] In Qaraghandy, one article fixed the number of architectural "objects" in the *oblast* at more than four hundred and estimated that more than ten times that number of sites deserved immediate attention for their historical value but remained unexcavated.[17] In Mangystau *oblast*, a region of profound archaeological interest, there was a call for restoring the mausoleums and necropolises of various figures dating to the ninth century.[18] In Semei *oblast*, the descendants of Toghybai *batyr* (hero) erected an "interesting and unique monument" in his honor.[19] In Taldy-Qorghan, a fund was established to build a monument to Eskeldi *batyr*.[20] In Aqtobe, a funeral repast (*as beru*) was held for Eset *batyr* of the Shekti clan (Younger Umbrella Clan).[21] Qyzylorda *oblast* celebrated Zhanqozhy *batyr*, a prominent warrior against the Kokand Khanate and then Russian imperial expansion.[22]

Some historical figures were the subject of protracted, multievent celebrations, as in the case of Bogenbai *batyr* of the Qanzhygaly of the Middle Umbrella Clan in Akmolinsk *oblast*. As in other regions, the demise of Soviet symbols created an opportunity for renaming various objects of significance; accordingly, authorities elected to honor local notables. Thus, in the city of Aqmola, Five-Year Plan Street was renamed Bogenbai Street,[23] and the state farm "Peaceful" in Seletinsk district of Akmolinsk *oblast* was recast as Bogenbai Farm.[24] The region's papers carried innumerable articles covering the sacred history of Bogenbai and his efforts to stave off Zhungar advances in the early eighteenth century. In addition, a scholarly conference was convened,[25] and two monuments were erected in his honor in the *oblast*.[26]

This celebration had profound connotations for subethnic identities. One news account made a hero of a direct ancestor of Bogenbai who had kept Bogenbai's helmet in safe keeping, never surrendering it to the authorities during the Soviet period, and finally coming forth in time for the celebration of Bogenbai's three hundreth birthday.[27] During the birthday celebration, "the esteemed elders [present] . . . represented the legendary segment of the *batyr* Bogenbai. They told of the legends connected with Bogenbai *batyr* that had been carefully protected throughout the generations."[28]

Some regions lagged in their staging of such celebrations. Qyzylorda *oblast*, among the most poverty-stricken areas, encountered acute difficulties with funding and adequate building materials in its drive to restore mosques, towers, and other memorial structures. Local officials claimed that restorative efforts began "notably later" than in other *oblasts*.[29] Indeed, whether through press accounts or personal networks, many officials seemed clearly aware of the attention to historical figures lavished in the other administrative regions. One article from the official paper in Akmolinsk *oblast* lamented, "You get offended for our fellow countrymen [*zemliaki*] when you read in the papers or see on television how in the other *oblasts* people unveil monuments to their heroes and historical personalities. Can it really be that we cannot be proud of our history, that we will have nothing to show our children . . . ?"[30]

Given that most of the limited funding for restoring sites of cultural significance, as well as for publicizing the endeavors of almost forgotten heroes, came from Almaty (and with the move of the capital in late 1997, Astana), competition was keen. Regions therefore touted the significance of the sites in their jurisdiction as somehow central to Kazakh history. Thus, an official paper in Mangystau *oblast* claimed with optimism in 1998, "It would not be surprising if the Mangyshlaq [peninsula] turned into a Mecca for archaeologists and tourists."[31]

Why would local authorities stage a semipublic battle over resources to conduct celebrations of their local heroes? Why were these resources considered worth the effort? While some state officials probably desired to line their pockets under any available pretext, funding was not the only good in scarce supply. The attributes understood

to underlie Kazakhness—language, genealogical knowledge, and connection to events or personages of historical significance—were
sorely lacking, especially among the members of a largely Russified
political elite. To embrace the markers of Kazakh identity (or at minimum to become the rhetorical champion of those markers) was part
of a bidding war in the context of a society widely understood to be
bi-ethnic. Distinguishing oneself from the ethnic other was a political tool, and widespread attention to local heroes and historical sites
honed the instrument. Although embracing Kazakh traits did not
always translate directly into material rewards, it did hold the promise of future gains in the context of an increasingly ethnic Kazakh
Kazakhstan.

These state-led attempts at ethnic redress served to reinvigorate
subethnic identities because of the activities of quasi-state actors who
implemented them. This was not what the state elite had intended.
If anything, state actors rather had preferred to unify ethnic Kazakhs
as a strategy of ethnic nation building. Instead, their actions lent political salience to the subdivisions among ethnic Kazakhs.

Reframing kinship and its significance, these regional actors were
involved in a metaconflict. While they seemed determined to portray subethnic divisions as the positive markers of Kazakhness and
themselves as the carriers of these identities, members of the opposition contested the notion that subethnicity could be progressive in
any sense.

THE OPPOSITION

In contrast to the quasi-state actors, the opposition used a discussion
of subethnicity to criticize officialdom. A diverse group invoked
subethnicity as a means of discrediting the regime for its lack of transparency and openness. Their central claim was that clan clientelism—
the privileged allocation of resources along subethnic lines—was rampant among the elite. In advancing this contention, the opposition
engaged the metaconflict by depicting subethnicity as negative—as
the wellspring of traditionalism and backwardness. These claims had
some empirical basis in patterns of official behavior, but they went
beyond descriptive accuracy; they were marshaled in exaggerated tones
for political effect.

As chapter 5 detailed, there is no question that clan identity continued to inform patronage networks in the 1990s. However, the extent of these networks was itself an object of contention. To what degree was clan patronage a central aspect of political life, and to what degree were claims about the pervasiveness of subethnic clientelism part of a larger metaconflict? Clan politics was behind-the-scenes; relationships were opaque. This opacity was not only a methodological obstacle for researchers; it was also an epistemological one for any outsider, be that person a researcher or a political actor.

Subethnic Criticism

Exaggeration for political effect is not the monopoly of the masters of "spin" in advanced industrial democracies. Central to these clan struggles was a powerfully resonant discourse on subethnic identities that was marshaled by a diverse political opposition intent on discrediting the Nazarbaev regime. Events dealing with Nurbulat Masanov, a prominent member of the liberal opposition, vividly illustrate how the regime viewed kin-based commentaries as a threat. The use of subethnicity as a way to criticize the regime, however, was not limited to liberals; rather, it was common across the broad spectrum of opposition groups. These criticisms had a clear empirical basis in observations of officialdom, but they went beyond simple descriptions of behaviors to render the polity as closed, primitive, and traditional.

Scholar and activist Nurbulat Masanov wrote a series of articles critical of the regime in which he used subethnicity to interpret political developments.[32] His deliberate marginalization by state officials from the scholarly community points to the threat perceived in his analyses. It is not merely that Masanov's critiques got too close to the truth by revealing patterns of subethnic politics. The very fact of marshaling such critiques based on clan divisions—identities that were stigmatized as backward and primitive in the context of modern statehood—implied a general criticism of the regime.

A composite of Masanov's scholarship will help to illustrate the controversy. In some senses, Masanov was a typical intellectual product of the Soviet period, combining elements of primordialism with a Marxian emphasis on evolutionary stages of development. He posited a stark dichotomy between the traditional (which he took to persist in forms unchanged from the pre-Soviet past) and the modern (which he idealized for its freedom of movement, social mobility, and complexity).

In other respects, Masanov stood apart from his colleagues. Broadly read, he commanded a wide audience as the end of Soviet dominance brought with it a renewed interest in pre-Soviet traditions. While his relatively poor knowledge of the Kazakh language did not endear him to Kazakh ethnonationalists, his erudition on nomadism remained unparalleled. More theoretically sophisticated than many of his peers, he was uniquely willing to marry the language of scholarship with the vehemence of political criticism. Moreover, unlike the vast majority of other scholars associated with the opposition, Masanov remained largely independent of domestic actors in Kazakhstan, opening him to the criticism of that he relied on foreign donor groups.

Taking a cue from traditions of structural-functional anthropology, he argued that the harsh climatic conditions of the Eurasian territory virtually determined the essential cultural patterns and modes of behavior that he considered hallmarks of Kazakhness.[33] While milder climatic conditions allowed for greater variation in social structure and mode of economy in much of the world, the semi-desert, desert, and steppe severely limited such variation in the territory of what is now Kazakhstan. Instead, capital accumulation was negligible, so one of the prime engines of social change was largely absent.[34]

What the nomads lacked in capital accumulation, Masanov argued, they made up for in knowledge accumulation: "the very survival of the nomad was possible only given the possession [*ovladenie*] of special knowledge accumulated and passed on by generations of ancestors."[35] He contended that under such conditions, if this knowledge as well as limited property were made diffuse, this would heighten competition for already scarce resources (pasturage, water). Therefore, nomads would instead transmit their knowledge and property through patrilineal channels. While "social organization could become significantly more complicated under the influence of other principles . . . the high consistency [*ustoichivost'*] of the genealogical principle does not raise any doubts."[36]

Gradually, Masanov became a political critic, authoring an alternative constitution for the republic and participating in various weak opposition movements, such as Citizen, People's Front (*Narodnyi front*), the Republican People's Party, and Democratic Choice of Kazakhstan. His articles appeared with increasing frequency on the pages of Kazakhstan's relatively liberal press, and while they never lost their tone of scholarly authority, they demonstrated an increasingly clear criticism of the current regime. The Kazakh-language press, which received generous operational subsidies from state agencies, routinely singled out Masanov for being a Russified Kazakh who ostensibly did not respect his own people, preferring instead to travel to Europe and to forge ties with the Soros Foundation.[37]

As a critic of the regime, Masanov was one of many. His criticism, however, was deemed unusually threatening in official circles. In 1996, Masanov published an article entitled "Kazakh Political and Intellectual Elite: Clan Membership and Intra-Ethnic Competition" in a Moscow-based journal. In this article, he used clan and umbrella clan backgrounds broadly to analyze Soviet and post-Soviet political developments.[38] About Nazarbaev, in particular, he noted the pattern of appointments from the village of Chemolgan (Nazarbaev's birthplace), which gave rise to depictions of the *Chemolganizatsiia* (Chemolganization) of the power structures. Part of his conclusion contended that

> competition of the umbrella clans on the elite level played and plays an extremely important role in the life of Kazakh society. Notwithstanding, we should not forget that no clan is monolithic, since among Kazakhs intraclan competition is also widespread. Much depends on the concrete region and concrete people, but it is quite well-known, for example, that some Arghyns, Naimans, and Qypshaqs cannot stand each other. In the Younger Clan, Alimulins and Vailulins condescend to the Zhetiru. In the Elder Clan, the Shaprashts and Dulats are more influential than others, often hampering the advancement of representatives of other clans.[39]

Observers of Kazakhstani politics, both casual and professional, will recognize this mode of analysis as common in post-Soviet Kazakhstan. Rumor, innuendo, and private conversation routinely centered on speculation about the umbrella clan and clan-based machinations understood to underlie patterns of political appointments. Masanov differed from others in that his analysis that listed individual names from across officialdom saw publication, and this posed a particular threat to the Nazarbaev regime.

The issue came to a head in March 1998 when President Nazarbaev summoned members of the cultural intelligentsia to hear him speak about the "Moral and Political Choice of the Intelligentsia."

In this session, he admonished those present for "not taking into consideration . . . the historical and social responsibility of the Kazakh intelligentsia" to "demonstrat[e] restraint and wisdom, not allowing [themselves] to succumb to emotional calls to arms."[40] After a long excursus on the historical role of the intelligentsia, he called upon those present to, among other things, "preserve not only interethnic [*mezhnatsional'nyi*] but also intraethnic [*vnutrinatsional'nyi*] peace in the country. The whole history of our defeats, the whole history of our victories, is connected to ethnic [*natsional'nyi*] unity."[41]

Nazarbaev likened subethnic analysis on the part of the intelligentsia to an ostensible desire to divide Kazakhs, singling out Masanov's article. According to Masanov's description of the events, the president said: "He has divided [*raspisal*] all of you sitting here by your kin background [*rodovoi priznak*]."[42] Several weeks later, Masanov was removed from his tenured position at Kazakh National State University. Even before these events, as a Russia-trained and linguistically Russified Kazakh, Masanov had already engendered a degree of opposition. Masanov's article convinced his opponents that he was merely the latest in a string of outsiders—everyone from tsarist administrators to Stalin himself—who exploited clan divisions to divide and rule the Kazakhs. Nazarbaev's words had given Masanov's critics ammunition in their long-standing struggle. While it is impossible to say whether or not the president personally sanctioned this action, his position on Masanov's article encouraged those inclined to make a move.

Part of the reason that the Masanov critique was effective is that it accurately captured empirical patterns about clan networks. Had his depictions of subethnicity-based politics been totally off the mark, officials might have summarily dismissed them as irrelevant and unthreatening. But perhaps the effectiveness of clan-based critiques lay not in their ultimate truth or falsity (neither of which could, in any event, be established conclusively). The specific claims about patterns of clan clientelism notwithstanding, the regime faced a more general criticism—based on accusations of traditionalism, patrimonialism, and secretiveness.

Criticism across the Political Spectrum

The Masanov controversy was a particularly vivid illustration of how the regime viewed subethnic analysis as threatening, but similar cri-

tiques were offered across the political spectrum. Liberals, ethnonationalists, the technocratic elite, ethnic Russians, and even some external actors used the language of clans to discredit the regime. The
diversity of ultimate ends that actors pursued through use of this criticism highlights its broad resonance. The invocation of subethnic identities was not merely a specific way to comment on observed patterns
of political behavior; it was a more general political tool used against
the regime.

Who constituted this opposition? Opposition to the regime was poorly
reflected in organized politics. Political parties encountered myriad problems of organization, resources, and legal and extralegal restrictions.
The opposition is better characterized not according to formal organizations but rather by the political agendas pursued, which included
(1) a liberal agenda of human rights and political freedoms, (2) a cul-
turalist agenda to promote the Kazakh culture and language, and (3)
a technocratic agenda of preparing the state for international economic
competitiveness.[43] Subethnic criticism spanned all three agendas.

Masanov and other political liberals took as their central goal to
democratize politics and establish guarantees against the arbitrary exercise of power. Among them, the claim that elite politics turned on
clan clientelism achieved wide sweep. This claim potentially included
both kin and non-kin, leaving no political actor fully immune to its
taint. The criticism allowed political liberals to construct a broad criticism that suggested a closed, premodern, exclusive, authoritarian
polity, in which patrimonialism was rampant.

An erstwhile coauthor with Masanov and a prominent liberal critic
of Nazarbaev, Nurlan Amrekulov, marshaled subethnic criticisms in
ways similar to Masanov.[44] In a 1998 interview published in a newspaper known for engendering controversy, he remarked,

> We Kazakhs began our movement to the market essentially from pre-
> feudal positions, from kin-tribal structures. Our kin-tribal (clannic)
> construction of society persists; kinship governs the individual. When
> the republic received sovereignty, the clannic principle simply repro-
> duced itself. Deterrent mechanisms, checks on power that in other
> countries, for example, are the parliament, were absent. And, if some-
> thing was divided up, it was divided in the closest of surroundings,
> among faithful people. In order to gain a position, one must have a
> patron.[45]

What is notable about this criticism is how easily the author moves from descriptions of kin-tribal (*rodoplemennye*) ties to the language of close family circles; for the liberal opposition the language of family and the claim of clan clientelism allowed the criticism to be extended beyond those with formal kin ties. Nonrelatives were routinely described as ensnared in these networks; the logic was that even though they were not technically part of a family (or clan) network, by their behavior they might as well have been. Amrekulov added in a full-length, self-published monograph that "traditionalism, ethnocentrism, an orientation to a dead-end resource strategy, skepticism about the power and creative potential of the people is what distinguishes this high-level, predominantly Kazakh *nomenklatura* that groups itself around the president."[46]

At the other end of the political spectrum, Kazakh ethnonationalists, with a political agenda that centered on strategies for reviving Kazakh culture and language, also marshaled this critique. This is noteworthy, since the political force of this group was particularly dependent on state resources. Unlike their Russian-language counterparts, those whose education, training, and socialization were in Kazakh-language environments were not the recipients of Soviet-era skills that translated well into independent political power in the post-Soviet era. To the contrary, ethnonationalists largely pursued their agenda through state agencies such as *Qazaq tili* and the Ministry for Information and Social Accord, which sponsored programs promoting Kazakh language and culture.[47]

Largely dependent on state structures, ethnonationalists used the subethnic critique more rarely but in ways similar to their liberal colleagues. Unlike the liberals who referred to traditional practices and the pre-Soviet era as a way to discredit the regime, many ethnonationalists viewed pre-Soviet traditions—including broad knowledge of genealogies—with nostalgia. The criticism from this group cited the regime for using family circles to satisfy particularistic agendas, rather than to provide public goods of broad use for all Kazakhs. Khasen Qozhaakhmet, a prominent member of this group, in an interview depicted clan identity as the domain of the *nomenklatura* class. Ordinary people were not interested in these issues, he claimed; they were more interested in national unity.[48] Thus, the ethnonationalists used the subethnic criticism to depict a corrupt regime bent on sowing disunity among Kazakhs to its own private gain.

Evidence from the ground level suggests that such critiques were common among ordinary Kazakh speakers, that is, those most likely to support an ethnonationalist agenda. In private gatherings, especially traditional ones where subethnicity played a role, such as wedding rituals (*qyz alu, betashar*), funeral repasts, and other events defined by family ties, private conversations that turned to political issues often viewed developments in similar terms. In such settings, stereotypes about the assumed characteristics of other subethnic groupings were reinforced, especially through jokes and witticisms.[49]

As a matter of fact, actors excluded from access to power may have suffered their fates for a variety of reasons. Their lack of proper kin ties was only one possibility among many. In the rapidly changing configurations of Kazakhstani politics, other reasons for exclusion included lack of access to foreign investors, to ready domestic capital, to cheap domestic resources, to powerful press actors, or the existence of close connections to Islamic groups, foreign human rights organizations, or informal groups of ethnic Russians or Cossacks.

Nonetheless, the most powerful metaphor of exclusion was the clan. It indexed a whole series of notions about the backwardness of tradition. The criticism was a powerful way by which a political outsider—whatever that person's agenda—could decry the regime for its particularism, for its exclusionism, for distributing benefits to a certain few insiders rather than to a broader array of groups.

On an everyday basis, ethnic Russians made similar claims, although published accounts of such critical voices are relatively rarer. Typical were the comments of one thirty-eight-year-old taxi driver in Almaty, who suggested that the umbrella clans always fight among themselves. When pressed on how he knows this, he replied that "It just seems to be so."[50] On the level of ordinary discourse, many Russians expressed the opinion that subethnic politics was one of many negative manifestations of a more general trend of Kazakhification.

For ethnic Russian critics locked out of access to power, the subethnic criticism derided Kazakhification as a return to the primitive. Calling Kazakhstan an historically "quite uninhabited [*pustynnoe*] space between Russia and China," one Russian member of the opposition asserted,

> Kazakhstan is always prone to separatism because it is an artificial formation. . . . And, the Kazakhs now in power try to carry out the idea

[of nation-statehood] —that we are on the age-old land of our ancestors, and so on. . . . We understand that Kazakhstan does not have the
possibility to return to some traditional history, to a pre-Soviet history,
and to build on that basis some—perhaps not a very modern, but a relatively balanced—state like Uzbekistan has. . . . We must build a civil
society and attempt to cross the bridge from the kin-tribal to the modern, but we have neither the time, nor the possibility, nor the material
to conduct all these transformations.[51]

In a similar fashion, Piotr Svoik, a vocal and critical Russian who
took up the mantle of political liberalism to defend the rights of Russians living in Kazakhstan, published an article in the weekly tabloid
Karavan that generated much controversy and created legal troubles
for the paper. (Because of this article, the newspaper was being inves-
tigated in 1998 for violating article 20, section 3 of the Constitution,
which prohibits "propaganda or agitation . . . of social, racial, national,
religious, class, or tribal superiority. . . . "[52]) About pre-Soviet Kazakhstan, Svoik claimed, "In essence, the single thing that among
nomads was fortified and passed down through inheritance was [their]
mentality based on the sanctity of kinship and the right of power." He
continued, "Corruption, incompetence and treachery are the ancestral markings [*rodovye priznaki*] of the current system of power." The
author here played on the double meaning of *rodovye*, which denotes
both "ancestral" and "kin-related."[53] Criticism of this sort allowed Russians disgruntled with the loss of status (or even with the demise of
the USSR) to render the post-Soviet regime as backward and traditional. It was a broadly resonant way to discredit the regime for being
unable to perform up to the standards of modern states.

Russians were not the only citizens with nostalgic visions of the
Soviet period. The dislocations caused by plummeting industrial out-
put, the collapse of state-sector employment, and other strains of economic transformation lent resonance to nostalgic visions of the Soviet
period among broad swaths of the population, regardless of ethnicity.
At the level of ordinary people, one Kazakh fisherman in his early for-
ties from the Arys region in South Kazakhstan *oblast* directed his ire
against local elders, claiming that they were responsible for encouraging subethnic divisions. He recalled that during the Soviet period,
people of all cultural backgrounds lived together and that the economy was also much better. This reasoning that made a connection

between an imagined cultural harmony and visions of economic stability remained fairly common.[54]

Technocrats also marshaled these sorts of claims. The rapid insertion of Kazakhstan into the world economy, which began in 1994 with the introduction of the national currency (*tenge*) and a subsequent austerity plan, was accompanied by a state-led effort to train economic managers, both abroad and in local institutes. This stratum of usually young technocrats took up the critique as a way to address economic inefficiency and back-room deals with high transaction costs. Akezhan Kazhegel'din, before being disqualified from participating in the 1998 presidential elections on a state-crafted technicality, offered a soft rhetorical version of this argument, writing, "The following variant is possible: when an authoritarian political regime is formed at the stage when market relations are just being established, the illegal assimilation of power and property by a concrete high official, his family, his relatives and friends, his clan [*klan*] is all too probable. Is this not what we now observe in Kazakhstan?"[55]

Interestingly, the criticism was also issued from beyond the borders of Kazakhstan. While it is difficult to know the extent of external actors who used the critique, those who linked their well-being to the shape of the regime found it effective. For example, the ultranationalist Russian politician Vladimir Zhirinovsky and his inaccurately named Liberal Democratic Party (LDP) focused attention on Kazakhstan because of the presence of six million diaspora Russians "stranded" there with the Soviet collapse. Known for hyperbole and clownishness, Zhirinovsky demonstrated real political acumen in his surprising performance in the 1993 elections to the Russian Duma, leading to concern in Kazakhstan over whether his widely quoted dream of Russian soldiers "washing their boots in the Indian Ocean" was not a threat to the territorial integrity of Central Asian states. Especially in the context of 1990, during Aleksandr Solzhenitsyn's claim on the northern regions of contemporary Kazakhstan, the rhetoric of such neoimperialists was taken seriously. While it is difficult to ascertain the LDP's actual interests in Kazakhstan, there was no question that depicting neighboring states in unflattering terms for their treatment of ethnic Russians residing there was part and parcel of its approach.

In 1997, with borders more normalized both politically and in the imaginations of ordinary people, neoimperialist visions from the north were no longer highly politicized matters, but they were still a concern. Under such circumstances, the LDP began publishing a "scholarly" series called the "Imperial Collection" (*Imperskii sbornik*), and the first volume was dedicated to Kazakhstan.[56] The volume's preface, while not calling into question Kazakhstan's right to sovereign statehood, did emphasize that its territory was "populated by the very same Russian people [as those in Russia], but who by the criminal will of unlucky politicians were torn away from the maternal body of the country."[57]

The *Imperskii* volume described the "battle for oil in Kazakhstan," in which a "narrow group of the closest relatives of Nursultan Nazarbaev and the clan-tribal leaders" of the Elder and Younger Umbrella Clans monopolized the sector.[58] Accordingly, besides Nazarbaev, a network involving the director of the State Committee on Investments (Akhmetzhan Esimov), the husband of Nazarbaev's daughter Dinara (Timur Kulibaev), and the husband of Nazarbaev's other daughter Dariga (Rakhat Aliev) represented the "basic principle of the functioning of the Kazakhstani economy."[59] These relationships were entrenched through an alliance with foreign (especially American) capital.

While the *Imperskii* volume was written by capable analysts with a largely plausible rendering of the high-stakes politics of oil in the region, and while there was substantial evidence that the depiction of the increasing concentration of power in the hands of Nazarbaev's family was accurate, there is no question what other purposes the language of subethnicity served. A regime to Russia's south that was understood to be deeply corrupt and wildly clientelistic was a regime incapable of defending the rights of its citizens, especially ethnic Russians. The publication was an effort to legitimate the political agenda of the LDP, insofar as it extended beyond the borders of the Russian Federation.

Opacity and the Political Use of Available Data

The politics of subethnicity as criticism was made resonant because it allowed various actors, on the basis of incomplete evidence, to depict the regime in unflattering terms. As outsiders, they could make judgments about opaque relationships, judgments that were subject to profound political forces. This is not to imply that oppositionist depictions were necessarily inaccurate; in fact, there is much to recommend them.

It is to suggest that, as outsiders, such actors' conclusions were also related to their political agendas.

This should not be surprising. Many who used the subethnic critique first identified a group of people with common subethnic background and only then described the political position of these people relative to one another. This recalled the "sharpshooter" who riddles the side of a barn with bullets and only afterwards superimposes a bull's-eye target where the holes have clustered.[60]

By contrast, as we saw earlier, if one first selected the domain of political activity and afterwards examined subethnic backgrounds, the picture was less determinate. Take, for example, South Kazakhstan region, predominantly ethnic Kazakh and consisting of Kazakhs predominantly from the Elder Umbrella Clan; one would expect this predominance to be reflected in the composition of appointments. In fact, of the seventeen local *akims* in December 1997, seven were from the Elder Umbrella Clan, six were from the Middle, one was Korean, one Russian, and one was of unidentified background.[61] Similarly, according to a key informant from a university in Taraz, where one would expect to find a similar predominance of Elder Clan Kazakhs, leading university administrators in early 1999 were three from the Elder Clan, two from the Middle, two from the Younger, one Uzbek, and one Tatar.[62] In these cases, the picture was not one of obvious clan clientelism.

There was not much consensus over the specific shape of subethnic politics, even among those who studied the question closely. The 1997 move of the capital from Almaty to Astana is illustrative. Observers named many possible factors explaining the move, one of which was clan politics. Among those who singled out the clan factor, there was striking divergence of opinion. Some, for example, viewed the move as a way to appease the Middle Clan Kazakhs, historically locked out of the ruling coalition between the Younger and Elder Clans, by giving them closer access to the resources of state. Others took the opposite viewpoint, believing this a step toward further Elder Clan domination by enabling a closer watch over the affairs of Middle Clan Kazakhs. To be clear: this is not to suggest that clan was not a critical criterion in this policy decision. Rather, it is to argue that whether one took one viewpoint versus the other in the face of inconclusive evidence was itself a political question.

Moreover, the knowledge of genealogies was a growth industry in the 1990s, given renewed popular interest in pre-Soviet forms of identity. Books purporting to be the authoritative *shezhire* of one or another subethnic division graced bookshelves in most homes, even in urban areas. The rapidity of publication to meet demand led to the possibility of serious mistakes. In addition, a widespread normative expectation that Kazakhs must possess genealogical knowledge led to feverish attempts to obtain that knowledge. While informants insisted that falsification of one's own genealogy was impossible—that any such attempt would be discovered rather quickly—the possibility that one would come to hasty conclusions about the *shezhire* of those in opaque relationships, especially those in the distant seats of political power, was omnipresent.

THE REGIME RESPONDS

The regime's response suggests that the subethnic criticism worked to good effect. A myriad of articles appeared in the state-run press and official academic journals that, attempting to co-opt the discussion of subethnicity, stressed the positive features of subethnic identity for Kazakhs. One article in the semi-scholarly journal *Aqiqat* attempted to recast *traibalizm* as *zhuzizm*, linguistically distancing the assumed consequences of divisions in Kazakhstan from that in other, tribal contexts.[63] Another article in the same journal went further, suggesting, "There is no need to fear umbrella clan and clans. It would be appropriate to see knowledge of genealogy [*shezhireni zertteu, bilu*] as the duty of every rooted [in his or her culture] Kazakh."[64] A semi-official research institute published an anonymous report on "Kazakh Tribalism" that described supposed tribalism as a limited problem that could be overcome by the "continuing modernization" of society.[65]

A common point emphasized in official versions was that divisions among Kazakhs served to preserve the integrity of the Kazakh people.[66] One response to Piotr Svoik's controversial article from *Karavan* stated,

> It seems that P. Svoik likes constantly to play on the supposedly weak chord of our people—our tradition of remembering and respecting our ancestors up to the seventh generation. This tradition, no matter the exotic clannic coloring "experts" like P. Svoik try to lend it, helped to

maintain the strong gene pool of the nation, since it excluded marriage within the clan. The kinship system allowed [us] to distribute pasturage and water fairly and accurately. . . . If it were not for kinship
unions, our ancestors would not have been able to keep control over
the expanses in which we live today and those borders of Kazakhstan
which are recognized by all of the world community.[67]

Official discourse emphasized historical moments of ethnic unity.
Accordingly, events such as the alliance of the three umbrella clans
in 1726 at Ordabasy to counter the threat of a Zhungar invasion from
the East were the subject of state-sponsored anniversary celebrations
in the mid-1990s. In 1998, when the new capital, Astana, was officially
dedicated, a sculpture of three prominent judges from each of the three
umbrella clans was unveiled in front of the Supreme Court building
with great fanfare and official press coverage. The symbolic fusion of
the new state apparatus with the ethnic unity of the clans was made
complete.

Essentialized depictions of pre-Soviet cultural traits and the pur-
ported origins of umbrella clan divisions were designed to defuse the
issue. In the context of a resurgent interest in Kazakh customs and
history, as many searched for the "real" character traits of Kazakhs,
such depictions had an effect. One article, written in English for a
foreign audience involved in energy development, downplayed the
contemporary significance of subethnic divisions, saying, "The four-
century existence of the culture of the *zhuz* has had a strong influence
on the ethnic self-consciousness of the Kazakh people. Undoubtedly
in the near future its role will be limited by national identification
and one's identity as a member of a klan [*sic*] or *zhuz* will gradually
become no more than historical property."[68]

While official publications allowed some diversity of opinion,
clear limits were imposed on discussion. Any suggestion, for example, that clan divisions be incorporated institutionally into political
life was officially unacceptable. One political observer whose commentaries had previously passed muster with state censors was told in
1995 that his article proposing parliamentary set-asides for each
umbrella clan could not be published.[69] Likewise, a prominent member of the legislature in 1993 was able to publish a provocative article
in *Aqiqat* in 1994 that suggested a need to clarify the "new rules of the
game" between the umbrella clans.[70] He gradually found himself mar-

ginalized from official political life and by 1999 was organizing a liberal opposition group called Progress (*Orleu*) that explicitly opposed tribalism.[71]

The regime also attempted to counter this critique through making very public an "anticorruption" campaign. Article 11 of an anticorruption law proscribed family members from being in superior-subordinate relationship in state structures.[72] Suddenly, the removal of *akims* from office—a frequent occurrence under any conditions—was accompanied by publicized reasons, which often included preferential access to economic and power structures given to relatives. Except for these highly publicized cases, enforcement was weak. One official engaged in the campaign privately lamented that were he to confront subethnic networks directly, his life would be worth about a hundred dollars.[73]

If the activities of the opposition generated such responses from officialdom, critics of subethnic influence were part of a broader metaconflict with those who sought to depict subethnicity in positive terms. Whereas regional actors sought to promote subethnicity as a virtuous attribute of Kazakhness, the opposition strove to portray it as a backward and negative attribute that hampered reform efforts in the newly independent state. The opposition accomplished this by depicting, for political effect, clan clientelism as rampant.

This chapter's arguments have certain implications. To be effective, subethnic criticism requires opacity; those engaged in opaque relationships and who were criticized for conducting clan clientelism were at pains to *deny* such activities. Were the regime to open the polity and make the bases for political relationships more transparent, the effectiveness of this criticism would likely wane. Such a move—unlikely under the leadership of Nazarbaev—might defuse the metaconflict about subethnic divisions and remove it as an explosive issue from the political agenda.

PART THREE

Managing Clans

7

A Vicious Cycle? Kinship and Political Change

[W]ith the reproduction of the Kyrgyz [Kazakh] people, the number of new subdivisions among them increases, and the initial names of generations slowly but surely are consigned to oblivion. . . . From this we can conclude that in about 100 years, the greater part of the names of subdivisions of the Kyrgyz people we have enumerated will remain only in our archives and in the memory of a few old men. —*Aleksei Iraklievich Levshin*

Not to know one's genealogy is unthinkable. —*Kazakh proverb*

USUALLY UNDERSTOOD TO BE DEEPLY ROOTED IN FACE-TO-FACE interaction, clan identities in the modern world are in fact constructed, in large part by state action. No longer the paramount wellspring of social and cultural belonging, they were simultaneously transformed and promoted in particular niches by Soviet rule. The shortage economy, which persisted for ordinary people into the 1990s, gave ongoing impetus for clan identities and for the conflict and metaconflict that they inspired.

In this sense, state practices give shape to the political role of clans. But this characterization creates a theoretical tension. To the extent that the members of clan networks privilege their own kind, they in a sense *manufacture* shortages for those who are outside of the clan network. That is, the very practice of clan clientelism by one set of actors itself gives impetus for other sets of actors to rely on their clan background. Clan behaviors by some can reproduce clan behaviors by others. Is clan politics a permanent feature of political life in such states? Is political change possible, or is it "unthinkable" that clans might be relegated to the "memory of a few old men"?

Such a line of inquiry returns us to primordialism. Does not primordialism capture the essential continuity of clan politics over time? Perhaps conceding that her theory cannot explain the particular *form* that clan politics assumes, a primordialist might argue that her approach nonetheless accounts for the *sources* of this politics. Primordialists might ask, "Does not a description of deeply rooted affiliations help to account for (1) the raw material that is used in diverse attempts to craft and construct subethnic identities, and (2) the popular resonance of subethnic identity politics?"

To what extent can the politics of subethnic identities be seen as percolating bottom-up from closely held group affiliations or, alternatively, as moving top-down from powerful state political agents? This chapter shows that ordinary Kazakhs from ethnically homogenous regions, and especially those from rural locales, attribute important social and political meaning to subethnic identities. But deeply rooted affiliations are not sufficient to explain clan politics. Even rural Kazakhs from predominantly ethnic Kazakh regions (cohorts that, following the logic of both identity modernization *and* primordialism, might be the "carriers" of clan identities) are subject to the normative logic of the state.

To make this argument, this chapter turns to the spatial dimension. After sketching the historical reasons for in-country variation along the lines of ethnic diversity and rurality, I consider the perspectives of urban migrants, who are uniquely situated to shed light on the question of closely held affiliations. Relatively untransformed by the Soviet experience, Kazakhs who recently migrated from rural and largely mono-ethnic (i.e., homogeneously Kazakh) milieus should manifest strong subethnic identities. This is an easy test for primordialism: if there are limits to the bottom-up significance of clan identities among ordinary people from rural, mono-ethnic regions, then we can infer dramatic limits in urban and multi-ethnic milieus.

PARTIAL TRANSFORMATION:
THE ORIGINS OF RURALITY AND ETHNIC DIVERSITY

At the onset of Soviet power, Central Asia was one of the most rural of regions in a generally preindustrial Soviet space. Relying on Russian and Ukrainian labor (a pattern which would be replicated in the Soviet era), tsarist authorities in the nineteenth century began to mine for copper, lead, silver, coal, and oil, to develop agricultural process-ing plants, and to manufacture cotton and silk. Hampered by poor transportation infrastructure over long distances, industry had achieved limited scope before Soviet rule.[1] As a consequence, the region had largely avoided the broad-scale disruptions to traditional identity for-mations that accompany urbanization and industrialization.

Blueprints for the construction of Soviet socialism included plans for identity transformation across Soviet territory. A population with a local and rural consciousness, rather than a national proletarian one, was of little use to a state undergoing consolidation and dedicated to a particular high-modernist vision.[2] Accordingly, authorities in Cen-tral Asia took quite seriously their attempts to fight manifestations of pre-Soviet identities, constructing public ceremonies to "liberate" Muslim women from the veil, conducting censuses to propagate new population categories, and sending so-called *agittrains* into the region to agitate for the virtues of Soviet power.[3]

The massive industrialization and collectivization drives were fur-ther vehicles for such identity transformations. Soviet efforts appeared to work to genuine social effect, even if they failed by their own cri-teria.[4] As Rakowska-Harmstone describes, "The impact was massive, the changes irreversible, and the result has been the emergence of a hybrid society in which traditional elements have been inextricably interwoven with the characteristics of a *Homo sovieticus*."[5] Especially in Kazakhstan, education levels rose dramatically, literacy became near universal, and the workforce became increasingly specialized. In 1979, population mobility in Kazakhstan was 4.5 times higher than in Azer-baijan, 3.5 times higher than Uzbekistan, 3 times higher than Turk-menistan, and 2.1 times higher than Tajikistan.[6] By 1970, some 63 percent of Kazakhs were formally considered members of the "work-ing class," although what this designation meant in practice was not clear.[7] This brought urbanization, but urbanization with a peculiar cast. It was comprised largely of professionals rather than manual labor-ers, and of non-Kazakhs rather than Kazakhs.[8]

The state intervened to temper these processes. While large-scale migration generally accompanies industrial change, several factors lim-ited the scope of migration in Central Asia. First, labor was often imported from the Slavic regions of the USSR, thus resulting in the construction of culturally Slavic cities on a Central Asian landscape. The cultural and linguistic gap that emerged was often a barrier against the movement of indigenous groups from rural areas.[9] This was also true of massive agricultural transformations, such as the 1950s' Virgin Lands project to bring under the plow the grazing lands of northern Kazakhstan, which disproportionately relied on external specialists. Second, Soviet authorities kept cotton prices artificially high and hesitated to push the mechanization of agriculture. In part this was a political decision to avoid the potential for destabilization that Soviet authorities feared would accompany large-scale rural-to-urban migration.[10]

Third, urbanization efforts in Soviet Central Asia faced the mediating effects of regional authorities, whose position was enhanced by the administrative structure of the Soviet state. The de facto delegation of significant authority to the *oblast* level was a characteristic of the polity from its very inception.[11] Especially in the agricultural parts of Central Asia, regional leaders were given critical decision-making autonomy. As long as they fulfilled Moscow's directives, local officials were given wide berth to conduct politics in the territories they administered.[12] Moreover, Moscow fostered rivalries between Party secretaries at the regional level, thus structuring competition along these lines. Any Union-wide policies designed to have transformative effects were subject to the tempering influences of *oblast* first secretaries.

The Soviet-era immigration of non-Kazakhs (especially Slavs) into the republic left Kazakhstan with multi-ethnic terrain that transformed the arena for identity politics. In 1999, Kazakhs constituted a majority of the population in only seven of fourteen regions, and their numbers rose above 80 percent in only two of these regions. Ethnic heterogeneity characterized not only the north and northeast, where the Slavic presence was most pronounced, but also the south, where Meskhetian Turks, Germans, Uzbeks, Uyghurs, North Caucasian peoples, and others neighbored Slavs and majority Kazakhs. Among ordinary people in the 1990s, southerners would frequently deride northern Kazakhs as "Russified," and northerners would label southerners as "Uzbeks." The popular recognition of the cultural influence of non-Kazakhs was thus widespread.

No disaggregated data on ethnic composition at the village level are published, but one local ethnographer described multi-ethnic locales as "rather numerous in contemporary Kazakhstan."[13] These villages were numerous enough that when the state conducted "eth-nocultural expeditions" in 1998 to highlight the cultural traditions of ethnic Kazakhs, local administrators had to be instructed specifically to identify "real" (i.e., mono-ethnic) Kazakh villages where ethnog-raphers would be asked to conduct their research. Left to their own devices, these ethnographers might otherwise have selected from among the country's numerous multi-ethnic villages.[14]

In such a culturally and economically variegated landscape, one would expect the primordialist perspective to remain most apt in rural, mono-ethnic locales. These are the milieus that were relatively least transformed by Soviet rule.

URBAN MIGRANTS: A KEY COHORT

To gain purchase on subethnic attachments in rural, mono-ethnic areas, rural-to-urban migrants aged twenty to twenty-eight were invited to participate in focus groups in three *oblasts*. Focus groups offer advan-tages for identity research. First, they reconstruct a group context for a discussion by assembling members of a single cohort. Individual inter-views, by contrast, extract participants from the interactive context in which identities find everyday expression. Second, focus groups allow greater agenda setting by participants than do more structured inter-views, since the moderator is instructed to allow discussion to evolve without excessive guidance. Focus groups were complemented by non-participant observation and individual interviews that took place within everyday contexts. The intention was to use several ethno-graphic strategies to triangulate the manifestations of subethnic iden-tities in rural areas; a combined approach offers better purchase than a single methodological strategy could in isolation.[15]

Migrants were chosen for two reasons. First, a cohort of migrants from various regions provides a window into the social salience of iden-tities across broader territory than would an intensive study of just a few rural sites.[16] The results are therefore potentially more general-izable across space. Second, by definition, migrants are located at the juncture of the urban and the rural. They therefore offer an indica-tion of the processes by which subethnic identities—if they are best understood as percolating bottom-up from ordinary rural residents—moved into urban milieus and onto the political stage. Thus, to the extent that these migrants were the "carriers" of clan affiliations, any large-scale migration could be expected to increase further the salience of these attachments in urban areas.

By the late 1990s, migrant communities were a potent social force. Many of the Soviet-era political, economic, and cultural obstacles to mobility evaporated with the Soviet collapse. Where the Soviet system had strictly limited urban migration through its system of resident permits (*propiska*), the post-Soviet state could only poorly enforce existing rules for residence. The possession of such a permit continued to bolster one's opportunities in education, employment, and housing, but its absence was no longer an insurmountable impediment to migration. Moreover, given the state's broad promotion of the Kazakh language and culture, the cultural gap between the predominantly Kazakh-speaking countryside and the largely Russian-speaking cities began to narrow. Greater acceptance of rural culture in the cities made migration easier.

The economic motivation to leave rural areas was the plummet in agricultural production. The livestock sector, for which most of the country is ecologically suited, was hardest hit. Producers rapidly butchered their stocks to pay for consumer goods whose prices had soared. The retreat of the state had worsened health and sanitary conditions, calling into question the medium-term viability of this mode of economy. According to one local expert, as a percentage of 1991 levels, the 1998 numbers had declined precipitously for all types of stock—cattle (42.7 percent), sheep (28.1 percent), horses (62.1 percent), and camels (66.6 percent).[17] The consequent rural depopulation stretched the social fabric of affected areas in crucial ways. Where once there were large and tight-knit families, now rural populations were disproportionately elderly and female, since younger people and men readily moved to cities. Kin networks now spanned the rural-urban divide.

Urban opportunities were marginally better. Many former industrial towns in the north had come to a standstill by the mid-1990s, but the country's largest cities—Almaty and Qaraghandy—continued to offer disproportionate socioeconomic opportunities. Competition for urban jobs was also keen, but the out-migration of a large portion of the Slavic population (especially to Russia, but also to other destinations) lowered its intensity. Gradually, foreign capital found its way to the smaller cities as direct investment, and many state enterprises that had stood idle in the mid-1990s were privatized and resumed oper-

ations. Thus, most urban areas found themselves attracting noteworthy migrant populations.

The visual transformation of cities' outskirts was unmistakable, as
many migrants took up residence in substandard or jerry-built housing. Official unemployment statistics provide one indication of the
migrations' scale. Theoretically, in the absence of urban migration,
job losses in rural areas should swell the ranks of the rural unemployed.
In fact, as the agricultural economy of post-Soviet Kazakhstan con-
tracted, rural unemployment levels fell. When in 1996 more than
200,000 agricultural jobs were lost, official rural unemployment rose
only by 63,362. In 1997, 263,000 more agricultural jobs were lost, and
rural unemployment actually shrunk by 42,366. Assuming that official
record keeping in rural and urban areas did not change in these years,[18]
these data suggest a significant urban migration of out-of-work rural
residents. As a consequence of this population shift, the relative composition of the unemployed changed as well. In 1995, 54 percent of
those officially registered as unemployed resided in rural areas. In 1996,
49 percent did, while in 1997, the number was 38 percent.[19] All of
these changes occurred in a context in which the largely urban Slavic
population was dwindling; the scale of the rural-to-urban migration
may have been underreported, as the urban milieu could absorb large
numbers of migrants without this fact being reflected in urban population statistics.

In an absolute sense, the scale of these migrations did not rival that
of migrations, for example, to Latin American cities in the second
half of the twentieth century. The relative social impact was perhaps
comparable, however, given Kazakhstan's population of about fifteen
million in 1999. One local scholar, lamenting the influx of migrants,
contended that the process was not urbanization and assimilation of
migrants into the urban milieu, but the "ruralization" of the city.[20]

Among ordinary people, the population movement brought an
increasing popular awareness of the cultural and linguistic gap
between migrants and longtime city dwellers. The frequent use of two
pejorative terms attests to the social distance between rural and urban
Kazakhs. On the one hand, rural Kazakh speakers decried the Soviet-
era Russification of urban dwellers by calling them *manqurt* (one who
does not know his or her roots); on the other hand, urban Kazakhs
increasingly depicted their country co-ethnics as uncivilized by calling them *mambet* (roughly: country bumpkin).

This was the context in which focus groups were conducted in three regions. Table 7.1 locates these regions according to two factors that could be expected to alter the social salience of subethnic identities: ethnicity and rurality. Ethnicity is the percentage of the region's population that is ethnically Kazakh. Rurality is the percentage of the region's population that resides in rural areas.

Table 7.1
Oblasts by Percent Kazakh and Percent Rural Populations

Oblast	% Kazakh	% Rural
Qostanai	29.5	49.7
Aqmola[a]	30.8	44.6
North Kazakhstan	31.4	56.5
Qaraghandy	36.5	17.7
Pavlodar	36.8	37.5
Almaty[a]	39.3	42.2
East Kazakhstan	48.3	42.6
Zhambyl	62.3	54.0
West Kazakhstan	64.9	58.8
South Kazakhstan[a]	65.4	62.1
Aqtobe	67.8	46.1
Mangystau	72.8	19.8
Atyrau[a]	87.4	41.5
Qyzylorda	92.8	40.4

Source: Komitet po statistike i analizu, *Regional'nyi statisticheskii ezhegodnik* (Almaty: Statkomitet, 1997), 5–47, 54.

[a] Primary research sites

If we begin with assumptions about deeply rooted clan affiliations, we can expect that in predominantly ethnic Kazakh regions (such as Atyrau and Qyzylorda), where assimilative pressures are more limited, clan identities would be strongest, while in less Kazakh regions (such as Aqmola and Qostanai), they would be less salient. Likewise, one would expect that the more rural Kazakh *oblasts* (such as West Kazakhstan and South Kazakhstan), where the potentially transformative effects of urbanization were limited in scope, greater still would be the manifestations of these identities.

The *oblasts* selected for study were Atyrau, South Kazakhstan, and Almaty. By comparing Atyrau and South Kazakhstan, we evaluate variation from urban to rural, while providing a rough control for ethnic balance. By comparing Almaty and Atyrau, we vary the ethnic composition, while roughly maintaining levels of urbanization.[21]

NO IDENTITY IS PRIMORDIAL

Focus group participants from rural and mono-ethnic regions had relatively stronger kin networks than did those from more urban and multi-ethnic *oblasts*.[22] Figure 7.1 summarizes the results of a questionnaire, in which respondents were asked upon whom they expected to rely for assistance in the future. Each possible basis for an assistance network received a score from respondents' rankings. These scores establish how strong each network basis was reported to be; the scores here are depicted as percentages of the total possible score.[23] The strongest networks among the respondents were based on relatives. Indeed, these extended families in all three *oblasts* studied were clearly more important than the bases for other relationships. Adding clan-based networks to these networks of extended family, the picture is a clear one: kinship mattered to these migrants. Tighter kin units (extended family) were important across the three regions; looser kin aggregates (clans) were more important in rural, largely mono-ethnic South Kazakhstan *oblast*. In no case did clan networks completely preclude other types of relationships.

The quantitative variation—itself suggestive rather than statistically significant—is consistent with aspects of modernization theories; those areas more affected by urbanization and increased cultural diversity saw clan ties that were marginally weaker vis-à-vis alternative bases for assistance networks. Urbanization and cultural diversity bring the individual into contact with an array of other individuals with a variety of backgrounds. A person need not rely solely on kinship for assistance in such diverse contexts. Rather, bonds forged on the basis of common interest, rather than common origin, may proliferate. These factors play a role in affecting the salience of kinship.

But the differences in assistance networks across regions should not obscure what is common across them. Urbanization and cultural

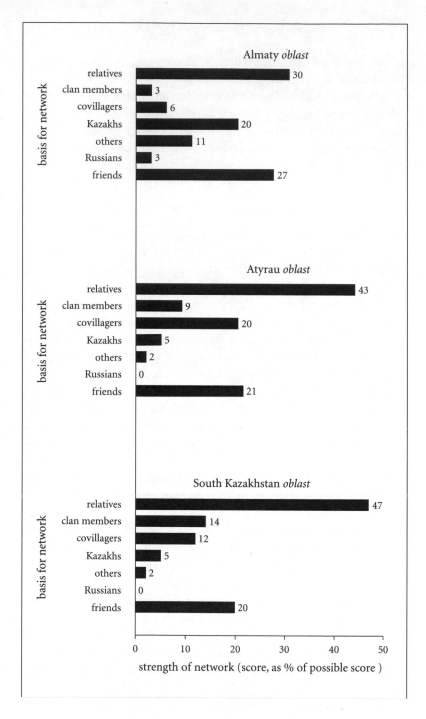

Figure 7.1. Assistance Networks by Region

diversity are not the *only* factors that influence kin relations. Commonalities across regions are revealed by the particular meanings that migrants attributed to the networks. Their perspectives went beyond the neat concepts and tidy, macrolevel categories of modernization-based analysis. Much variation lay beneath the surface. By elaborating on some of this complexity, we view subethnicity as a dynamic feature of life in Central Asia, whose direction is shaped critically by the state.

Clans in Context

To ask, as primordialist approaches do, which identities are primary "when the chips are down" or "in the final analysis" is to eschew context. Rather than assuming that certain identities are fundamental while others are secondary, focus-group participants pointed to the need to contextualize identities. In the course of discussion, religious, ethnic, and rural/urban identities sometimes reinforced, sometimes competed with, subethnic sentiments. These migrants could not discuss clans in isolation; the divisions were intertwined with many related affiliations.

For some, subethnicity was entangled with religious identity as a Muslim.[24] Originally from the Zhambyl region in southern Kazakhstan, Zhumabek proclaimed his concern that the focus group would be conducted by foreign religious missionaries: "When Saulesh [native research collaborator] came to me, I thought, 'There are Buddhists and Baptists in the city now. Sort of "societies," where they ask you to come, listen, and have a look.' I told her, 'I am a Muslim [*musylman balasymyn*],[25] but if it is a religious meeting, then I will not attend.'"[26] If Zhumabek harbored such a religious identity, Timur, with whom he sparred on several occasions during the Almaty focus group, expressed profound concern that clans were traditionalistic and therefore a hindrance to the functioning of a market economy.[27] In response, Zhumabek contended, "I think that Kazakh youth are coming to [Kazakh] culture and are accepting the faith of Muslimness [*musylmandyq*] and Islam. One must give oneself up to religion. We must know ourselves." For Zhumabek, clans were like religious divisions; they distinguished titular Kazakhs from the historically dominant Russians.[28]

Islam was sometimes seen as the wellspring of subethnicity. Religious authorities were often the possessors of detailed genealogical knowledge in rural communities. In Shaulder, South Kazakhstan region, for example, a local mullah of prominent social status offered an expansive oral history of the region based on the genealogies of dominant groups. In it, he assimilated non-Kazakh Muslims as also kin-related; he understood them as simply one further degree removed from Kazakhs on a genealogical tree.[29] A focus-group participant in Shymkent offered a similar logic, saying, "In the Muslim faith, you may not marry a girl related to you within seven generations. This is what medicine says, too: that marrying within seven generations can lead to sick children."[30]

For others, discussion of subethnicity naturally led to questions of ethnic belonging. For many informants, ethnicity was akin to subethnicity in the sense that it was experienced by degree.[31] Slavs were the most distinct "other" and were often simply called "Europeans." Uzbeks, Kyrgyz, Tatars, and Uyghurs were generally considered less different, given their Turkic and Muslim background. Here, too, much depended on the situation. Uzbeks and Kazakhs, who might understand themselves as fellow Turkic peoples vis-à-vis Russians or other Europeans, often found themselves in competition in South Kazakhstan, where the Russian population was only getting smaller.[32]

The distinction by which Kazakhs had clan identities while Slavs did not led to a related discussion during the focus groups of the rural-urban divide. Common was the refrain that the village was where the "authentic" Kazakhs lived; cities were "European." To migrate meant to face all the pressures of dress, culture, and habit that were of alien origin. One participant used the example of his having a seizure on public transportation in a way that intertwined several related identities:

> Once when I was riding a bus, I had an attack (Russian: *pristup*). All the people [on the bus] simply went about their own business. "This person is young, drank a lot of vodka, and must be an alcoholic," they said as they got off the bus. But, if this happened in the village, people, having preserved the essence of Islam, would help. "This is a Kazakh child [*bala*], after all," they would say, asking how they could help. But, in the city it is not like that. I got off at the bus stop, and no one paid attention. They call that humanity! If you die, no one even notices. This is why I am bitter about city people. City life is like that.[33]

Given the number of related identities with which subethnicity was intertwined, and given the variety of ways in which this occurred, the independent valence of closely held subethnic affiliations in animating political competition is difficult to establish. No longer the overriding organizing feature of social and political life that it had been before Soviet rule, it intersected with a striking number of other identifications.

Further Axes for Variation

Beneath the patterns of macrolevel variation, the strength of clan networks also was influenced by microlevel settlement patterns, personality factors, the monetarization of the economy, and the application of performance criteria.

If the quantitative data above considered variation in levels of ethnic diversity and rurality by *oblast*, each region was itself diverse along these two lines. Much of the importance of kin networks depended on the particular locale in which ordinary people built their relationships. That is, micro settlement patterns had a critical impact on how Kazakhs structured their everyday affairs.

Two examples illustrate the wide array of social and cultural milieus in which clan networks were contextualized. On the one hand is Shaulder, a village of 8,300 residents in South Kazakhstan *oblast*. This *oblast* is composed overwhelmingly of Elder Clan Kazakhs; Shaulder residents, however, are overwhelmingly from the Middle Umbrella Clan. In fact, almost all residents are from the Qongyrat subdivision among Middle Clan Kazakhs. In this largely homogenous Qongyrat context, the subdivisions among Qongyrats assumed social salience, with Zhetimder, Bozhbandar, Mangytai, and Sanghyl residents living in separate areas relatively clearly defined by the main streets, the local irrigation canal, and the Arys River. Place of residence on this micro scale coincided with genealogical subdivisions.[34]

A second example shows that, even where subethnic divisions were significant for villagers, they were not necessarily the dominant division. In rural Taldy-Qorghan region, the most salient cleavage crosscut umbrella clan lines. On the one hand were Kazakhs from the Younger and Elder Umbrella Clans who remained in the area continuously under Soviet rule. On the other hand were those Kazakhs from the Middle and Elder Umbrella Clans who had fled to China in the late 1920s, returning to their original villages in the 1950s and 1960s. The main cleavage was between "Sovietized" Kazakhs and "Hanified" ones.[35]

Qualitative inquiry reveals another point that the numbers presented above do not: directionality. If in villages such as Shaulder, clan divisions defined residence patterns throughout the Soviet period, in many others such patterns were more recent in origin. The privatization of state and collective farms in the mid-1990s provided impetus. While some farms were transformed into joint-stock companies and cooperatives, many broke down into small-scale private operations run by clusters of related families. Had state-led privatization not privileged small farms, clans would not have been promoted in this way.[36]

Second, restrictions on ownership moved settlement in the direction of clan-based patterns. Whatever type of land tenure emerged on any particular site, legal ownership was largely reserved to farm workers. As chapter 5 suggested, this excluded those professionals who had been a central part of the rural community during the Soviet period— especially doctors, teachers, and nurses—but who were not technically members of the farm. Cultural outsiders defined by some degree of ethnic or clan difference, these people were often compelled to move; the state now considered their services to be nonessential and eliminated their positions. In those cases where clan outsiders were entitled to land, they often received parcels of inferior quality.[37] Thus, even those areas where Soviet-era settlement had not been structured along clan lines, post-Soviet agricultural privatization promoted clan-based settlement.

The overwhelming perspective in the focus groups was that clan networks were pervasive and important. The consensus was that society's power holders provided benefits (especially access to scarce economic and political resources, as well as employment) to their kin. A common refrain was that such actors "bring in their blood" (qanyn tartady). To emphasize this point, one Kazakh-speaking migrant switched to Russian—the language of science and education—to highlight that such kin behavior is a scarcely alterable sociological fact: "That is life. It is a law-like regularity [Russian: zakonomernost']."[38] One participant in Almaty explained how this logic dominated thinking among ordinary Kazakhs: "I was raised in the Kazakh way, as I told you. . . . For example, would you like it if your relative was poor?

Or, you are a rich person and occupy a position as a boss [*bastyq*]. Would you like it [better] if [your relative] was a poor vagrant, or if he/she was rich?"³⁹

At the same time, many participants sought to illustrate the limits to these networks, even among the economic and political elite. For example, with regard to the bases for political appointments made by *akims* and other local officials, one participant remarked, "If one clan takes over a high-level position, it does not take care of [benefit] only this clan, but in truth take a look at how many other people start to work there! If I were to help only my own clan, this would force out all the other people. If someone wants to help [his/her own clan], let him/her do so. . . . It seems that you can divide [Kazakhs] into clans, but you can also divide [them] into individuals."⁴⁰

On a more personal level, migrants often claimed that others used clan ties to find employment or gain admission to universities but glossed over similar behavior in themselves. Almagul, a recent migrant who ran a small stand at a local bazaar in Shymkent, claimed to have come to the city not for economic reasons, but because she preferred the excitement and anonymity of the city. After some probing, she admitted that her husband found a job at a local factory through a clan connection, but maintained that she herself did not know her clan or umbrella clan background. She reported that people talked about these divisions in her village but that she had no interest in them.⁴¹

If many of these migrants availed themselves of kin networks, such connections had limits. According to participants, networks were limited in at least two ways: (1) by bribery and other manifestations of the monetarization of interpersonal relationships, and (2) by the application of performance criteria in some spheres. Once a relationship was established—whether through kinship or not—that relationship had some chance of enduring. Citing a Kazakh proverb, a participant in Atyrau summed up the limits to kin connections: "A person once met is recognizable. A person twice met is reliable."⁴²

The partial and uneven monetarization of the economy allowed cash to provide some access to political, economic, and social goods. Suddenly, those with financial resources found it possible to forge relationships through easy payment, a practice that could be used to complement or in some cases replace the exchange of favors or the ties of kinship. One participant in Shymkent, in response to a question of whether or not she had ever thought to herself, "This boss [*bastyq*] is from my own clan. He will offer me help," offered the following conclusion: "Today, if you give someone money, then you will have your support. It is all about money."[43]

Kin and market relations, of course, were not mutually exclusive but rather intertwined in a variety of ways. One respondent's comments suggested that the principles often operated simultaneously. A self-promoter would be wise to consider the use of both:

> Now, everything is in the riches, in the money. Only if you have a *koke* [roughly: sponsor],[44] if you have the money, then things are good. We do not have money; we do not have a *koke*. If we were to get one, then we would become rich. Here is what we think: if the factories and plants were working, if there were salaries, then no one would be having trouble. Now, everyone is moving from the village. They are coming because there is no work, no money. For example, one family [I know] was given five hectares of land. They planted it, but they needed water. But, water is expensive. Will they be able to get two or three tonnes of harvest? It is no use. Water, a tractor, a cart—none of them are worth it [the expense]. If you can come to the city and get work from your *koke*, great. There isn't any bread to eat in the village.[45]

One recombination of these principles mentioned in chapter 5 bears repeating. Kin networks served as a mechanism to identify those non-kin who sought to offer payments, often bribes, for access or protection. The husband of one informant from Almaty, a low-level state bureaucrat, regularly solicited payments from non-kin for state-issued licenses, the greater part of which was passed to higher-level members of his kin network.[46] As we saw earlier from another informant, in higher education in Shymkent the kin of instructors were often recruited to act as the instructors' "long ear," to be on the lookout for poor-performing, non-kin students who might seek to pay a bribe in exchange for passing a course.[47]

Another informant from the area of higher education in Shymkent had a different experience with this problem. He claimed that having a relative in a high position provided critical information about which officials might accept a bribe for services. If such an official was from the same subethnic division, the informant insisted, he or she still required payment. The distinction he made was that members of a clan shared and distributed information about how and to whom to make such payments. Non-kin—for lack of information—were forced to resort to the inefficiencies of formal institutional channels.⁴⁸

Much of my ethnographic data suggest that a neoliberal, free-market orientation for the state did nothing to limit the salience of kin networks. Rather, market-based poverty strengthened existing networks. To survive the exigencies of such poverty, rural Kazakhs intensified the reciprocal exchange of gifts within kin groups.⁴⁹ When I asked one informant how he could gain the favor of a well-placed relative, he replied that it was a slow, gradual process. He would first try to make the relative's acquaintance at a celebration (*toi*) or circumcision ceremony (*sundet toi*). Then, he would regularly make himself visible in the relative's imagination by purchasing presents at various family celebrations and presenting them with great ceremony. By becoming centrally involved in the exchange of gifts, he was sure, he would gain the confidence of the relative whose help he sought.⁵⁰

Kin ties were reaffirmed on a regular basis through ceremonies such as weddings, funerals, and other family occasions. Urban Kazakhs traveling to the countryside were expected to visit all major families in the area, even if only for a short time. At each visit to a home, it was obligatory to stop and have at least a small meal. The belief was that hospitality had not been extended unless food had touched the lips of the guests (*auyz tiiu*). A relative who did not offer such hospitality, or a visitor to a locale who did not visit to receive it, were seen as seeking to sever the kin bond.⁵¹

In the late 1980s, patrilineally defined agnatic kin in rural areas began conducting regular meetings called *gap*. Celebrated as family holidays, the meetings provided a venue and reason for relatives to gather once per month. Moreover, they usually served as rotating credit-giving circles. During one such *gap* in the small town of Shayan, South Kazakhstan region, the group of relatives maintained a rather strict hierarchy within the family. Every new guest to arrive was seated the appropriate distance from the head of the table, depending on his or her status within the group of agnatic kin. At this particular *gap*, the kin subdivisions of those present became the subject of ongoing jokes and puns.⁵²

Such reiteration of kin connections, however, was only one side of a complex picture. While some kin networks preserved their integrity in the face of monetarization, others did not. The latter fate was especially common in small-scale commercial operations. Whereas in the beginning of the 1990s, having a moderately distant relative in a service industry or in the consumer-goods sector would guarantee privileged access, by the late 1990s, such a relative would often charge for services provided. Thus, one informant from Almaty who routinely received free photo-development services in the early part of the decade reported being turned away by a relative in the latter part.[53] Likewise, those entrepreneurs who enjoyed some commercial success received steady streams of relatives seeking favors, but the economic pressure to turn away favor seekers was strong. One successful hotel owner in Shymkent elected to assist certain kin and not others. While the criteria used to make such selections were not evident, the need to limit assistance was clear to such an entrepreneur.[54]

Performance criteria, usually considered conceptually distinct from kin-based networks, also interacted with kinship ties. Frequently, blood links prevailed over professional ones. One informant described how a prominent official at a local institute, who was the "head" [Russian: *glava*] of his "clan" [Russian: *klan*], could not bring himself to fire a poor-performing secretary because she was a blood relative.[55] In other cases, some degree of performance, or promise of performance, was required even among kin. This lies at the core of one focus group participant's comment: "In essence, I came [to the city] to rely on my relatives, but, in order to go to my relatives, I had to show [prove] myself, which I did. . . ."[56]

To sum up: The importance of clan divisions was a variable, not a constant, in the 1990s. Levels of rurality, cultural homogeneity, patterns of settlement at the micro level, aspects of monetarization, and the application of performance criteria all had an impact on the degree to which clan connections were used. On occasion, individual preferences played a role. One migrant to Almaty penned the word "myself" in his questionnaire about assistance networks, apparently asserting that he faced the challenges of city life alone.

Constant, however, was the role of the state in making clan identities politically and socially relevant.

The Never-Absent State

In the pre-Soviet past, an individual was normatively expected to commit to memory his ancestry to avoid intermarriage among close kin groups. In the 1990s this practice of marital exogamy was not uniformly observed; in some locales, the members of close kin groups married with regularity. While the prospect for instant recall of elaborate genealogies was diminished, a normative drive to know one's background persisted. Its source was the state.

Reacting to this normative directive, many migrants claimed to have such knowledge, describing it as an essential aspect of everyday life, especially in the villages. When asked if villagers know their genealogies, one participant responded, "Of course they do. There is no one who does not know it. Children are fed it like mother's milk."[57] Follow-up questions, however, revealed that this was an ideal that few villagers could achieve. One participant responded with an evasiveness that was suggestive: "Many know, they know. Especially the older people, they know. They teach the children. There are people who know other people's clan. In our village there are people who have been around and who know their seven generations [*tanydy, korgenderi bar*]."[58]

In reality, many found it difficult to recite their background beyond four or five generations. According to one participant explaining this phenomenon, villagers would approach local experts who would recite elaborate genealogies for transcription onto paper. Most no longer committed to memory their background, instead preserving it in written form.[59] In interviews of migrants in Qaraghandy and Almaty conducted by Esenova, interviewees often knew their umbrella clan background and the largest subdivisions, but knowledge seldom went further. Moreover, "migrants named with difficulty the tribal identifications of their best friends or relatives, such as the husbands of their sisters, etc."[60] In a follow-up interview, one participant contended that, "Even among Kazakh speakers, many do not remember. They know that they are supposed to know their seven generations. . . . They remember what umbrella clan they are from, but not necessarily any further. Some even do not know what umbrella clan they are from." He added that many know the lowest clan subdivision as well, but ancestry between umbrella clan and this lowest subdivision was often unknown.[61]

It was not even clear that command of genealogy was stronger in rural than in urban areas. While most participants believed that villagers knew their genealogies better than their city counterparts, one respondent disagreed, saying, "No, I watch these city children. We have a competition . . . and when the school kids [gather], the city kids get to know each other and introduce themselves around . . . they know it [their seven generations]. They come [to the competition] knowing it, and how they introduce themselves to each other! They introduce themselves through songs and do a really powerful job."[62]

While ancestry was not necessarily at the tip of these respondents' tongues, this does not mean that the normative drive to know it was no longer operative. To the contrary, it simply had another source: the state. As chapter 6 illustrated, state discourse stressed traits that were understood to distinguish ethnic Kazakhs from non-Kazakhs. Most critical, Kazakhs had a subethnic identity, while Slavs did not. Thus, it is not surprising that migrants scarcely could disentangle issues of subethnic identity from issues of ethnicity. In one rapid-fire exchange in the South Kazakhstan *oblast* focus group, the moderator asked whether urban Kazakhs knew their *shezhire*:

> *Moderator:* So, what about young people in the city?
> *Bolat:* They have taken on Russian behavior.
> *Moderator:* What exactly is Russian behavior?
> *Bolat:* In the city, parents teach their genealogy, but they don't give it much significance.
> *Moderator:* Why does one need to know their clan [background]?
> *Bolat:* Each person needs to know his/her own blood and the land from which he/she comes.
> *Moderator:* In the city, are there people who don't know their own clan?
> *Bolat:* Yes, there are.
> *Anonymous:* No, there are not.

This perspective conflated urbanization with Russification and Russification with loss of genealogical knowledge. The sense that renewed attention to genealogies was a way to revive ethnic pride pervaded comments in the Atyrau focus group:

> *Meiran:* . . . if someone knows it [seven generations], they can call themselves a Kazakh.
> *Zhanybek:* You prove that you are a Kazakh.
> *Meiramgul:* . . . your nationality [*ulttyq*] . . . like everyone . . . that you are a nation.
> *Meiran:* Yes, that you are a nation. You have to be an individual, you have to be true to your nation. . . .

Erlan: For example, to prove that you are a Kazakh . . . let's say, you go to another place, and they ask, for example, what sorts of things do you know from your Kazakhstan? . . . Do you know, for example, customs and traditions of Kazakhstan? If you do not know, shame on you. What kind of a Kazakh are you here, how is this so? What kind of a Kazakh is this? This person doesn't know his/her recent history, so what kind of a Kazakh [is he/she], they ask. . . .

Indeed, the final comment above suggests that genealogical knowledge positions Kazakhs relative to other peoples of the world; it is a tradition whose revival and full realization would ensure entrance into the world community as a distinctive nation. Zhuldyz in Almaty put it most succinctly: "Every person who knows him/herself to be a Kazakh, as a matter of obligation, has to know seven generations. It is a sign of the nation [*ulttyng tangbasy*]."

The need to assert ethnic nationhood had its roots in state discourse; it had no parallel in pre-Soviet Kazakhstan (i.e., before statehood). In fact, if we trace the language used by participants, we see the clear imprint of state discourse on clan identities. Even rural Kazakhs were linked to the state through print and broadcast media; they were literate and active consumers of information that the state provided. Not necessarily the passive recipients of state-generated information, they nonetheless assimilated the vocabulary that the state chose to provide.

State-led discourse on ethnic and subethnic identities filtered to these migrants in various ways. One indication is the use of terms, such as "tribalism," that originated not in the vocabulary of ordinary people, but rather in the discourse of scholars and elites on cultural and political identities. One participant who had come to Almaty to study in a local institute commented about clan divisions: "[First,] I think that tribalism [*traibalizm*] is not significant. I do not descend to that level and do not make my choices through clan divisions. Second, under market conditions tribalism cannot live for very long."[63] Timur was the first to introduce this term "tribalism" to the discussion; he was not prompted by the moderator's questions, which used the terms umbrella clan (*zhuz*) and clan (*ru*) exclusively. Moreover, his logic that opposed tribalism and market conditions was a common one in state discourse: the idea was that such subethnic divisions would inevitably lose their political significance just as soon as Kazakhstan completed its much proclaimed transition to the free market.

Another participant in Almaty showed her awareness of the Masanov affair, in which a member of the liberal political opposition published in Moscow an article on umbrella clan divisions that presented a frontal challenge to the legitimacy of the Nazarbaev regime.[64] She commented, "Tribalism is exaggerated as a problem. A scholar of sorts—who in fact went to Moscow to promote his own name— wrote in an article that there is tribalism in Kazakhstan. [switches to Russian] Russians look at us as if [back to Kazakh] everything were still tribal in Kazakhstan. . . ."[65]

The example of a participant in South Kazakhstan is suggestive. In conversations before the focus group began, this young man called himself ethnically "pure," using the Russian word for "pure" in an otherwise Kazakh conversation. The switch to Russian is worth considering. The code switch suggests that the speaker had internalized this notion of purity in the Russian, rather than the Kazakh, language. The need to assert one's purity emerges only with the appearance of a significant ethnic other and pressures to assimilate.[66] The notion of purity is marked linguistically Russian because linguistically Russified Kazakhs face scrutiny about their qualifications for membership in the community of Kazakhs.

To distinguish themselves from ethnic Russians, these Kazakhs developed Russian-language notions of purity to play out vis-à-vis their Kazakh-language co-ethnics. Thus, among the sources of this participant's notion of ethnic purity is a highly Russified state elite that was constantly defending itself against charges of ethnic impurity. Interestingly, this participant introduced himself at the outset of the focus group this way: "I come from the Sovetskoye village [Russian: *selo*] in Tole Bi region of South Kazakhstan region. [I graduated from] M. Auezov school. I study in the State University. I am a student. I am from the Elder Umbrella Clan." He was one of two participants who volunteered their umbrella clan attachment by way of introduction, thus highlighting a connection between genealogical divisions and notions of ethnic purity.

In Almaty, a participant who had introduced himself as a member of the ethnonationalist group Azat, and who had been concerned that the focus group might be conducted in Russian, "rather than in the state language [Kazakh]," showed an awareness of scholarly discourse on cultural identities (transmitted in the media) when he commented, "I read in a newspaper that German scholars have been studying our Kazakh people [*khalyq*]. Our own scholars and our guest Edward here from America are studying our customs and traditions, too. The German scholars apparently said that twenty years from now the Kazakh people will vanish."[67]

In the context of a broadly literate rural population, state discourse on subethnic identities was particularly visible to these migrants. Even if the extent to which they took behavioral cues from this discourse is an open question, closely held affiliations were not sufficient to build the social salience of these identities.

And, just as ordinary people were aware that the state played a role in this process, they tended to view the state as the sole arena in which clan divisions mattered. It was something that defined not the lives of ordinary people, but the political maneuvering among the political elite. In the village of Mikhailovka, in rural South Kazakhstan region, for example, informants uniformly dismissed the notion that subethnicity played a role in everyday life. Clan, one villager claimed, was important only for those with influence; their village was too remote from centers of power to be susceptible to clan relations. Another resident responded with belligerence to the same question, behaving as if he had been accused of a heinous crime. After being assured that he was not being thus accused, he retorted that these divisions matter for administrators and politicians, but not for ordinary people.[68]

STATE ACTION AND POLITICAL CHANGE

State action was the critical variable in shaping clan identities in the 1990s, just as it had been crucial in fueling clan relations in the Soviet period. Even for those relatively removed from its reach, the state was always a force in producing change or stasis in identity relations. It was the engine behind variation that could diminish the import of clan politics, as well as variation that could lend it significance. States construct clans as regressive or not, divisive or not, and disruptive or not, to modern politics.

In one sense, this conclusion is not surprising. Compared to its counterparts in Tajikistan, Georgia, and Kyrgyzstan, Kazakhstan's state capacity began to improve dramatically in the late 1990s. Shored up by oil receipts, an extensive system of patronage, and later a privileged position in the U.S.–led "war on terrorism," this was an impressive state indeed. The Nazarbaev regime could project power to the far reaches of its vast territory, co-opt challengers, and crush opponents. It inherited the agencies of coercion and propaganda from the Soviet period and put them to effective use, with increasing ruthlessness, in the early years of the new century. State action constructed clans, much as it influenced other aspects of social and political life.

On the other hand, the conclusion is surprising for the study of identity politics. It undercuts the primordialists' expectation that clan divisions change or persist *in spite of the state*. To the contrary, the reach of the post-Soviet state was impressive; even those apparently distant from the state and its initiative in fact took cues from the state. Is clan politics a permanent feature of political life in states such as Kazakhstan? Much depends on the character of state action. In this sense, there is much potential for state elites to craft institutions and policies that will transform clan politics into something less explosive, more manageable, and less likely to fulfill the stereotype of primitive, antimodern social relations.

Conclusions:
Kinship and "Normal" Politics

THIS STUDY BEGAN WITH THE WEBERIAN *PROBLÉMATIQUE* OF
traditional bonds and statehood. Based on the Central Asian experience, it arrives, however, at a different end point. While Weber was
correct to observe that clan and other particularistic affiliations may
impede the creation of ideal-typical bureaucracies, it is also true that
state action shapes clans. Causal arrows move not only from clans to
state (the assumption of Weberians), but also from the state to clans.
Across the southern tier of the ex-USSR, clans and states construct
each other in an ongoing dialectic. The image that modern statehood
and clan operate by mutually exclusive logics, that they are situated
at a fundamental separation, and that they are necessarily at odds with
one another is misleading. Even kinship-based divisions are (re)pro-
duced by the state.[1]

State action may be—as it was in the Kazakhstan case—the core
reason for the persistence of clans. There, the political significance
of clans was not the result of sticky attachments that resist attempts
to transform them. Nor was their significance the natural consequence of a lack of state penetration. The character of a state that
penetrates society may in fact be critical. To be sure, state action is
not the *only* theoretical reason why clans might persist. After all, clan
systems predate the rise of the modern state, and in some contexts
the state simply fails to penetrate societies deeply enough to undermine preexisting modes of behavior and forms of identity. This is
probably the story of parts of the ex-USSR (notably, mountainous
Tajikistan and the northern Caucasus), among the nomadic groups
of the Horn of Africa, and in the Moroccan "zone of dissidence."
But state action *can reproduce* clans. When similar end points can

be reached through different causal paths, we must grapple with new theoretical possibilities.[2]

Weber casts the problem of states and clans in stark relief, setting out the ideal-typical logic governing each and suggesting the irreconcilability of these social forms. Although he is careful to provide reasons for using ideal-typical categories, which deliberately accentuate the common aspects across various cases to make comparative analysis possible, once created, the categories take on a life of their own. Reified, these (originally analytic) constructs become inscribed in the exercise of power. States that seek to transform societies according to perceived modern imperatives use the vocabulary of Weberian modernity to attack practices described as premodern.

Ironically, the foregoing chapters suggest that the Weberian problem — how to reconcile kinship-rich societies with effective state institutions — can be addressed if we relax some of Weber's assumptions. If states and clans construct each other, as I have suggested, then the two operate not according to essentially different, mutually exclusive logics, but rather share important potentialities. We have seen in previous chapters that these potentialities are not all desirable; state action that privileges limited segments may lend additional salience to clan divisions, and these clans may in turn contribute to patrimonialism on the part of the state. Below, I will suggest areas in which a selective symbiosis could prove developmentally useful.

Second and related, we must find ways—*contra* the simplified schematics of Weber and others—to theorize the complexities of multiple social and political attachments. We have seen how the promotion of Soviet internationalist, Kazakh ethnonationalist, and class-based identities did not supplant kinship divisions. Rather, these affiliations developed into a partially interlocking set of communities. That they were interlocking is critical to note, for a change in one collectivity gave rise to important, if not always predictable, changes in the other collectivities. If we begin explicitly to theorize these interrelationships, we carve out a conceptual space for various affiliations—premodern, modern, postmodern, and those unrelated to modernity—to be a part of contemporary political and social life. Weber's language, like that of other scholars of identity modernization, is an awkward fit with this complex, multilevel nature of identities.

CRAFTING SOLUTIONS

If the Soviet state played a critical role in sustaining clan relations, it would nonetheless be a mistake to equate the demise of the USSR with a return to an equilibrium path of "normal" modernization; we should not hastily conclude that clan politics will shortly fade away under the pressures of market-style urbanization and industrialization.[3] Just as Stalin replaced one mechanism for reproducing clans (nomadic pastoralism) with another (the shortage economy), actions of the post-Soviet state have served to sustain clan relations. By drawing our attention to the role that the Soviet state played, I do not imply that states may only become involved in constructing clan politics in the "Soviet" way. Neither kinship as a social phenomenon nor the state's relationship with it is likely to disappear, but its role in political life is open to state-directed management.

Whether designed to address kin divisions or not, state institutions have an effect in making them a normal or abnormal part of political life; deliberately or not, states manage or mismanage clan affiliations. The Soviet case is one example (though not the worst) of mismanagement: state action activated the concealable nature of clan divisions, thereby enhancing their political content. Mismanagement is, of course, only one possibility. Little prevents state elites from being self-conscious in their efforts to "craft" solutions to the challenges of clan politics.

To be effective in managing clan divisions, states must stitch new practices into the fabric of political life — practices that are tailored to the peculiarities of kinship. Doing so may ultimately prove to be a more successful and enduring means of preserving stability, enhancing state performance, and ensuring representative government than attempts to undermine preexisting identity relationships. Since states typically take the opposite approach, viewing clans as a threat worth marginalizing or eradicating, the remainder of this chapter will necessarily take on a speculative tone. In social scientific language, there is too little variation on the dependent variable (states' approaches to clans) to come to firm conclusions. Nonetheless, my speculation is rooted in the empirics of the Kazakhstan case and the logic that I provided to analyze it.

To "craft" institutions is to make a self-conscious attempt to

influence behavior. The fact that effective statehood has proved problematic in many cases where kinship divisions run deep should coun-
sel caution, but not pessimism. As Di Palma puts it, "Hard facts do
not mean necessity. In political matters . . . causal relationships are
probable and outcomes uncertain." Carving out a space for the contingent policy choices that individuals make, he offers: "It is a dismal
science of politics (or a science of a dismal politics) that passively
entrusts political change to exogenous and distant social transformations."[4] As globally momentous an outcome as the collapse of the
USSR may be attributed, in significant part, to the "tidal force" of contingent events that generated their own causal structure.[5] Macrostruc-
tural variables are not fate; we must reserve conceptual space for the
crafting efforts of individual agents.

To minimize the challenges that kinship-rich societies play, the state
must become more involved in managing these divisions by shaping
their meaning, function, and role in contemporary political life. Students of ethnic pluralism have long known that diversity presents challenges but that it does not seal a society's fate. Accordingly, they have
sought to develop institutional solutions to manage cultural pluralism. They were not always thus preoccupied. In the heyday of the
modernization paradigm in the 1950s and 1960s, ethnic minorities
were expected to become culturally assimilated at the hands of all-
powerful, state-driven high culture. The view proved unjustified; students of ethnicity quickly faced the reality that ethnic diversity requires
accommodation within unified institutional frameworks.[6] Because no
one—notwithstanding the doctrine of ethnic nationalists themselves—
could expect an isomorphism between political boundaries and the
contours of each of the world's countless culturally defined populations, ethnic pluralism came to be viewed as a fact of domestic political life. The state availed itself of a vast repertoire of policies to manage
this diversity: affirmative action, ethnically defined federalism, regional
autonomy, inclusive citizenship laws, consociational arrangements,
transferable voting, rules on political party formation, electoral rules,
liberal human rights protections, and language-promotion schemes—
to name a few.[7]

The policy prescriptions that emanate from these analyses of ethnic divisions require refinement if we are interested in clan divisions.
One-size-fits-all advocacy obscures the fact that identity cleavages vary
widely. Differences in the ways that ethnic, gender, regional, religious,

and subethnic divisions operate should not be elided in an effort to offer general prescriptions. We know that distinctive cleavages require distinctive approaches; institutions must be crafted with an eye to the specific affiliations that require managing.

INSTITUTIONS FOR CLANS

Before state structures emerged, societies where kinship divisions ran deep had nonstate institutions that governed the behavior of groups. As an alternative to accepting a Leviathan, societies developed elaborate practices that reined in would-be destabilizing forces before such forces could have that effect. The fissure and fusion of groups, an ability to deliver swift "justice" through punitive action on neighboring groups, as well as an ecologically driven imperative for cooperation, all supplemented the authority of local elders and extralocal chiefs. Such indigenous institutions for managing societal divisions typically went into demise when states expanded into kinship-rich territory.

The demise, however, was not total. The residue of these indigenous practices remained for decades. To the extent that clan balancing was practiced (see chapter 5), the state's supreme authority figure attempted to avoid fundamental inequities among clan groupings, even as he could often simultaneously find ways to privilege his own kind. In the contemporary context, however, this was an inadequate mechanism for managing clans, since it essentially relied on the goodwill of an individual or a narrowly circumscribed elite to maintain a balance. The residue of premodern institutions is not terra firma for managing clan divisions.

What is needed is an institutional framework that directly addresses the peculiar features of kin-based politics. A three-pronged initiative would move in this direction. A drive toward transparency in governance, a push toward mechanisms for equitable distribution of wealth, and efforts to selectively embrace (rather than reject and stigmatize) kin divisions would go a long way toward deactivating clan divisions' explosive potential.

A drive toward transparency in governance would counteract the concealable nature of clan divisions. Transparency has several effects on clan politics. Generally, transparency means diminished control over flows of information. In information-constrained environments, kinship divisions become especially useful, readily acting to channel information from user to user. In environments where actors receive information from a variety of sources that are not censored or manipulated, kinship networks no longer may claim a near monopoly on information transmission. While the trend in Central Asian states in the late 1990s and early years after 2000 was quite in the other direction (i.e., toward greater control over flows of information), a relaxing of control would bolster efforts to rein in clans.

More specifically, transparency could mean making available the clan background of prominent political and social actors—or, at a bare minimum, not stigmatizing public discourse on the matter. The weakened knowledge of the kin background of others spells trouble for political life in two ways. First, it renders it impossible for outsiders to scrutinize, and thereby perform an external check on, the behavior of insiders. Observers' knowledge of insiders' kin background would give insiders pause to develop kin-based networks, for fear of being known. This could occur by making kin background a part of a published and widely available public record. Second, a weakened knowledge of kin background leads outsiders to politicize kinship deeply, by using the broad language of stigmatized societal divisions to make political hay. A published record on the score would force them to use alternative rhetorical strategies that would not politicize clan identities.

Transparency on clans is about publicly acknowledging the nature and existence of kin-based ties. It is a prescription that stops short, however, of advocating that the state deliberately build clan divisions into its institutional edifice. That is, state actors should be wary of consociational arrangements, parliamentary set-asides for different clan groupings, and other schemes that would elevate clan divisions above others of society's cleavages. Such schemes—diverse as they may be—have a tendency to reify the very categories that they set out to manage. They would require a comprehensive nationwide census on kin groups, which itself would be difficult to conduct. They would require that institutions inscribe a formula with regard to the role of clans—a formula that itself would become the topic of hot political debates. I suspect that going this far would be neither necessary, nor desirable.

Rather, the solution would be simpler: allow meaningful elections at the regional and local levels. Heretofore, Central Asian leaders have not conducted free or fair elections at any level and have been particularly reluctant to entertain even the facade of electoral competition in local areas. Combined with a published public record of clan background, meaningful elections at all levels would provide a mechanism for individuals to know (rather than to speculate and politicize) the extent to which they are being represented by their authorities. A politics that were aboveground and open would render the raw material for a mechanism of clan self-regulation. The prescription applies for bureaucratic posts as well; published information on kin background would force actors to be explicit about avoiding imbalances among clan groupings.

Transparency in the legal system would also defuse clan politics. In situations such as the command economies of state socialism, exchange of goods is delayed rather than immediate. Kinship networks are effective in orchestrating such delayed exchanges, as they provide the diffuse relationships that nonetheless link individuals remotely. Kinship is promoted under such conditions. The shift to effective and open enforcement of contracts is an alternative way to protect individuals engaged in such transactions. In the early years after 2000, the trend in Central Asia was precisely the opposite: toward weakened protections of existing contracts (especially with foreign multinationals) in an effort to become less reliant on foreign capital. Whether or not this devaluing of contracts was justified, it can be expected to result in an enhanced role for kin-based networks.

Transparency would represent a dramatic change from existing practices. Such a change would emanate from the goodwill of the state elite or, alternatively, pressure from the international community to compel reform—neither of which materialized in the context of Central Asia's ongoing participation in the U.S.-led "war on terrorism." More modest steps in the direction of transparency, however, could be imagined. A regime that was reluctant to introduce regional and local elections might still be encouraged to publish the minutes of all administrative proceedings at the regional and local level, allowing members of the media and any political group to access this record. A regime that found it difficult to create an impartial judicial system that would enforce contracts could invite outside auditors to create an effective ombudsman or anticorruption office to investigate allegations of corruption. It might be run through international nongovernmental or governmental organizations. The regime would begin by adhering to both the letter and the spirit of the state's constitution, thus itself taking the law seriously.

A push toward mechanisms for equitable distribution of wealth would undermine the role of clans further. Because networks in general and clan networks in particular thrive under conditions of shortage, ensuring that there is no unreasonable concentration of wealth would deprive networks of the shortages that give them full flourish. Moreover, an equitable distribution of wealth (at least in oil-rich states such as Kazakhstan) would move individuals beyond the subsistence-based practices that privilege barter-type transactions rather than cash payment. Under state socialism, barter was widespread and common because money lost meaning when goods (that money could theoretically buy) were not available. In monetarized situations, individuals avail themselves less often of kin connections, as goods become available through alternate means. But this requires that every segment of society—not just a privileged elite—experience monetarization in the sense of having surplus and being engaged in market transactions. Doing so could only erode clan divisions' economic importance in goods acquisition.

A regime that, either for self-interested reasons or because of an embrace of neoliberal economic philosophy, was unwilling to strive for greater equity in social and economic development could at minimum take the step of fighting the corruption that plagues the system and creates further inequities. This would necessarily involve bringing in outside anticorruption agencies, which the elite might abhor for its implication that the local state is itself incapable of combating the problem; but doing so would have important implications for clan politics.

At the same time, selective efforts should be made to embrace (rather than reject and stigmatize) kin divisions, since clan can be used for developmentally useful purposes.[8] In addition to their concealability, a further distinguishing feature of clans is their multilevel nature. Under conditions of systemic or local shortages, such a peculiarity is an advantage for access networks. It allows individuals to avail themselves of a multitude of ties at a variety of levels of aggregation. It allows individuals to pool and mobilize their resources at low cost, since the state is not involved. Resource pooling occurs when groups of extended kin enter into rotating credit circles. Mobilization occurs when kin connections provide the transmission belt for information about the need for labor to contribute to a local, regional, or national public good.

Kin ties were not much used for such purposes in Central Asia in the 1990s, as states continually drove these affiliations underground.

This was a mistake. Much potential exists for kinship to serve developmentally useful purposes. Kenya's *harambee* (self-help) movement under Jomo Kenyatta successfully involved local institutions and individuals in public works projects. The state elite provided special access to national-level resources and offices to those who contributed financially to local *harambee* projects.[9] Similarly, Central Asian states should develop strategies that would restructure kinship-based competition: instead of a competition among kin networks to *extract* from the central state, a contest among kin units to *contribute* to national development could ensue. Central Asian states are in a propitious position to do so, since in no way does affiliation to a local clan or a regional umbrella clan preclude attachment to a larger community. To the contrary, to serve the developmental needs of one level of community is, potentially, to bolster the development of the next level of community.

To develop strategies that depoliticize clan divisions is a laudable goal, but in the first years of the new century, Central Asian states moved precisely in the opposite direction: toward greater opacity in governance; away from meaningful elections; toward increasing crackdowns on independent media; and toward greater disparities in wealth. The distance of existing state practice from what could be expected to defuse clan as a hot political issue is precisely the point: the more that Central Asian states continue the trends of the late 1990s and early years after 2000, the less likely it is that clan will disappear as a political phenomenon.

RELEGITIMIZING CLAN

At root, to fight clan politics, states must selectively and in limited fashion relegitimize kinship as a basis for social organization and political life. Finding developmentally useful purposes for kin groups is a start. Further, clearly defining and strictly enforcing laws regarding the use of kin ties in the private and public sectors is crucial, since clarity and nonarbitrary enforcement allow individuals to bring kinship into the open—at least insofar as they do not contravene the law.

Even a state elite that endeavored to religetimize clans would face a hostile international normative environment that could undermine the effort. Taylor captures the line of thinking that undergirds inter-

national norms when he claims, "The search for a categorical identity, to answer the call to difference, and be the bearer of the sought-
for dignity, can take many forms. It is understandable that the
discrediting of some must strengthen the appeal of others."[10] I have
made it plain that I prefer to view human beings as the possessors
of multiple, layered identities with an astounding capacity to, when
no sanctions are levied against doing so, proclaim membership in
various, overlapping collectivities. Nowhere is this clearer than with
multilevel kinship divisions.

But there is little recognition of multiple identities in the structure
of international politics. Rather, some divisions receive international,
and hence state, legitimacy, while others do not. Subethnic divisions
occupy a peculiar place in contemporary configurations of international politics. Just as they are seldom on the conceptual map of political analysts, neither are they on the political map for modern states.
Take ethnicity, for a contrast. There is an implicit norm by which the
nation-state—still the dominant cultural-political organization in
today's world, notwithstanding globalizing trends—is understood to
have an ethnic core. Although the myth is to the contrary, even self-
proclaimed "civic" polities have a cultural component.[11] The logic
of ethnic cleansing is the heinous face of this norm; the logic of ethnic partition—presumably to separate warring ethnic groups and allow
their full independent flourish—is its more benign face. Either way,
ethnic groups are tapped as legitimate political actors that either enjoy
sovereign statehood or seek to gain it. Their level of aggregation appears
appropriate in order for them to be in legitimate competition for control of existing states. Liberal advocates of civicness are understandably distraught by the trend, but they would nonetheless agree that
ethnic groups receive recognition and, hence, legitimacy from international political norms.

The same cannot be said for subethnic divisions, which are rendered illegitimate by the logic of the modern state system. In the
extreme forms, as we have seen, they are stigmatized as backward and
regressive and targeted for elimination. In the less extreme forms, they
simply go unrecognized by state institutions. This neglect, however,
is not entirely benign. Liberals purport to treat other cultural divisions
similarly (the "race-blind" movement in the United States comes to
mind, at least for its theoretical sustenance), but even where liberal
norms reign, the terms of debate are set: ethnic categories are those

which the state is to ignore, move away from, and not countenance. Subethnic divisions, by contrast, simply go unrecognized; as long as this is the case, they are likely to retain the potential for subversiveness. Given the retrenchment of the nation-state in the early years of the new century, after a decade of globalizing trends, the lifeline for a vibrant clan politics remains intact.

Appendix: Methods

I used a wide array of strategies to discern patterns of clan politics. The central premise guiding me was that identity is largely (though not exclusively) a subjective phenomenon. That is, while ascription by outsiders or circumstances is an element in all forms of group affiliation, insider perspectives lie at its core. Here, I elaborate on ethnographic methods, interviews, in-depth interviews, focus-group methods, and strategies for generating a database on personnel appointments.

ETHNOGRAPHIC METHODS

Taking emic perspectives seriously means listening to people and making note of their views. The meanings that insiders attribute to group identities are crucial in any study of such identities' effect on political life, although this is not the same as uncritical acceptance thereof. In no way would I seek to ascribe a "false consciousness" to people with whom I talked, but neither was I willing to embrace their views prima facie. I sought to listen, but with a critical ear.

Ethnographic approaches excel in making such voices audible in everyday life. As a matter of research practice, this means that the researcher cannot control the contexts in which voices are heard. This presents challenges. In a social-scientific version of the Heisenberg uncertainty principle, the researcher's very presence may alter the context and thereby change the character of insider perspectives that are gleaned. Western researchers—who are likely to look and act in ways that can only be described by locals as "alien"—are at exceptional pains to know that their presence is not fundamentally shaping the results they get. There is no easy solution to the problem. All one can do is strive to be accepted by local actors and cross-refer-

ence every conclusion, however small, about the texture of local identities and behaviors.

To do so requires an intensive approach. As someone who sought
to characterize politics across a vast and varied state, I chose not to
proceed with a fully ethnographic study. An intensive study of one
village, for example, would develop a descriptively accurate picture
of a single locale but risk ignoring just how varied local environments
may be across space. An extensive approach could capture variation
in local environments but mischaracterize the phenomenon under
study, for lack of familiarity with local contexts and lack of acceptance by local actors.

In the end, I sought to combine intensive and extensive ethnographic methods. Based in Almaty and the surrounding region, I also
lived in Shymkent and traveled in South Kazakhstan region for
upward of two months, Atyrau and region for almost a month, and
Astana and region for almost a month. I had countless conversations
with ordinary people and recorded notes about those interactions.
These encounters were the product of much happenstance. Given
this, I sought neither to embrace them as unbiased nor to dismiss them
as irrelevant. I viewed it as my task to strip away the perspectives—
based on cultural, gender, class, clan, and other features—to reveal
any useful information. In some cases, I found nothing. In many more,
I found much of use. This was a strategy guided by a common-sense
question: "What, if any, are the biases that influence this person's
engagement of me and my topic?"

In these interactions, I never directly approached the questions that
interested me. I quickly found that direct questions about the politics
of kinship ties elicited direct, but problematic answers. Many respondents would take some offense at the line of questioning, affronted
that this American researcher would assume that local people were
"backward." At the other end of a rather polarized spectrum, others
would enthusiastically describe kinship as all-determining, especially
in the higher echelons of power. This told me much about the vis-
ceral nature of the topic, but as a true-to-life depiction of politics, it
left much wanting.

Rather, I broached the topic indirectly. I never had a rigid series of
questions, since each situation required maximal flexibility. I would
begin by turning the conversation toward matters of goods distribution,
matters of family and extended family, and matters related to Kazakh

language and culture. Since I could converse in Kazakh, language became a natural discussion topic. After some initial conversation, my respondents and I would often—though not always—switch to Russian, with which we (often both!) had greater facility. If, after several attempts to guide conversations to benefit my research, my partner resolutely refused to bite, I would willingly discuss most things under the sun. I viewed this as both ethically and methodologically justified. It was ethically justified because my informants were full-fledged human beings and not merely fonts of information. It was methodologically justified b'ecause in a number of cases, it paid dividends: minutes after I had abandoned the effort to use the conversation for research purposes, the informant raised issues of direct relevance to the project.

Although I used ethnographic methods, this was not my sole fieldwork strategy. The intention was to use several strategies to triangulate the manifestations of subethnic identities; a combined approach offers better purchase than a single methodological strategy could in isolation.

INTERVIEWS

Interviews were likewise conducted in a flexible rather than a structured way. Had I adhered closely to a set list of questions, I would have sacrificed internal validity. This would have been ill suited to penetrate an opaque phenomenon. Instead, I began with a range of issues that I sought to cover but—if I calculated that it would be useful—I allowed the interviewee to shift the direction of the conversation. The final product in most cases bore a stamp both of the interviewees' interests and my own. The fluency usually generated by this approach more than justified it as a research strategy.

Interviewees spanned a wide spectrum—from ordinary people, to state officials, to members of the opposition, to the cultural intelligentsia. I sought to represent the widest array of perspectives possible without sacrificing the depth needed to elicit meaningful responses. See the bibliography for a complete list of interviews cited.

IN-DEPTH INTERVIEWS

For the narrow purpose of learning the character of individuals' access networks during the Soviet period, I faced the daunting task of reconstructing everyday life. I availed myself of all written material I could find about the mundane details of Soviet-era Kazakh life, but this material left considerable gaps. There was, however, an entire generation old enough to recall much of the Soviet period and lucid enough to do so in detail. In-depth interviews were designed to use these individuals as a source of information on the subject.

If the ethnographic and interview approaches (above) attempted to combine intensive with extensive strategies for data gathering, these in-depth interviews were decidedly more intensive. The calculation was threefold. First, older interviewees need more time to recall their lives in detail and may lack the strength for a short, intense session. Second, they were reconstructing the mundane, which is not an easy task. It is far easier to remember the exceptional, the unusual, and the surprising than the ordinary. Since it was precisely the ordinary that interested me, I allotted much time. Third, I was attempting to consider kinship ties, so an indirect approach to the subject was needed to gain valid insights. The average duration (cumulative, over several sessions) for these interviews was between five and six hours.

Selection was made along a number of criteria. First, because I was interested in the kinship divisions among ordinary Kazakhs, eight interviewees were Kazakh and two were non-Kazakh. All respondents were more than sixty years old. Six were men, four were women. Six were from rural areas, four from urban areas. While the interview pool was not large enough for this variation to hold statistical significance, it still made good sense to vary the profile of interviewees. Beyond these criteria, I allowed interviews to be conducted with people with whom research assistants (see below) were already acquainted; this allowed greater receptivity on the part of the interviewees.

In contrast to the other fieldwork done for this project, these in-depth interviews were conducted by research assistants. Assistants were trained in the methods for conducting such interviews, supplied with a list of issues to be covered, and instructed to take as long as necessary to gain good information. Almost all interviewees were more comfortable speaking Kazakh than Russian, so I selected assistants who were both schooled in sociological methods and fluent in Kazakh. I am convinced that, had I conducted the interviews in Kazakh by myself (or through a Russian-Kazakh translator), my less-than-fluent facility in Kazakh would have disrupted the flow of information and jeopardized recollections. Serik Aidossov of the Sociological Resource

Center in Shymkent was crucial in organizing the team of research assistants.

After the interviews, each interviewer transcribed the audio recordings. I held meetings with each interviewer, going over each transcript in detail, and inviting him or her to reflect on nonverbal or otherwise subtle aspects of the interviews that might not find reflection in the written transcript. As a routine matter, interviewees were told that their names would be withheld. I have thus used pseudonyms in the text. I preferred to protect their identities rather than make difficult judgments about whether particular details from their interviews were or were not compromising.

Relying on interviewers other than myself, I drew up a protocol to guide their decisions. It appears here in English translation.

Location

In the home environment of the person being interviewed.

Duration

These conversations should make the participants feel comfortable. Therefore, six to eight hours of total time should be enough. This time should be spent over several different conversations, since *no one should be expected to speak for six to eight hours straight.*

Transcription

Transcribe everything that the participant says. Do not summarize. Do not make any decisions about whether to include something or to exclude something else. *Include everything in the transcription.* If something occurs during the conversation that you would like to make a note of, please indicate. For example, if someone walks into the room and the participant begins speaking to him or her, please note this in the written transcript.

Beginning the Interview

1. Introduce yourself: You have been asked to have a conversation about daily life under Soviet rule. You believe that _____ will have a good perspective on daily life and much to say about it. You hope that _____ will be willing to share his or her personal experience in the Soviet period.

2. Tell about the American scholar: An American scholar, who

speaks Kazakh, is trying to interview as many Kazakhs as possible, but he cannot be everywhere at once! So, he has asked you to conduct some of these conversations. He is writing a scholarly book, in which the experiences of _____ in the Soviet period are very important. He wants to get a picture of how people lived then.

3. Ask for permission to record: You would like to ask for permission to record the conversations on cassettes—to make sure that it is an accurate representation of what _____ wants to convey. This is not required of _____, but it will help the scholarly process. Would _____ be willing to help?

Conducting the Interview

1. Style: The conversation should be free, relaxed, and open-ended. Some questions (below) are provided for you, but if you want to add questions of your own, please do so. Do not skip questions that are provided for you; they are important.

2. Order of questions: You may ask questions in any order that seems logical. Do not feel that you must ask the questions in the order given. Be sure, however, to ask the questions provided.

3. Ask for elaboration and examples: If the participant says something interesting, ask them to say more about it, or ask them to offer examples from their personal life about what occurred.

4. Interruptions: If the conversation is interrupted, that may be good. Be sure, however, to establish a time and a place to continue the conversation.

5. Prematurely ended conversations: The participant may end the conversation for any reason (or without reason). If this happens, we will find a suitable alternative participant.

Fundamental Questions

1. Date of birth
2. Ethnicity
3. Umbrella clan
3. Subdivisions
4. Clan background of parents
5. Profession
6. Place of residence
7. Place of residence during Soviet period

8. Did extended family live nearby in the Soviet period?

Sample Questions about Daily Life under Soviet Rule

1. During the Soviet period, life was difficult. Was it easier then than it is for your children today? Please explain what is easier and what is more difficult.

2. During the Soviet period, the term *blat* (connections) and *po blatu* (via connections) were often used. How important was *blat*?

3. Was *blat* important for getting a job? Do you remember any specific examples of someone using *blat* to get a job?

4. Was *blat* important for getting produce? Do you remember any specific examples of someone using *blat* to get produce?

5. Was *blat* important for getting consumer goods? Do you remember any specific examples of someone using *blat* to get consumer goods?

6. Was there a specifically Kazakh variant of *blat*?

7. Was *blat* among Kazakhs different from *blat* among Russians? Please explain the differences.

8. Kazakhs are well known for their hospitality and their strong families. During the Soviet period, could Kazakhs count on their families to help?

9. Could they count on their families more than Russians could count on theirs?

10. Can you think of examples?

11. Do Kazakhs still count on their families today? Why, or why not?

12. Let's say that you wanted to get a new apartment. In the Soviet period, how would you have done it?

13. Today, how would you do it?

14. Who could you rely on for help during the Soviet period?

Sample Questions on Contact with Kin

1. Can you think of examples when a close relative came to you for help in the Soviet period? Could you help? How?

2. Can you think of examples when a distant relative came to you for help in the Soviet period? Could you help? How?

3. If a relative whom you previously didn't know came to you for help in the Soviet period, would you help him? Examples?

4. Kazakhs often help each other—to the extent possible. What sorts

of requests were made by relatives in the Soviet period that you simply could not satisfy?

5. What requests were easier to satisfy? What requests were harder to satisfy?

6. Give examples.

FOCUS GROUPS

Focus groups are a way to reconstruct group interaction. If individual interviews extract people from their social contexts, focus groups generate discussions that are, by nature, dynamic. Assuming that people's perspectives are not static, but rather "in process," this is critical to discerning their attitudes and patterns of behavior. Such groups also allow greater agenda setting by participants than do more structured interviews, since the moderator is instructed to allow discussion to evolve without excessive guidance.

As with in-depth interviews, I invited local sociologists to assist in the project, in this case as focus-group moderators. I personally screened and instructed them in the methodology. Central among their instructions was to let participants, within reason, set the agenda for the discussion. That is, we were to begin with themes but allow ourselves to deviate from them, before resuming with the next theme. They were to conduct the sessions in the Kazakh language but to let anyone who preferred to speak Russian do so. I participated in the events, acting as occasional moderator myself. Sessions were recorded on audiotape and transcribed.

Three focus groups were conducted—one each in Almaty, Shymkent, and Atyrau. Each had ten to twelve participants who were selected along several criteria. They ranged in age from twenty to twenty-eight. This cohort represented the core of the recent migrant population, whose experience interested me. They were all from rural areas, and thus this was an easy test for a bottom-up primordialist perspective. By focusing on migrants (rather than villagers) I could assemble a group of individuals from various surrounding rural areas (rather than just a few), making the results a better reflection of the whole countryside. Besides, migrants undergo a particularly acute process of relying on assistance networks. They were thus generally more conscious of the relationships they had than were their villager counterparts, who rarely stopped to think about the matter. Migrants came to urban areas either for work or for school. We sought an equal number of people with each motivation. We also sought an even gender distribution.

DATABASE ON PERSONNEL

In the 1990s, there was a virtual explosion of Who's Who? books in Kazakhstan. Many of them, informants reported, were derivative at best, inaccurate at worst. I used Ashimbaev's *Kto est' kto v Kazakhstane,* the most accurate and comprehensive such work, as a primary source for the database on personnel appointments.

Because I was interested in the political and economic elite, I wanted to select those who enjoyed some economic or political status in Kazakhstan, not moral, cultural, or social standing. I thus included (n=481) anyone who met any of the following criteria for either 1997 or 2001 or both: (1) occupied a national-level post (upper midlevel to high level), (2) was a prominent member of a prominent business group (high-level only), (c) occupied a top regional post (high-level only), or (d) was a prominent member of the opposition. Inclusion in the database was based on the answer to the question, Is there some indication that this person was in a position of national influence?

Each entrant's position in 1997 and 2001, ethnicity, and birthplace were recorded. Positions were then grouped into larger categories: presidential administration, regional administrator (*akim*), business, diplomatic corps, education, finance, general government, judiciary, legislature, central ministry, press, internal security, military, and other.

Birthplace was recorded as a proxy for umbrella clan background among ethnic Kazakhs. If an entrant was urban-born, then his or her umbrella clan background could not be reliably discerned. On the other hand, the background of rural-born Kazakhs could be reliably predicted from the location of their birth. There was some margin for error, the extent of which I regret I cannot know, but most local scholars agreed that this was a reasonable strategy. After doing so, I asked local scholars who follow kin background to check the entrants' backgrounds for validity. Of 481 entrants, I changed the kin background of 5 of them at the suggestion of local scholars. These scholars preferred to remain anonymous, since they knew that collecting information on kinship was an explosive issue.

Notes

INTRODUCTION

The chapter's epigraph is from Carl B. Landé, "Kinship and Politics in Pre-Modern and Non-Western Societies," in John T. McAlister Jr., ed., *Southeast Asia: The Politics of National Integration*, 229 (New York: Random House, 1973).

1. I use the male pronoun here, since the metaphor is based on shoes more likely to be worn by men.

2. Anatol Lieven, *Chechnya: Tombstone of Russian Power* (New Haven: Yale University Press, 1998), 335–45.

3. Sergei Poliakov, *Everyday Islam: Religion and Tradition in Rural Central Asia* (Armonk: M.E. Sharpe, 1992); and Demian Vaisman, "Regionalism and Clan Loyalty in the Political Life of Uzbekistan," in Yaacov Ro'i, ed., *Muslim Eurasia: Conflicting Legacies*, 105–21 (London: Frank Cass, 1995).

4. Vladimir Kushlubayev, "Tribalism and the State Formation in Kyrgyzstan" (thesis, Central European University, 1995); and Kathleen Collins, *Clans, Pacts, and Politics: Understanding Regime Transition in Central Asia* (Ph.D. diss. , Stanford University, 1999, and book ms., 2002).

5. Shahram Akbarzadeh, "Why Did Nationalism Fail in Tajikistan?" *Europe-Asia Studies* 48, no. 7 (1996): 1105–29; and Barnett Rubin, "Russian Hegemony and State Breakdown in the Periphery: Causes and Consequences of the Civil War in Tajikistan," in Barnett R. Rubin and Jack Snyder, eds., *Post-Soviet Political Order: Conflict and State Building* (London: Routledge, 1997).

6. On state weakness in the region, see Vanelin Ganev, "Postcommunism as an Episode of State-Building: A Historical-Sociological Approach" (working paper, Miami University, 2002); and Mark R. Beissinger and Crawford Young ,eds., *Beyond State Crisis?: Post-Colonial Africa and Post-Soviet Eurasia in Comparative Perspective* (Washington, DC: Woodrow Wilson Center Press, 2002).

7. I wish here only to note the broad use of the term, not to revisit the debates surrounding its use. See Carl J. Friedrich and Zbigniew K. Brzezin-

ski, *Totalitarian Dictatorship and Autocracy* (Cambridge: Harvard University Press, 1956); and Hannah Arendt, *The Origins of Totalitarianism* (1951; repr., New York: Harcourt Brace and Company, 1979).

8. Chapter one offers an in-depth introduction to *zhuz* and *ru* attachments among ethnic Kazakhs. For now, I would merely like to note that these identities are rooted in precise (if sometimes fictive) genealogical knowledge. In chapter one, I also justify the use of the terms "clan" and "subethnicity," which I interchange freely.

9. *Holos Ukrayiny*, 13 October 1993, translated by the Foreign Broadcast Information Service (FBIS-SOV-93–198).

10. D. Satpaev, "Tainye rychagi vlasti: lobbi i institut lobbizma v Kazakhstane," *Mysl'* 6 (1996): 34. All translations from Russian and Kazakh are the author's (unless otherwise indicated). When the particular rendering of a thought in one language (rather than another) carries nuances that are important for this study, I specify the original source language.

11. Donald L. Horowitz, *Ethnic Groups in Conflict* (Berkeley: University of California Press, 1985).

12. Max Weber, *On Charisma and Institution Building*, ed. Samuel N. Eisenstadt (Chicago: University of Chicago, 1968).

13. Kathleen Thelen, "Historical Institutionalism in Comparative Politics," *Annual Review of Political Science* 2 (1999): 369–404; and Kathleen Thelen and Sven Steinmo, "Historical Institutionalism in Comparative Perspective," in Sven Steinmo, Kathleen Thelen, and Frank Longstreth, eds., *Structuring Politics: Historical Institutionalism in Comparative Analysis*, 1–32 (Cambridge: Cambridge University Press, 1992).

14. See Stephen Van Evera, "Primordialism Lives!" *APSA-CP* 12, no. 1 (Winter 2001): 20–22.

15. Dennis Galvan, *The State Must be the Master of Fire: Syncretism and Sustainable Development in Senegal* (Berkeley: University of California Press, forthcoming).

16. James C. Scott, *Seeing Like a State: How Certain Schemes to Improve the Human Condition Have Failed* (New Haven: Yale University Press, 1998).

17. Scott, *Seeing Like a State.*

18. The quotation is from Weber, *On Charisma,* 69.

1 / KINSHIP AND MODERNITY

The chapter's epigraph is from Charles Lindholm, "Kinship Structure and Political Authority: The Middle East and Central Asia," *Comparative Studies in Society and History* 28 (1986): 337.

1. The term "lower aggregate" addresses the relative size of the referent group. In this sense, nations and ethnic groups are usually higher aggregate,

while tribes, clans, and other local identities are understood to be lower aggregate. In a number of African cases, as well as in parts of the northern Caucasus, many ethnic groups are quite small in number and therefore lower aggregate.

2. Siobhan Harty, "The Institutional Foundations of Substate National Movements," *Comparative Politics* 33, no. 2 (January 2001): 191–210.

3. See the contributions to John A. Hall, ed., *The State of the Nation: Ernest Gellner and the Theory of Nationalism* (Cambridge: Cambridge University Press, 1998), as well as H. D. Forbes, *Ethnic Conflict: Commerce, Culture, and the Contact Hypothesis* (New Haven: Yale University Press, 1997).

4. John Waterbury, *The Commander of the Faithful: The Moroccan Political Elite—A Study in Segmented Politics* (London: Weidenfeld and Nicolson, 1970).

5. Ernest Gellner, *Nations and Nationalism* (Ithaca: Cornell University Press, 1983), 37–38, emphasis in original.

6. Ernest Gellner, "Tribalism and the State in the Middle East," in Philip S. Khoury and Joseph Kostiner, eds., *Tribes and State Formation in the Middle East,* 114 (Berkeley: University of California Press, 1990).

7. Gellner, *Nations,* 38

8. Karl Deutsch, *Nationalism and Social Communication: An Inquiry into the Foundations of Nationality* (New York: Wiley, 1953); and "Social Mobilization and Political Development," *American Political Science Review* 55, no.3 (1961): 493–514.

9. Benedict Anderson, *Imagined Communities: Reflections on the Origin and Spread of Nationalism* (London: Verso, 1983), 6, emphasis added.

10. For an insightful discussion, see Joel Migdal, *States in Society* (Cambridge: Cambridge University Press, 2001).

11. I do not wish to revisit the shortcomings of functionalism, since anthropology has moved demonstrably beyond these early assumptions. For a discussion of the subfield of kinship studies, see Michael G. Peletz, "Kinship Studies in Late Twentieth-Century Anthropology," *Annual Review of Anthropology* 24 (1995): 343–72.

12. Robert M. Emerson, Rachel I. Fretz, and Linda L. Shaw, *Writing Ethnographic Fieldnotes* (Chicago: University of Chicago Press, 1995), 139.

13. Peter Berger, Brigitte Berger, and Hansfried Kellner, *The Homeless Mind: Modernization and Consciousness* (New York: Vintage Books, 1974), 9.

14. I borrow the metaphors "noisy" and "quiet" from Mark R. Beissinger, *Nationalist Mobilization and the Collapse of the Soviet State* (Cambridge: Cambridge University Press, 2002).

15. Walker Connor, "Nation-Building or Nation-Destroying?" *World Politics* 24, no. 3 (April 1972): 337

16. See René Lemarchand, "Political Clientelism and Ethnicity in Tropical Africa: Competing Solidarities in Nation-Building," in Steffen W. Schmidt et al., eds., *Friends, Followers, and Factions* 100–123(Berkeley: University of California, 1977); S. N. Eisenstadt and L. Roniger, *Patrons, Clients, and Friends: Interpersonal Relations and the Structure of Trust in Society* (Cambridge: Cambridge University Press, 1984); Mark S. Granovetter, "Economic Institutions as Social Constructions: A Framework for Analysis," *Acta Sociologica* 35, no. 3 (1992): 3–11.

17. Janet Tai Landa *Trust, Ethnicity, and Identity: Beyond the New Institutional Economics of Ethnic Trading Networks, Contract Law, and Gift Exchange* (Ann Arbor: University of Michigan Press, 1994).

18. Robert Putnam, *Making Democracy Work: Civic Traditions in Modern Italy* (Princeton: Princeton University Press, 1993). Putnam's analysis shows that the same institutions created in northern Italy perform better than those in southern Italy. His research does not address the possibility that state institutions crafted differently for each context could perform equally well in each region.

19. Empirically, these principles intersect, as Granovetter famously illustrates. Nonetheless, as ideal types, they are competing principles. See Mark S. Granovetter, "The Strength of Weak Ties," *American Journal of Sociology* 78, no. 6 (1973): 1360–80.

20. Popular perception of immutability notwithstanding, in fact the salient lines of kinship—what Stevens calls "regimes of kinship"—are in large part the product of state practices. See Jacqueline Stevens, *Reproducing the State* (Princeton: Princeton University Press, 1999).

21. E. E. Evans-Pritchard, *The Nuer: A Description of the Modes of Livelihood and Political Institutions of a Niolitic People* (Oxford: Oxford University Press, 1940).

22. I. M. Lewis, *A Modern History of Somalia* (Boulder, CO: Westview Press, 1988) and *Blood and Bone: The Call of Kinship in Somali Society* (Lawrenceville, NJ: Red Sea Press, 1994); Abdi Ismail Samatar, "Destruction of State and Society in Somalia: Beyond the Tribal Convention," *Journal of Modern African Studies* 30, no. 4 (1992): 625–41; A. Nizar Hamzeh, "Clan Conflicts, Hezbollah and the Lebanese State," *Journal of Social, Political and Economic Studies* 19, no. 4 (1994): 433–45.

23. David D. Laitin, *Hegemony and Culture: Politics and Religious Change among the Yoruba* (Chicago: University of Chicago Press, 1986); and Collins, *Clans, Pacts, and Politics.*

24. Amatzia Baram, "Neo-Tribalism in Iraq: Saddam Hussein's Tribal Policies 1991–96," *International Journal of Middle East Studies* 29 (1997): 1–31.

25. Waterbury, *Commander of the Faithful.*

26. Lewis, *Blood and Bone.*

27. Andrew Shryock, *Nationalism and the Genealogical Imagination: Oral History and Textual Authority in Tribal Jordan* (Berkeley: University of California Press, 1997).

28. Max Weber, *From Max Weber: Essays in Sociology,* trans. and ed. H. H. Gerth and C. Wright Mills (New York: Oxford University Press, 1946), 81–82.

29. Max Weber, *The Theory of Social and Economic Organization,* trans. and ed. A. M. Henderson and Talcott Parsons (New York: Free Press, 1947), 332.

30. Making a distinction between goal-rationality and value-rationality, Weber suggests that a bureaucracy that is effective and efficient is not necessarily one that creates a greater good. On how models of efficiency are—ironically and tragically—implicated in the twentieth century's major atrocities, see Zygmunt Bauman, *Modernity and the Holocaust* (Ithaca: Cornell University Press, 1989).

31. Catherine Weaver points to organizational features within the World Bank that hampered efforts to create the "rule of law" on the ground. She covers the irony of an organization that, for lack of internal goal-rationality, was unable to foster such rationality in the target societies of ex-Soviet space in her *Hypocrisy of International Organizations: The Rhetoric, Reality and Reform of the World Bank* (Ph.D. diss., University of Wisconsin–Madison, 2003).

32. Max Weber, *Economy and Society,* vol. 3, ed. Guenther Roth and Claus Wittich (Berkeley: University of California Press, 1968), 1002

33. Harold Isaacs, *Idols of the Tribe: Group Identity and Political Change* (New York: Harper and Row, 1977); Walker Connor, *Ethnonationalism: The Quest for Understanding* (Princeton: Princeton University Press); and Alexander J. Motyl, *Revolutions, Nations, and Empires: Conceptual Limits and Theoretical Possibilities* (New York: Columbia University Press, 1999)

34. Anderson, *Imagined Communities;* Eric Hobsbawm and Terrence Ranger, *The Invention of Tradition* (Cambridge: Cambridge University Press, 1983); Peter L. Berger and Thomas Luckmann, *The Social Construction of Reality: A Treatise in the Sociology of Knowledge* (Garden City: Doubleday, 1966); and David D. Laitin, *Identity in Formation: The Russian-Speaking Populations in the Near Abroad* (Ithaca: Cornell University Press, 1998).

35. This is the unfortunate direction in which Huntington moves us by essentializing and homogenizing world "civilizations." The consequent picture of such reified groupings is misleading; while cultural differences can become politicized, political significance does not inhere in difference itself. See Samuel P. Huntington, "Clash of Civilizations?" *Foreign Affairs*

72, no. 3 (Summer 1993): 22–49. As one student of Japan has demonstrated, what appears to the outsider as homogeneity is rarely so simple; the absence of relatively politicized difference is not the same as the absence of difference itself. See Dorinne K. Kondo, *Crafting Selves: Power, Gender, and Discourses of Identity in a Japanese Workplace* (Chicago: University of Chicago Press, 1990).

36. Contrast Anderson's depiction of national identity in *Imagined Communities* with Landa's picture of clan in *Trust, Ethnicity, and Identity*.

37. Collins, *Clans, Pacts and Politics*, 108. Although Collins departs from primordialism on other points, her reasoning is consistent with it on this one.

38. Kathleen Thelen, "Historical Institutionalism," 397.

39. Ibid.

40. William Fierman, ed., *Soviet Central Asia: The Failed Transformation* (Boulder, CO: Westview Press, 1991). By common practice of Soviet scholars and Western Sovietologists, Kazakhstan was left out of discussions of Central Asia precisely because its socioeconomic profile had come to differ critically from the other republics. See, for examples, Leslie Dienes, *Soviet Asia: Economic Development and National Policy Choices* (Boulder, CO: Westview Press, 1987); and Boris Z. Rumer, *Soviet Central Asia: A Tragic Experiment* (Boston: Unwin Hyman, 1989).

41. Kenneth A. Shepsle, "Studying Institutions: Some Lessons from the Rational Choice Approach," *Journal of Theoretical Politics* 1, no. 2 (1989): 131–47.

42. James C. Scott, *Seeing Like a State: How Certain Schemes to Improve the Human Condition Have Failed* (New Haven: Yale University Press, 1998).

43. Ronald Grigor Suny, *The Revenge of the Past: Nationalism, Revolution, and the Collapse of the Soviet Union* (Stanford: Stanford University Press, 1993); Yuri Slezkine, "The USSR as Communal Apartment, or How a Socialist State Promoted Ethnic Particularism," *Slavic Review* 53, no. 2 (1994): 414–52; and Rogers Brubaker, *Reframing Nationalism* (Cambridge: Cambridge University Press, 1996).

44. Ethnic categories in Central Asia were not entirely a Soviet-era creation, as chapter two describes.

45. For brevity's sake, I refer to this as the "shortage economy," although a fuller characterization might be "political economy of shortage," since political processes and goods were central to its operation.

46. Chapter two details the clan system.

47. Donald L. Horowitz, *A Democratic South Africa?* (Berkeley and Los Angeles: University of California Press, 1991); René Lemarchand, *Burundi: Ethnocide as Discourse and Practice* (Cambridge and New York: Woodrow Wilson Center Press and Cambridge University Press, 1994).

48. Stevens, *Reproducing the State*, 24.

2 / NOMADS, DIFFUSE AUTHORITY, AND SOVIETIZATION

The chapter's epigraph is from Barrington Moore, *Social Origins of Dictatorship and Democracy*, repr. with a new foreword by Edward Friedman and James C. Scott (Boston: Beacon Press, 1993), 486.

1. Thus, we minimize what methodologists call an "endogeneity" problem; Kazakhs traditionally lacked state structures of their own. Statehood was a Soviet creation, so the impact of state structures emanated not from indigenous institutions that predated Soviet rule but rather from Soviet efforts themselves.

2. Thomas Hobbes, quoted in H. D. Forbes, *Ethnic Conflict: Commerce, Culture, and the Contact Hypothesis* (New Haven: Yale University Press, 1997), 13.

3. George Herbert Mead, *Mind, Self, and Society from the Standpoint of a Social Behaviorist* (Chicago: University of Chicago Press, 1934); and Erving Goffman, *Strategic Interaction* (Philadelphia: University of Pennsylvania Press, 1969). See Dorinne K. Kondo, *Crafting Selves: Power, Gender, and Discourses of Identity in a Japanese Workplace* (Chicago: University of Chicago Press, 1990) for a powerful exposition of these themes in the Japanese context.

4. The reference is to the emphasis Durkheim places on the "collective consciousness." See Emile Durkheim, *The Division of Labor in Society*, trans. W. D. Halls, with an introduction by Lewis A. Coser (1893; repr., New York: Free Press, 1984).

5. Samuel P. Huntington, "Clash of Civilizations?" *Foreign Affairs* 72, no. 3 (Summer 1993): 22–49.

6. For a game-theoretic argument that ethnic difference produces conflict, see Forbes, *Ethnic Conflict*.

7. Fredrik Barth, ed., *Ethnic Groups and Boundaries: The Social Organization of Culture and Difference* (Boston: Little, Brown and Company, 1969).

8. David D. Laitin, *Identity in Formation, Identity in Formation: The Russian-Speaking Populations in the Near Abroad*, (Ithaca: Cornell University Press, 1998), 368.

9. Donald L. Horowitz, *Ethnic Groups in Conflict*, (Berkeley: University of California Press, 1985), 64.

10. Philip S. Khoury and Joseph Kostiner, eds., *Tribes and State Formation in the Middle East* (Berkeley: University of California Press, 1990), 5.

11. Edmund R. Leach, *Political Systems of Highland Burma* (London, 1954), quoted with emphasis added in Richard Tapper, "Anthropologists, Historians, and Tribespeople on Tribe and State Formation in the Middle East," in Philip S. Khoury and Joseph Kostiner, eds., *Tribes and State Formation in the Middle East*, 51 (Berkeley: University of California Press, 1990).

12. Kenneth Christie, "Introduction: The Problem with Ethnicity and 'Tribal' Politics," in Kenneth Christie, ed., *Ethnic Conflict, Tribal Politics: A Global Perspective* (Surrey: Curzon Press, 1998), 5.

13. Michael Walzer, "The New Tribalism: Notes on a Difficult Problem," *Dissent* 39, no. 9 (Spring, 1992): 164–71

14. Natalia Dinello, "Clientelism, Corruption and Clans in Hungary and Russia" (working paper, University of Pittsburgh, 1999). The pejorative connotation is central to its meaning. When Russian speakers use *klan* and *traibalizm* to evoke images similar to those associated with the English terms, it shows that this normative baggage travels with the terms as they enter into use in other languages.

15. Durkheim, *Division of Labor*, 127.

16. E. E. Evans-Pritchard, *The Nuer: A Description of the Modes of Livelihood and Political Institutions of a Niolitic People* (Oxford: Oxford University Press, 1940); Durkheim, *Division of Labor*; Dru C. Gladney, "Relational Alterity: Constructing Dungan (Hui), Uygur, and Kazakh Identities Across China, Central Asia, and Turkey," *History and Anthropology* 9, no. 4 (1996): 445–77.

17. Subethnic clan identity is a relational affiliation, depending on the existence of higher-aggregate categories as a referent. The terminological link between subethnicity and ethnicity highlights what we know is an empirical link: forms of identity are often best understood in relation to each other. This project returns with frequency to the link between identity forms.

18. For convenience, I refer to the territory as "Kazakh" or "Kazakhstan," even though the terms did not enjoy wide use until well into the twentieth century.

19. All translations are the author's unless otherwise indicated.

20. Evans-Pritchard, *The Nuer*.

21. Aleksei Iraklievich Levshin, *Opisanie kirgiz-kazach'ikh, ili kirgiz-kaisatskikh, ord i stepei* (1832; repr., Almaty: Sanat, 1996), 289n.

22. After Soviet-forced sedentarization, *aul* comes to mean "village."

23. S. G. Kliashtornyi and T. I. Sultanov, *Kazakhstan: letopis' trekh tysiacheletii* (Alma-Ata: Rauan, 1992). An exception was the desert terrain of what today is central Kazakhstan, where extreme water scarcity and heat militated against the possibility of larger summer encampments.

24. Nurbulat Masanov, *Kochevaia tsivilizatsiia Kazakhov* (Almaty: Sotsinvest, 1995), 42. Masanov's book title translates as "the nomadic civilization of the Kazakhs," which hints at his larger structural-functional argument. What emerges in this territory, he argues, is not simply a mode of economy, particular worldview, or political system, but a civilization that is organic to the region. Overstating the case, Masanov's perspective nonetheless captures the

essential features of the relationships between social structure and nomadic pastoralism.

25. Anatoly Khazanov, *Nomads and the Outside World*, 2nd ed. (Madison: University of Wisconsin Press, 1994).

26. M. M. Ishchenko, I. S. Kazbekov, I. V. Larin, and B. K. Shchelokov, *Osobennosti sel'skogo khoziaistva Adaevskogo uezda*, Materialy komissii ekspeditsionnykh issledovanii, issue 13, Seriia Kazakhstanskaia (Leningrad, USSR: Izdatel'stvo Akademii Nauk SSSR, 1928), 44, quoted in Khazanov, *Nomads*, 51; clarification by Khazanov.

27. For a rendering of major clan emblems, see Kun Fu Chzhen, *Geopolitika Kazakhstana: mezhdu proshlym i budushchim* (Almaty: Zheti zharghy, 1999), 88–89.

28. "Kazakh Customary Law," *Central Asian Review* 5, no. 2 (1957): 127–44; Z. Zh. Kenzhaliev et al., eds., *Qazaq adet-ghyryp quqyghynyng materialdary* (Almaty: Zheti zharghy, 1996); Virginia Martin, "Law and Custom in the Steppe: Middle Horde Kazakh Judicial Practices and Russian Colonial Rule, 1868–1898" (Ph.D. dissertation, University of Southern California, 1996); Virginia Martin, "Barimta: Nomadic Custom, Imperial Crime," in Daniel R. Brower and Edward J. Lazzerini, eds., *Russia's Orient: Imperial Borderlands and Peoples,1700–1917*, 249–70 (Bloomington: Indiana University Press, 1997).

29. Elizabeth E. Bacon, *Central Asians Under Russian Rule: A Study in Culture Change* (Ithaca: Cornell University Press, 1966), 38.

30. Russian ethnographers and travelers referred to these nomads as "Kyrgyz." The term can be read as "Kazakh." See Daniel Brower, "Islam and Ethnicity: Russian Colonial Policy in Turkestan," in Brower and Lazzerini, eds., *Russia's Orient*, 115–37 (Bloomington: Indiana University Press, 1997).

31. B. Iuzefo, "O byte Kirgizov Turgaiskoi oblasti," *Russkii vestnik*, (April 1880), reprinted in F. M. Orazaev, *Tsarskaia kolonizatsiia v Kazakhstane: po materialam russkoi periodicheskoi pechati XIX veka*, 336–66 (Almaty: Rauan, 1995). This traveler also observed the emergence of modest "lending pools" [*ssudnye kassy*] in Turgaiskaia *oblast* that apparently helped to temper such economic downturns (353).

32. Russian colonization fundamentally weakened the position of this whitebone stratum, largely absorbing it into the segmentary structure. See Zh. O. Artykbaev, *Kazakhskoe obshchestvo v XIX veke* (Karaganda: Poligrafiia, 1993). Whitebone identity did not constitute the dense web of kinship relations that cut across other social divisions. Rather, it was limited in scope and therefore lacked resilience.

33. The author's translation from the proverb reported in Russian in Igor Savin, "O kategoriiakh gruppovogo soznaniia u kazakhov-kochevnikov" (working paper, Shymkent branch, Kazakhstan Academy of Sciences, 1998),

9. *Sart* was the ambiguous term used by Russian ethnographers (and by some portions of the agricultural populations themselves) to refer to inhabitants of Central Asia's oases cultures. See Brower, "Islam and Ethnicity."

34. Quoted in A. Namitov, *Perezhitki rodovogo byta i Sovetskii zakon* (Moscow: Gosizdatel'stvo, 1929), 49.

35. The occasional alternative translation of *zhuz* as "tribal confederation" is encumbered by some of the same issues that bedevil "tribe."

36. V. V. Vostrov and M. S. Mukanov, *Rodoplemennoi sostav i rasselenie Kazakhov: konets XIX - nachalo XX v* (Alma-Ata: Nauka, 1968); Khazanov, *Nomads*; and Masanov, *Kochevaia tsivilizatsiia*.

37. Martha Brill Olcott, *The Kazakhs*, 2nd ed (Stanford: Hoover Institution Press, 1995), 11.

38. Ibid., 13.

39. Bacon, *Central Asians*, 37–38.

40. I use the spelling *qazaq* (a more accurate phonetic rendering of Kazakh or Kazak) in this context to distinguish it from the latter terms, for purposes that will be clearer below.

41. For a summary of the historiography on this question, see M. Viatkin, *Ocherki po istorii Kazakhskoi SSR* (Leningrad: Gospolitizdat, 1941).

42. Kliashtornyi and Sultanov, *Kazakhstan: letopis'*, 249.

43. Levshin, *Opisanie kirgiz-kazach'ikh*, 153.

44. Mukhamedzhan Tynyshpaev, "Genealogiia Kirgiz-Kazakhskikh rodov" (1925), reprinted in Mukhamedzhan Tynyshpaev, *Istoriia Kazakhskogo naroda*, ed. A. Takenov and B. Baigaliev, 104–5 (Almaty: Sanat, 1998).

45. The description "Kyrgyz-Kaisak" was designed in part to avoid calling them Kazakh, which might confuse them with the Cossacks.

46. Schoeberlein-Engel has made this point most clearly for the agricultural parts of Central Asia. See John Schoeberlein-Engel, "Identity in Central Asia: Construction and Contention in the Conceptions of 'Ozbek,' 'Tajik,' 'Muslim,' 'Samarkandi' and Other Groups" (Ph.D. diss., Harvard University, 1994).

47. David Lowenthal, *The Past is a Foreign Country* (New York: Cambridge University Press, 1985). For a skillful interweaving of documentary and oral folk material to describe the popular anticolonial uprising of Kazakhs led by Kenesary Kasymov, see Yermukhan Bekmakhanovich Bekmakhanov, *Kazakhstan v 20–40 gody XIX veka* (Alma-Ata: Qazaq Universiteti, 1992).

48. For a broader overview of Kazakh history than this chapter can provide, see Olcott, *The Kazakhs*.

49. The changes brought by Russian colonization were not entirely without precedent in the steppe. Attachment to territory, which would later be strengthened with increasing sedentarization and the creation of colonial administrative boundaries, had already been forged by seasonal nomadic

migrations along identifiable routes. Agricultural cultivation, later promoted by colonial structures and encouraged by emergent commercial opportunities, had already achieved significant scope; wheat and other grains occupied a prominent position in the nomad's diet.

50. On what the Russian military stood to gain by the Central Asian conquest, see Firuz Kazemzadeh, "Russia and the Middle East," in Ivo Lederer, ed., *Russian Foreign Policy*, 489–530 (New Haven: Yale University Press, 1962).

51. Russian rule gradually eliminated the political power of the khans, but identification with these umbrella clans persisted. Well into the Soviet and post-Soviet periods, myths continued to circulate about the when and how each umbrella group was incorporated into the empire. Historians and laypeople debated whether the Younger and Middle clans' accession to Russian rule was voluntary or forced. Was it the product of far-sighted ruling elites seeking to protect their peoples or shortsighted ones interested only in personal gain? Had the Younger Umbrella Clan put up a stiffer resistance, would it have saved the Central Asian steppe and oases from Russian encroachment entirely? Had the Elder Umbrella Clan offered more substantial support in anticolonial uprisings (especially that of Kenesary Kasimov in the 1830s–40s), would this have forged interclan unity and prevented rapid colonization? Questions such as these manifested themselves in a variety of ways through Soviet and post-Soviet historiography, but the simple fact that they were posed in an idiom of clan divisions suggests the ongoing resonance of umbrella clan as an identity formation. (Interview, Irina Erofeeva, professor of history, Institute of History and Ethnography, Kazakhstan Academy of Sciences, 1 October 1998).

52. *Ustav o sibirskikh kirgizakh*, in Levshin, *Opisanie kirgiz-kazach'ikh*, 400. "Kyrgyz" here refers to Kazakhs.

53. Olcott, *The Kazakhs*, 58–59.

54. For a contemporary view of the resultant uprising among the Adai subdivision of the Younger Umbrella Clan, see P. Iudin, "Adaevskii bunt na poluostrove Mangyshlak v 1870 godu," *Russkaia starina* 7 (1894), reprinted in F. M. Orazaev, *Tsarskaia kolonizatsiia*, 79–100. On subsequent uprisings of the Adai in the early Soviet period, see Mukash Omarov, *Rasstreliannaia step': istoriia Adaevskogo vosstaniia 1931 goda; po materialam OGPU* (Almaty: Ghylym, 1994).

55. See document no. 96, reprinted in F. N. Kireev and F. I. Kolodin, eds., *Rabochee i agrarnoe dvizheniie v Kazakhstane v 1907–1914 godakh: sbornik dokumentov i materialov* (Alma-Ata: Kazakhskoe gosizdatel'stvo, 1957).

56. Iuzefo, "O byte Kirgizov," 339.

57. On the acute shortage of high-quality land by the early twentieth century, see the original source material in Kireev and Kolodin, *Rabochee i agrar-*

noe dvizheniie, especially document nos. 44, 48, 96, 109, 116, 135, 175, and 222. See also Martin, "Law and Custom," 162–197.

58. Bekmakhanov, *Kazakhstan v 20–40 gody*.

59. Olcott, *The Kazakhs*, 89–96.

60. Iuzefo, "O byte Kirgizov," 343.

61. Kireev and Kolodin, *Rabochee i agrarnoe dvizheniie*, document no. 248.

62. S. E. Tolybekov, *Kochevoe obshchestvo Kazakhov v XVII-nachale XX veka* (Alma-Ata: Nauka, 1971).

63. Kireev and Kolodin, *Rabochee i agrarnoe dvizheniie*.

64. Artykbaev, *Kazakhskoe obshchestvo*, 26–27.

65. Bekmakhanov, *Kazakhstan v 20–40 gody*, 279–86.

66. Steven Sabol, "Kazak Resistance to Russian Colonization: Kenesary Kasymov and His Revolt, 1837–1847" (paper presented at the meeting of the Association for the Study of Nationalities, Columbia University, New York, 15–17 April 1999), 1.

67. The totalitarian perspective is offered by Hannah Arendt, *Origins of Totalitarianism* (1951; repr., New York: Harcourt and Brace, 1979; Carl J. Friedrich and Zbigniew K. Brzezinski, *Totalitarian Dictatorship and Autocracy* (Cambridge, MA: Harvard University Press, 1956). Alternatives are offered by Merle Fainsod, *Smolensk under Soviet Rule* (Cambridge, MA: Harvard University Press, 1958); and Jerry F. Hough, *The Soviet Prefects: The Local Party Organs in Industrial Decision-Making* (Cambridge, MA: Harvard University Press, 1969).

68. See Terry D. Martin, "An Affirmative Action Empire: Ethnicity and the Soviet State, 1923–1938" (Ph.D. diss., University of Chicago, 1996).

69. Kuchkin adopts the language of class warfare in his richly empirical account of the processes of Sovietizing the Kazakhs. See Andrei Pavlovich Kuchkin, *Sovetizatsiia Kazakhskogo aula: 1926–1929 gg.* (Moscow: Akademiia Nauk SSSR, 1962).

70. On the uneasy application of Marxist categories to nomadic populations, see Ernest Gellner, foreword to Khazanov, *Nomads*, ix–xxv.

71. For an insightful look at how the Soviet construction of the trans-Siberian railroad was a site for attempts to create a working-class consciousness among Kazakhs where it had not existed, see Matthew J. Payne, "Turksib: The Building of the Turkestano-Siberian Railroad and the Politics of Production During the Cultural Revolution, 1926–1931" (Ph.D. diss., University of Chicago, 1995).

72. Olcott, *The Kazakhs*, 162.

73. Kazakhs tend to offer hospitality as a matter of course to any guest to their home. As Kuchkin points out, the hospitality extended to these guests was exceptional, signaling an unusually cozy relationship that involved the mutual exchange of favors (Kuchkin, *Sovetizatsiia Kazakhskogo aula*, 128).

74. Kuchkin, *Sovetizatsiia Kazakhskogo aula,* 242.

75. Ibid.

76. Quoted in ibid., 132.

77. Ibid., 133.

78. Central State Archives of the Republic of Kazakhstan, f. 769, o. 1, d. 11, l. 86. Post-Soviet archives are divided into *fondy,* subdivided into *opisi,* then into *dela,* and finally into *listy.* All subsequent references to archival documents are abbreviated as above. The *kishlak* was the village settlement among Uzbeks.

79. Quoted in Kuchkin, *Sovetizatsiia Kazakhskogo aula,* 149.

80. Central State Archives, f. 769, o. 1, d. 3, l. 3. Fermented mare's milk is an essential part of the traditional Kazakh diet, and one of enormous symbolic value, as well.

81. Kuchkin, *Sovetizatsiia Kazakhskogo aula,* 216.

82. Central State Archives, f. 769, o. 1, d. 66, l. 17.

83. Central State Archives, f. 769, o. 1, d. 3, l. 10.

84. Kuchkin, *Sovetizatsiia Kazakhskogo aula,* 187.

85. Quoted in Kuchkin, *Sovetizatsiia Kazakhskogo aula,* 188.

86. Central State Archives, f. 74, o. 4, d. 6, l. 5.

87. Central State Archives, f. 74, o. 4. d. 133, l. 9.

88. Central State Archives, f. 74, o. 1, d. 1, l. 53.

89. See Central State Archives, f. 74, o. 4, d. 6, l. 78.

90. Payne, "Turksib."

91. See much of Central State Archives, f. 74, o. 4, d. 345.

92. Central State Archives, f. 74, o. 1, d. 129, l. 57.

93. Central State Archives, f. 74, o. 11, d. 26, l. 4.

94. Irene Winner, "Some Problems of Nomadism and Social Organization Among the Recently Settled Kazakhs, part one," *Central Asian Review* 11, no. 3) (1963): 255.

95. Martha Brill Olcott, "The Collectivization Drive in Kazakhstan," *Russian Review* 40, no. 2 (1981): 122–42.

96. Olcott, "Collectivization Drive," 137.

97. As chapter seven describes, in the 1990s the land question reemerged, centering on issues of farm privatization, land redistribution, as well as the possibility of full rights of land ownership.

98. Parallel campaigns against similar practices took place at the same time in the north Caucasus, parts of Siberia, as well as in other regions of Central Asia. See especially M. V. Vagabov, *Kalym—vrednyi perezhitok* (Makhachkala: Dagestanskoe knizhnoe izdatel'stvo, 1975).

99. Central State Archives, f. 1380, o. 2, d. 200, l. 215.

100. Central State Archives, f. 1380, o. 2, d. 200, l. 206.

101. Central State Archives, f. 1380, o. 2, d.12, l. 71.

102. Gregory J. Massell, *The Surrogate Proletariat: Moslem Women and Revolutionary Strategies in Soviet Central Asia, 1919–1929* (Princeton: Princeton University Press, 1974).

103. Olcott, *The Kazakhs*, 197.

104. Bacon, *Central Asians*; Irene Winner, "Some Problems of Nomadism and Social Organization Among the Recently Settled Kazakhs, part two," *Central Asian Review* 11, no. 4 (1963): 355–73.

3 / TWO FACES OF SOVIET POWER

The chapter's first epigraph is from Joel Migdal, *States in Society* (Cambridge: Cambridge University Press, 2001), 252, emphasis in original.

1. Mark R. Beissinger and Crawford Young, eds., *Beyond State Crisis?: Post-Colonial Africa and Post-Soviet Eurasia in Comparative Perspective*. Washington, DC: Woodrow Wilson Center Press, 2002; Steven Levitsky and Lucan A. Way, "Elections without Democracy: The Rise of Competitive Authoritarianism," *Journal of Democracy* 13, no. 2 (April, 2002): 51–65.

2. On the ways in which the Soviet experiment was a modernization project, see Joanne P. Arnason, "Communism and Modernity," *Daedalus* 129, no. 1 (2000): 61–90.

3. James C. Scott, *Seeing Like a State: How Certain Schemes to Improve the Human Condition Have Failed* (New Haven: Yale University Press, 1998).

4. Martha Brill Olcott, "The Collectivization Drive in Kazakhstan," *Russian Review* 40, no. 2 (1981): 141. As chapter six details, the symbolic importance of these identities is not merely a point for academics to ponder; it generates a real political dynamic that deserves attention.

5. Arendt, Hannah, *The Origins of Totalitarianism* (1951; repr., New York: Harcourt and Brace, 1979), 21.

6. Jerry F. Hough, *The Soviet Prefects: The Local Party Organs in Industrial Decision-Making* (Cambridge, MA: Harvard University Press, 1969).

7. This apt term is taken from John McGarry, "'Demographic Engineering': The State-Directed Movement of Ethnic Groups as a Technique of Conflict Regulation," *Ethnic and Racial Studies* 21, no. 4 (1998): 613–38.

8. See much of Central State Archives of the Republic of Kazakhstan, f. 74, o. 11, d. 20.

9. Chapter seven illustrates how this changed in the post-Soviet period, with a large-scale urban migration of Kazakhs, especially to larger cities.

10. Robert A., Lewis, Richard H. Rowland, and Ralph C. Clem. *Nationality and Population Change in Russia and the USSR: An Evaluation of Census Data, 1897–1970* (New York: Praeger, 1976), 138.

11. For a discussion of the potential for urbanization, see ibid.

12. Gosudarstvennyi komitet Kazakhskoi SSR po statistike, *Narodnoe khoziaistvo Kazakhstana za 70 let: statisticheskii sbornik* (Alma-Ata: Izdatel'stvo "Kazakhstan," 1990), 113.

13. Gosudarstvennyi komitet Kazakhskoi SSR, *Narodnoe khoziaistvo Kazakhstana za 70 let*, 161.

14. Quoted in Andrei Pavlovich Kuchkin, *Sovetizatsiia Kazakhskogo aula: 1926–1929 gg* (Moscow: Akademiia Nauk SSSR, 1962), 134.

15. On the origins of Soviet nationalities policy, see Richard Pipes, *The Formation of the Soviet Union* (Cambridge, MA: Harvard University Press, 1954); Yuri Slezkine, "The USSR as Communal Apartment, or How a Socialist State Promoted Ethnic Particularism," *Slavic Review* 53, no. 2 (1994): 414–52; and Terry D. Martin, "An Affirmative Action Empire: Ethnicity and the Soviet State, 1923–1938," (Ph.D. diss., University of Chicago, 1996). On the policy's evolution during the Soviet period and consequences thereafter, see Rogers Brubaker, *Reframing Nationalism* (Cambridge: Cambridge University Press, 1996); Ronald Grigor Suny, *Revenge of the Past: Nationalism, Revolution, and the Collapse of the Soviet Union* (Stanford: Stanford University Press, 1993); and Walker Connor, *The National Question in Marxist-Leninist Theory and Strategy* (Princeton: Princeton University Press, 1984).

16. In these senses, the Soviet effort approximates the Turkish example. See Kemal Karpat, "Stages of Ottoman History," in Kemal Karpat, ed., *The Ottoman State and Its Place in the World History*, 79–98 (Leiden, Netherlands: E.J. Brill, 1974). One further important fact distinguished the Soviet case. Even as the Soviets offered affirmative action to compensate ethnocultural populations for the injustices of tsardom (as Martin describes in detail in "Affirmative Action Empire"), it simultaneously committed further atrocities (propagating famines, displacing populations, executing purges) against the same ethnically defined populations. Notably, Martin's extensive data come from Russian archives, where the benefits of Soviet affirmative action may be overrepresented, and the ethnically marked atrocities may be underreported. As correctives to Martin's account, see Aleksandr M. Nekrich, *The Punished Peoples: The Deportation and Fate of Soviet Minorities at the End of the Second World War*, trans. George Saunders (New York: Norton, 1978); and Robert Conquest, *The Harvest of Sorrow: Soviet Collectivization and the Terror-Famine* (New York: Oxford University, 1986).

17. Martin, "Affirmative Action Empire," 45.

18. Ibid., 950.

19. Suny, *Revenge of the Past*; Brubaker, *Reframing Nationalism*; and Slezkine, "USSR as Communal Apartment."

20. Yack suggests that no polity can be culturally neutral, the myth of civic-

ness notwithstanding. See Bernard Yack, "The Myth of the Civic Nation," *Critical Review* 10, no. 2 (Spring 1996): 193–211.

21. Yu. V. Bromlei, "A General Description of Ethnic Proceses," *Soviet Ethnographic Studies*, no. 3 (1983): 8–30; Yu. V. Bromlei, *Theoretical Ethnography* (Moscow: General Editorial for Foreign Publications and Nauka Publishers, 1984), 76–91; and Yu. V. Bromlei, ed., *Etnicheskie protsessy v sovremennom mire* (Moscow: Nauka, 1987).

22. The category "culturally backward peoples" (*kul'turno-otstalye narody*) was an official one promulgated in the early 1920s. It was a designation that local elites accepted readily, as it implied that some material benefit would be forthcoming to locales to remedy their backwardness (Martin, "Affirmative Action Empire," 183–86).

23. See Crawford Young, "Ethnicity and the Colonial and Post-Colonial State in Africa," in Paul Brass, ed., *Ethnic Groups and the State* (London: Croom Helm, 1985), reprinted in John Hutchinson and Anthony D. Smith, *Nationalism*, 230 (London: Oxford University Press, 1994).

24. N. Kiikbaev, *Torzhestvo leninskoi natsional'noi politiki v Kazakhstane* (Alma-Ata: Izdatel'stvo "Kazakhstan," 1968).

25. On changes in Soviet scholars' views of nomadic pastoralism as the Soviet Union itself changed, see Ernest Gellner, foreword to Anatoly Khazanov, *Nomads and the Outside World*, 2nd ed., ix–xxv (Madison: University of Wisconsin Press, 1994).

26. Quoted in Martin, "Affirmative Action Empire," 891.

27. Quoted in ibid., 951.

28. Abde Bochinovich Tursunbaev, *Kazakhskii aul v trekh revoliutsiiakh* (Alma-Ata: Izdatel'stvo "Kazakhstan," 1967), 481.

29. D. Kshibekov, *O preodolenii perezhitkov kapitalizma v soznanii i bytu* (Alma-Ata, 1957), 17, 34, 36–37.

30. N. S. Sabitov, "Obshchestvennaia zhizn' i semeinii byt Kazakhov-kolkhoznikov (po materialam Alma-Atiinskoi i Dzhambulskoi oblastei)," *Trudy instituta istorii, arkheologii, i etnografii* (1956): 190–230; A. Altmyshbaev, *Nekotorye perezhitki proshlogo v soznanii liudei v srednei azii i rol' sotsialisticheskoi kul'tury v bor'be s nimi* (Frunze, USSR: Academy of Sciences Kyrgyz SSR, 1958); and Tursunbaev, *Kazakhskii aul.*

31. Altmyshbaev, *Nekotorye perezhitki*, 4.

32. M. V. Vagabov, *Kalym—vrednyi perezhitok* (Makhachkala: Dagestanskoe knizhnoe izdatel'stvo, 1975), 28–29). Why it was not specifically listed as such in the codes of Uzbekistan, Kazakhstan, or Azerbaijan, is not clear.

33. Vagabov, *Kalym.*

34. The reference is to Arendt's characterization of totalitarianism in *Origins of Totalitarianism.*

35. Altmyshbaev, *Nekotorye perezhitki*, 6–8.

36. Ibid., 5. With this shift, the blame for clan-related behaviors also shifted: from abstract developmental stages and their accompanying social structures to ordinary people. Now, Central Asians themselves were understood as the carriers of these identities and began to bear the stigma for the traditions they practiced.

37. Bekezhan Tilegenov, *Tuiyq omirding qupiiasy* (Almaty: Deuir, 1992), 77.

38. The original Kazakh is *"eskini angsaghan qauipti shygharma"* (Tilegenov, *Tuiyq omirding*, 70).

39. Interview, Kenges Nurpeisovich Nurpeisov, professor of history, Institute of History and Ethnography, Kazakhstan Academy of Sciences, Almaty, Almaty *oblast*, 10 March 1998.

40. Interview, Marat Sabitovich Mukanov, professor of ethnography, Institute of History and Ethnography, Kazakhstan Academy of Sciences, Almaty, Almaty *oblast*, 16 March 1998. His work includes Marat Sabitovich Mukanov, *Etnicheskii sostav i rasselenie kazakhov Srednego zhuza* (Alma-Ata: Nauka, 1974) and V. V. Vostrov and M. S. Mukanov, *Rodoplemennoi sostav i rasselenie Kazakhov: konets XIX–nachalo XX v* (Alma-Ata: Nauka, 1968).

41. Interview, Nurpeisov, 10 March 1998.

42. See, for examples, "Neispravlennaia oshibka (o rodoplemennykh otnosheniiakh)," *Dozhivem do ponidel'nika*, 26 April 1996, 9; and "Rodoplemennoe delenie: 'za' i 'protiv'," *Dozhivem do ponidel'nika*, 3 May 1996, 9.

43. Sabitov, "Obshchestvennaia zhizn'," 192.

44. Winner, "Some Problems of Nomadism and Social Organization Among the Recently Settled Kazakhs, part two," *Central Asian Review* 11, no. 4 (1963): 357. See also Olivier Roy, *The New Central Asia: Creation of Nations* (New York: New York University Press, 2000).

45. O. A. Korbe, "Kul'tura i byt kazakhskogo kolkhoznogo aula," *Sovetskaia etnografiia* 4 (1950): 71.

46. Suny, *Revenge of the Past*; Slezkine, "USSR as Communal Apartment"; and Brubaker *Reframing Nationalism.*

47. Katherine Verdery, *National Ideology Under Socialism* (Berkeley: University of California Press, 1991).

48. State-owned business enterprises would keep on the payroll a *tolkach* (literally, "pusher"), who was responsible for procuring inputs. See Joseph Berliner, *Factory and Manager in the USSR* (Cambridge, MA: Harvard University Press, 1957).

49. I use "gray market" rather than the usual "black market," since much of this shadow economy operated in connection with state enterprises and state distribution channels.

50. Sheila Fitzpatrick, *Everyday Stalinism: Ordinary Life in Extraordinary Times—Soviet Russia in the 1930s* (London: Oxford University Press, 1999).

51. Mark S. Granovetter, "The Strength of Weak Ties," *American Journal of Sociology*, no. 6 (1973): 1360–80.

52. Alena Ledeneva, *Russia's Economy of Favours: Blat, Networking and Informal Exchanges* (Cambridge: Cambridge University Press, 1998); Andrew G. Walder, *Communist Neo-Traditionalism: Work and Authority in Chinese Industry* (Berkeley: University of California Press, 1986); and Berliner, *Factory and Manager*. Walder's discussion of these networks at times suggests that they are premodern (26); I would contend that their shape can in large part be attributed to the structure of the state socialist political economy. In that sense, they are quite modern indeed.

53. János Kornai, *Economics of Shortage* (Amsterdam: North-Holland, 1980).

54. On the different ways in which formal and informal networks operated under Hungarian state socialism, see József Böröcz and Caleb Southworth, "'Who You Know': Earning Effects of Formal and Informal Social Network Resources under Late State Socialism in Hungary, 1986–87," *Journal of Socio-Economics* 27, no. 3 (1998): 401–25.

55. Ledeneva, *Russia's Economy of Favours*.

56. I discuss some axes for variation below.

57. Interview, Bakhyt Tulebaeva (psued.), Shymkent, South Kazakhstan *oblast*, June 2002.

58. Interview, Marat Besenov (pseud.), rural South Kazakhstan *oblast*, June 2002; interview, Zhyldyz Qarataev (pseud.), rural South Kazakhstan *oblast*, June 2002; and interview, Beibit Esenova (pseud.), Shymkent, South Kazakhstan *oblast*, June 2002

59. Interview, Zhumabek Zhandosov (pseud.), June 2002

60. Interview, Natalia Ivanova (pseud.), rural South Kazakhstan *oblast*, June 2002; interview, Tulebaeva, June 2002.

61. Interview, Zhandosov, June 2002.

62. Interview, Besenov, June 2002; interview, Nurlan Tekenov (pseud.), Shymkent, South Kazakhstan *oblast*, June 2002; and interview, Meiramgul Zhdanova (pseud.), rural South Kazakhstan *oblast*, June 2002.

63. Interview, Tulebaeva, June 2002.

64. Ibid.

65. Interview, Besenov, June 2002; interview, Zhandosov, June 2002; interview, Esenova, June 2002.

66. Interview, Tulebaeva, June 2002.

67. Interview, Esenova, June 2002.

68. Interview, Ivanova, June 2002.

69. Interview, Tulebaeva, June 2002.

70. Interview, Zhandosov, June 2002.

71. Interview, Zhaqsylyq Asqarov (pseud.), rural South Kazakhstan *oblast*, June 2002; interview, Zhdanova, June 2002.

72. In one case, the interviewer knew from her personal tie with the interviewee that the latter's responses were implausible and pressed the interviewee to concede certain examples (interview, Tulebaeva, June 2002).

73. Interview, Zhandosov, June 2002. I use the term "cousin" here loosely. The original Kazakh *inim* does not distinguish the level of blood relation. The *inim* could be anything from a brother to a quite distant male cousin.

74. Interview, Tekenov, June 2002.

75. Interview, Asqarov, June 2002.

76. Interview, Tekenov, June 2002.

77. Interview, Qarataev, June 2002.

78. Interview, Zhandosov, June 2002. Naumova gives one example wherein certain Kazakhs of the older generation mistakenly believed that they belonged to the Younger Umbrella Clan when their ancestors were clearly from the Middle Umbrella Clan. See Ol'ga B. Naumova, "Materialy k izucheniiu etnicheskogo samosoznaniia omskykh i bel'agashskikh kazakhov," in Institut etnografii, ed., *Polevye issledovaniia instituta etnografii, 1978*, 109 (Moscow: Nauka, 1980).

79. Interview, Tulebaeva, June 2002.

80. Interview, Esenova, June 2002.

81. Occasionally, it is difficult to discern the degree of kinship being utilized in a kin network. All respondents claimed that they would routinely assist relatives of any degree—distant or close—given the opportunity (*mumkinshilik bolsa*). Some kin networks were clearly truncated; the members of a nuclear and extended family assisted each other greatly, maintaining weaker contact with more distant relatives. Most informants used the language of close kinship to describe distant cousins; the Kazakh language makes no distinction between "brother" and male cousin of any degree. Nonetheless, the ethnographic work of Werner makes clear that it was normal for extended networks of kin to remain operative. See Cynthia Werner, "The Significance of Tribal Identities in the Daily Life of Rural Kazaks in South Kazakhstan" (paper presented at the conference of the Association for the Study of Nationalities, 24–26 April 1997).

82. Interview, Tulebaeva, June 2002.

83. Interview, Qarataev, June 2002.

84. Interview, Qarataev, June 2002. A Russian respondent who lived through the Nazi blockade of Leningrad described how extreme poverty

made *blat* of little utility for ordinary Leningraders (interview, Ivanova, June 2002).

85. Interview, Tulebaeva, June 2002.

86. Interview, Esenova, June 2002.

87. Interview, Zhandosov, June 2002.

88. Ibid.

89. Interview, Tulebaeva, June 2002.

90. Interview, Besenov, June 2002.

91. Interview, Tekenov, June 2002.

92. Ibid.

93. Interview, Zhandosov, June 2002.

94. The Uzbek community in southern Kazakhstan was more numerous than the Russian, less urban, and more likely to use networks of extended kin than their Russian counterparts. Since Uzbeks traditionally privileged location rather than kin ties, the Uzbek respondent enjoyed a less expansive network of kin relations than did his Kazakh counterparts. (Interview, Islam Ozbekov [pseud.], June 2002.)

95. Interview, Ivanova, June 2002.

96. Ibid.

97. I put this word in quotation marks, since corruption always implies a normative baseline from which practices are understood to deviate.

98. *Izvestiia*, 11 February 1987, translated by the Foreign Broadcast Information Service (FBIS-SOV-87-028).

99. *Pravda*, 12 January 1987, translated by the Foreign Broadcast Information Service (FBIS-SOV-87-007).

100. *Argumenty i fakty* (Moscow), 3–9 September 1988, 6.

101. Quoted in Lion Onikov, "Pervaia krov' perestroiki," *Nezavisimaia gazeta*, 17 December 1992, 5.

102. Suny, *Revenge of the Past*.

103. Dinmukhammed Kunaev, *O moem vremeni* (Alma-Ata: Yntymaq, 1992), 10–11.

104. Ibid., 279.

105. As the longstanding critique of functionalist logic makes clear, just because a phenomenon enjoys a functional advantage does not mean that it will necessarily thrive. Functional needs do not create their own fulfillment.

106. To argue that clan relationships offered functional advantages under state socialism is not to deny a space for emotion and affect. As Jowitt forcefully argues, *blat* always involved status relationships and thus people often sought to develop their connections (whether kin-based or not) for the social standing it accorded. Thus, while the functional advantages of kinship helped it to thrive under state socialism, state socialism did not deprive kinship of its affective content. The opposite is true: the shortage economy helped

to prop up kin divisions—in both their instrumental and affective aspects. See Ken Jowitt, "Neotraditionalism," in his *New World Disorder: The Leninist Extinction*, 121–58 (Berkeley: University of California Press, 1992).

4 / CONTINUITY AND CHANGE
AFTER THE SOVIET COLLAPSE

The chapter's epigraph is from Vladimir Tismaneanu, *Fantasies of Salvation: Democracy, Nationalism, and Myth in Post-Communist Europe* (Princeton: Princeton University Press, 1998), 3.

1. Giuseppe Di Palma, *To Craft Democracies: An Essay on Democratic Transitions* (Berkeley: University of California Press, 1990).

2. On Mongolia, see M. Steven Fish, "Mongolia: Democracy without Prerequisites," *Journal of Democracy* 9, no. 3 (July 1998): 127–41. On Russia, see Timothy Colton, *Transitional Citizens: Voters and What Influences Them in the New Russia* (Cambridge, MA: Harvard University Press, 2000). On Kyrgyzstan, see John Anderson, *Kyrgyzstan: Central Asia's Island of Democracy?* (London: Routledge, 1999).

3. Mark R. Beissinger and Crawford Young, *Beyond State Crisis?: Post-Colonial Africa and Post-Soviet Eurasia in Comparative Perspective* (Washington, DC: Woodrow Wilson Center Press, 2002), 25.

4. Mark R. Beissinger, "The Persisting Ambiguity of Empire," *Post-Soviet Affairs* 11, no. 2 (1995): 149–84.

5. Teresa Rakowska-Harmstone, "Soviet Legacies," *Central Asia Monitor* 3 (1994), http://www.chalidze.com/cam/41,3,4.htm (accessed 21 June 2000; site now discontinued).

6. Beissinger and Young, *Beyond State Crisis?*

7. Mark R. Beissinger, *Nationalist Mobilization and the Collapse of the Soviet State* (Cambridge: Cambridge University Press, 2002).

8. Pauline Jones Luong, *Institutional Change and Political Continuity in Post-Soviet Central Asia: Power, Perceptions, and Pacts* (New York: Cambridge University Press, 2002).

9. Jones Luong in *Institutional Change* limits her discussion of continuity to the legacy of Soviet efforts to produce regional identities. This is an important argument, but one that is restricted to a single dimension of the Soviet legacy.

10. Brubaker, *Reframing Nationalism*.

11. See David D. Laitin, *Identity in Formation: The Russian-Speaking Populations in the Near Abroad* (Ithaca: Cornell University Press, 1998); Katherine Verdery, *What was Socialism and What Comes Next?* (Princeton: Princeton University Press, 1996); Bhavna Davé, "The Politics of Language Revival: National Identity and State Building in Kazakhstan" (Ph.D. diss.,

Syracuse University, 1996); Victor A. Shnirelman, *Who Gets the Past? Competition for Ancestors among Non-Russian Intellectuals in Russia* (Baltimore: Johns Hopkins, 1996).

12. Rogers Brubaker, *Reframing Nationalism* (Cambridge: Cambridge University Press, 1996), 5 (emphasis in original).

13. Ronald Grigor Suny, *Revenge of the Past: Nationalism, Revolution, and the Collapse of the Soviet Union* (Stanford: Stanford University Press, 1993); Brubaker, *Reframing Nationalism*.

14. Chapter three discusses these Soviet-era categories.

15. Lev N. Gumiliev, *Drevnie Tiurki* (Moscow: Nauka, 1967).

16. Nursultan Nazarbaev, *Kazakhstan—2030: poslanie Prezidenta strany narodu Kazakhstana* (Almaty: Bilim, 1997), 104.

17. "Unity" is not an accurate description of the often tense relations between the nomadic Kazakhs and sedentary *sarts*. Moreover, the Silk Road was hardly a *Kazakh* trading corridor, since most Kazakhs were nomadic and marginal to commercial flows. Most important, the idea of a restoration of the Silk Road in the late twentieth century profoundly ignored how marginalized from international trade routes landlocked Eurasia had become with the advent of the steamship, a problem that inadequate overland transportation routes could not solve.

Edward Schatz, "What Capital Cities Say About State and Nation Building," *Nationalism and Ethnic Politics* 9, no. 4 (2003): 111–40.

18. Nursultan Nazarbaev, quoted in Jørn Hølm-Hansen, *Territorial and Ethno-Cultural Self-Government in Nation-Building Kazakhstan* (Oslo: Norweigan Institute for Urban and Regional Research, 1997), 65.

19. Al'bert Grigor'evich Levkovskii, "Qazaqstan—mening ekinshi otanym," *Turkistan*, 29 April–5 May 1998, 3.

20. Open-forum meeting, Ukrainian national-cultural center, Almaty, Almaty *oblast*, 7 October 1998.

21. For a comparison of the dynamics of the Chechen, Polish, Uyghur, and Meskhetian Turk centers, see Hølm-Hansen, *Territorial and Ethno-Cultural Self-Government*, 66–77.

22. Barbara Watson Andaya and Leonard Y. Andaya, *A History of Malaysia* (London: MacMillan, 1982). A dangerous economic contraction in the post-Soviet period, broad-scale privatization of state industries, the geographic contiguity of colonizing power and colonized region, among other factors, also distinguish the Kazakhstani case from the Malaysian case.

23. Nursultan Nazarbaev, *Piat' let nezavisimosti* (Almaty: Izdatel'stvo "Kazakhstan," 1996), 104–5.

24. M. Bazarbaev, "'Kazakhstanskaia pravda' seet vrazhdu?" *Kazakhstanskaia pravda*, 8 August 1992, 3.

25. See Laitin, *Identity in Formation,* for a comparative analysis of the politics of language revival in the former USSR.

26. *O iazykakh v Respublike Kazakhstan* (Almaty: Zheti zharghy, 1997), 25.

27. Ibid., 24.

28. Nurbulat Masanov and Igor Savin, *Model' etnopoliticheskogo monitoringa: Kazakhstan* (Moscow and Almaty: MOST, 1997), 71.

29. The data presented here on language use in education come from Zh. Nauryzbai, "Etnokul'turnoe obrazovanie v Kazazkhstane," *Mysl'* 9 (1997): 65–75.

30. Interview, Erbol Shaimerdenov, director, Department for the Development of Languages, Astana, Tselinograd *oblast,* 15 September 1998.

31. Report on Kazakhstan, Radio Free Europe/Radio Liberty—Kazakh Service, 20 January 1999.

32. Article 18 of the law On Languages in the Republic of Kazakhstan specifies that Kazakh broadcasts must constitute at least one-half of all broadcasts (*O iazykakh,* 28). One informant who ran the Kazakh-language broadcasts for the station Otyrar in Shymkent estimated that 15 to 20 percent of broadcasts on his station were conducted in Kazakh (interview, Asan Kelesbaev, employee at television station Otyrar, Shymkent, South Kazakhstan *oblast,* 26 May 1998).

33. Davé, "The Politics of Language."

34. Interview, Kenzhekhan Matyzhan, deputy, Department for the Development of Languages, Astana, Tselinograd *oblast,* 15 September 1998.

35. For a full account of how the large numbers of Russified Kazakhs significantly alter the dynamic of what otherwise might be viewed as a simple bi-ethnic linguistic "tipping game," see Davé, "The Politics of Language." Most of the data presented by Laitin's *Identity in Formation* on Kazakhstan come from Davé's field work.

36. Shaimerdenov, 15 September 1998.

37. Masanov and Savin, *Model',* 35.

38. Interview with the editors of *Iuzhnyi variant* newspaper, Shymkent, 25 May 1998.

39. Askar Kumakovich Tulegulov, "Rekrutirovanie politicheskoi elity v usloviiakh transformatsii Kazakhstanskogo obshshestva" (Kandidatskaia diss., Institut Razvitiia Kazakhstana, Almaty, 1998), 88.

40. Integrating diaspora Kazakhs proved problematic. Press reports in 1998 stressed that support in many cases never reached the new immigrants. In addition, their cultural adjustment to highly Russified milieus was difficult, thus creating an identifiable social stratum of non-Soviet Kazakhs.

41. See G. M. Mendikulova, *Istoricheskie sud'by Kazakhskoi diaspory* (Almaty: Ghylym, 1997); and Maqash Tatimov, *Qazaq alemi: qazaqtyng sany*

qansha? (Almaty: Atamura-Qazaqstan, 1993). Tatimov's projections for the future ethnodemographic balance depicted Kazakh growth in a wildly optimistic fashion. In 1998, he became a leading proponent of legalized polygamy as a strategy for restoring an irreversible numerical predominance of ethnic Kazakhs.

42. Kolstø insightfully highlights the symbolic significance of topping 50 percent. See Pål Kolstø, "Anticipating Demographic Superiority: Kazakh Thinking on Integration and Nation-Building," *Europe-Asia Studies* 50, no. 1 (1998): 51–69.

43. The internal divisions among Kazakhs, especially along linguistic lines, were routinely left out of this understanding of majoritarian democracy. See Davé, "The Politics of Language."

44. Masanov fixes the number of Russian emigrants at 160,833 for 1995, although his data may not be comparable to official data. See Nurbulat Masanov, "Migratsii v Kazakhstane: istoriia, problema i metod" (paper presented at Soros Foundation seminar on interethnic relations, Almaty, 25 March 1998), 19. The official statistics on 1993 and 1994 are from Goskomstat Respubliki Kazakhstan, *Statisticheskii ezhegodnik Kazakhstana* (Almaty: Goskomstat Respubliki Kazakhstan, 1995), 30–31. Figures from 1997 are from Natsional'noe statisticheskoe agenstvo Respubliki Kazakhstan, *Demograficheskii ezhegodnik Kazakhstana* (Almaty: Natsstatagenstvo, 1998), 127; 1998 figures are from Agenstvo Respubliki Kazakhstan po statistike, *Statisticheskii ezhegodnik Kazakhstana* (Almaty: Agenstvo Respubliki Kazakhstan po statistike, 1999), 25; 1999 figures are from Agenstvo Respubliki Kazakhstan po statistike, *Demograficheskii statezhegodnik Kazakhstana* (Almaty: Agenstvo Respubliki Kazakhstan po statistike, 2000), 57; 2000 figures are from Agenstvo Respubliki Kazakhstan po statistike, *Demograficheskii ezhegodnik Kazakhstana* (Almaty: Agenstvo Respubliki Kazakhstan po statistike, 2002), 99.

45. Conversations in 1997–98 with scholars affiliated with the Institute of History and Ethnography in Almaty, Almaty *oblast.*

46. For example, see K. Daniiarov, *Al'ternativnaia istoriia Kazakhstana* (Almaty: Zhibek zholy, 1998); and M. Abdirov, *Khan Kuchum: izvestnyi i neizvestnyi* (Almaty: Zhalyn, 1996).

47. *Novoe pokolenie,* 19–26 April, 1996, 11.

48. *Dzhezkazganskaia pravda* (Zhezqazghan), 19 November 1991, 3.

49. *Mestnoe vremia* (Aqtau), 9 December 1997, 3.

50. Interview, Kulgazira Nurlanovna Baltabaeva, researcher, Department of Social and Humanitarian Sciences, Academy of Sciences, Almaty, Almaty *oblast,* 28 September 1998.

51. Interview, expedition participant, Almaty, Almaty *oblast,* 29 September 1998.

52. For an insightful ethnography of such multi-ethnic rural locales, see Ol'ga B. Naumova, "Nekotorye aspekty formirovaniia sovremennoi bytovoi kul'tury Kazakhov v mnogonatsional'nykh raionakh Kazakhstana," in A. Zhilina and S. Cheshko, eds., *Sovremennoe razvitie etnicheskikh grupp Srednei Azii i Kazakhstana*, 5–50 (Moscow: Institut etnologii i antropologii, 1992).

53. N. Orazbekov, *Kontsepsiia stanovleniia istoricheskogo soznaniia v Respublike Kazakhstan* (Almaty: Natsional'nyi soviet po gosudarstvennoi politike pri prezidente Respubliki Kazakhstan, 1995).

54. Abish Kekilbaev, Secretary of State (Republic of Kazakhstan), "Vozrozhdenie istoricheskoi pamiati—put' k obshchestvennomu vozrozhdeniiu," *Kazakhstanskaia pravda*, 9 January 1998, 1.

55. *Kazakhstanskaia pravda*, 1 October 1998, 1.

56. Report on Russia, Transcaucasia and Central Asia, Radio Free Europe/Radio Liberty, 4 December 1999.

57. *Konstitutsiia Respubliki Kazakhstan*, art. 63, sec. 1, lines 4–7.

58. Zhanylzhan Kh. Dzhunusova, *Respublika Kazakhstan: Prezident, instituty demokratii* (Almaty: Zheti zharghy, 1996), 114.

59. The author's field notes, 12 June 1997.

60. Seisen Amirbekuly, "Chto predstavliaet soboi Assambleiia narodov Kazakhstana?" *Dat*, translated from Kazakh to Russian and reprinted in *XXI vek*, 4 September 1998, 4.

61. On the imperative to reduce the size of the state, see World Bank, *Kazakhstan: Transition of the State* (Washington, DC: The World Bank, 1997).

62. Sally N. Cummings, "Nursultan Nazarbaev and Presidential Power in Kazakhstan" (paper presented at the convention of the Association for the Study of Nationalities, Columbia University, New York, 15–17 April 1999); and Anuradha Bose, "The *krug Prezidenta* or a Professional Civil Service in Kazakhstan?" (paper presented at the International Studies Association Conference, Washington, DC, 16–20 February 1999). Thanks to Anu Bose for permission to cite her unpublished work.

63. Report on Russia, Transcaucasia, and Central Asia, Radio Free Europe/Radio Liberty, 12 February 1999. See also Schatz, "What Capital Cities Say."

64. Bose, "The *krug Prezidenta*," 5.

65. Interview, Gaziz K. Aldamzherov, politician and business leader, Almaty, Almaty *oblast*, 1 April 1998. Aldamzherov later became a prominent member of the oppositionist Republican People's Party.

66. Steve LeVine, "Why Do Kazakhs Keep Trying to Ship MIG's to North Korea?" *New York Times*, 27 August 1999, A12

67. Gul'mira K. Ergalieva, "Ekonomicheskaia rol' mestnykh gosudarstvennykh organov vlasti v Respublike Kazakhstan," *Saiasat* 7 (1996): 63–74.

68. Ibid., 72–73.

69. While Nazarbaev became an enemy of press freedom, he was not the

region's worst offender. His being named among the world's ten worst "enemies of the press" by the Committee to Protect Journalists (CPJ) in 2000 indicated how internationally active his domestic opposition had become. Presidents Karimov (of Uzbekistan) and Niiazov (of Turkmenistan)—neither of whom was included on CPJ's list—deserved higher placement than Nazarbaev. See Report on (Un)civil Societies, Radio Free Europe/Radio Liberty, 18 May 2000.

70. *Panorama*, 19 June 1998, 6. In 1999 Rakhat Aliev, son-in-law of President Nazarbaev, purchased *Karavan*.

71. *Dat* was reincarnated as *SolDat* in 1999 and continued to face pressures from the regime well into 2002.

72. United Nations Development Program, *Republic of Kazakstan: Human Development Report* (Almaty: United Nations Development Program, 1997), 34.

73. Cynthia Werner, "Household Networks and the Security of Mutual Indebtedness in Rural Kazakhstan," *Central Asian Survey* 17, no. 4 (1998): 597–612.

74. G. Akhmetzhanova and N. Makhanov, "Osnovnye napravleniia razvitiia bankovskoi sistemy Kazakhstana," in *Sbornik nauchnykh statei molodykh uchenykh*, 112–28 (Almaty: Qazaqstan damu instituty, 1997).

75. Calculated on the basis of *Statisticheskii ezhegodnik Kazakhstana, 1994–1997* (Almaty: Natsstatagenstvo, 1998), 561.

76. The author's field notes, Shymkent, South Kazakhstan *oblast*, 7 June 1998.

77. Interview, Toqzhan Kizatova, founder of labor movement at Tengizchevroil, Atyrau, Atyrau *oblast*, 25 October 1998.

78. Alexander A. Cooley, "Booms and Busts: Theorizing Institutional Formation and Change in Oil States," *Review of International Political Economy* 8, no. 1 (Spring 2001): 163–80.

5 / CLAN CONFLICT

The chapter's epigraph is from Katherine Verdery, *What Was Socialism and What Comes Next?* (Princeton: Princeton University Press, 1996), 204.

1. Thanks to Timor Nurpeisov for this metaphor, which dates at least to Winston Churchill.

2. See chapter six for an elaboration on how imperfect information changes the dynamic of clan politics.

3. See Max Weber, *Economy and Society*, vol. 3., ed. Guenther Roth and Claus Wittich (Berkeley: University of California Press, 1968), 342.

4. Steffen W. Schmidt et al., eds., *Friends, Followers, and Factions* (Berkeley: University of California, 1977).

5. On the key difference between individuals behaving as rational, utility maximizers and playing social roles, compare Douglass C. North, *Institutions, Institutional Change and Economic Performance* (Cambridge: Cambridge University Press, 1990) with Robert K. Merton, *Social Theory and Social Structure* (Glencoe, IL: Free Press, 1957).

6. See Fredrik Barth, ed., *Ethnic Groups and Boundaries: The Social Organization of Culture and Difference* (Boston: Little, Brown and Company, 1969) and Mary Douglas, *Purity and Danger* (New York: Praeger, 1966).

7. Thanks to Tobin Grant for suggesting ways to analyze and present the quantitative information in this section. Thanks also to Anna Gregg for help in creating the data set.

8. D. R. Ashimbaev, *Kto est' kto v Kazakhstane* (Almaty: Credo, 2001). The appendix details how this database was compiled.

9. Below, I discuss the ways in which Russians were understood to behave as a metaphorical "fourth umbrella clan."

10. Estimates are from Mukhamedzhan Tynyshpaev, "Genealogiia Kirgiz-Kazakhskikh rodov" (1925), reprinted in Mukhamedzhan Tynyshpaev, *Istoriia Kazakhskogo naroda*, ed. A. Takenov and B. Baigaliev, 104–5 (Almaty: Sanat, 1998), as reported in Cynthia Werner, "The Significance of Tribal Identities in the Daily Life of Rural Kazaks in South Kazakhstan" (paper presented at the conference of the Association for the Study of Nationalities, 24–26 April 1997), 13. Given the lack of census data on umbrella clan backgrounds, estimates are rough, a point to which I return below.

11. Kunaev had managed to weaken but not fundamentally undermine the Middle Umbrella Clan's position.

12. Aleksandr Solzhenitsyn, "Kak nam obustroit' Rossiiu?" *Literaturnaia gazeta*, 18 September 1990.

13. Ian Bremmer, "Nazarbaev and the North: State-Building and Ethnic Relations in Kazakhstan," *Ethnic and Racial Studies* 17, no. 4 (1994): 619–35; and Anatoly M. Khazanov, *After the USSR: Ethnicity and Nationalism in the Commonwealth of Independent States* (Madison: University of Wisconsin Press, 1995).

14. Edward Schatz, "Framing Strategies and Non-Conflict in Multi-Ethnic Kazakhstan," *Nationalism and Ethnic Politics* 6, no. 2 (Summer 2000): 70–92.

15. Author's field notes and interviews in Atyrau, October 1998. See also *Aq zhaiyq* (Atyrau), 19 June 1997, 8.

16. Based on Radio Free Europe/Radio Liberty daily reports, I reconstructed the duration in office for each *oblast akim* in the 1990s. In 1997 four *oblasts* were absorbed into others, losing their separate administrative status. The average tenure in office in these four regions was 29.7 months.

17. Jones Luong argues that fiscal decentralization occurred in the late

1990s, but political decentralization did not accompany fiscal decentralization. Quite the contrary: politically centralized rule meant that any degree of fiscal decentralization that did occur had little impact on the regime's power. See Pauline Jones Luong, "Economic Decentralization in Kazakhstan: Causes and Consequences" (working paper, Yale University, 2003).

18. By Kazakhstani criminal law, rape trials are closed proceedings if they involve an underage victim.

19. Interview, Sabyr Kairkhanov, editor-in-chief of *Aq zhaiyq*, Atyrau, Atyrau *oblast*, 12 October 1998.

20. L. T. Zhanuzakova, "Problemy vzaimootnoshenii akima oblasti s vyshestoiashchimi i nizhestoiashchimi organami ispolnitel'noi vlasti v usloviiakh unitarnogo Kazakhstana," *Izvestiia Akademii Nauk RK* 4 (1997): 14–18.

21. Interview, local journalist, Atyrau, Atyrau *oblast*, 16 October 1998.

22. *Dozhivem do ponidel'nika*, 29 March 1996, as reported in V. N. Khliupin, *"Bol'shaia sem'ia" Nursultana Nazarbaeva: politicheskaia elita sovremennogo Kazakhstana* (Moscow: Institut aktual'nykh politicheskikh issledovanii, 1998), 12.

23. Khliupin, *Bol'shaia sem'ia*, 12.

24. Temirtas Tileulesov, *Ordaly zhylan: korruptsiia turaly* (Shymkent, 1998). The author of this book on the region's corruption found himself on "trial" for its publication. In 2000 he was severely beaten by unknown assailants.

25. *Severnyi Kazakhstan* (northern Kazakhstan), 17 August 1998, 2.

26. Interview, Arykbai Amanovich Tekeev, businessman, Atyrau, Atyrau *oblast*, 14 October 1998.

27. Interview, Kairkhanov, 12 October 1998.

28. Interview, Bakhyt (pseud.), Shymkent *akimat*, South Kazakhstan *oblast*, 28 May 1998. Many of these informants preferred to have their identity protected.

29. Interview, Darkhan Kaletaev, director, Department of Youth Policy, Ministry of Information and Social Accord, Astana, Tselinograd *oblast*, 14 September 1998.

30. Information at this level unfortunately becomes more and more anecdotal, since the pretenses to transparency in state governance evaporate the farther one moves from the republican level.

31. Author's field notes, rural South Kazakhstan *oblast*, July 1997.

32. Interview, Pavel Borisov (pseud.), Shymkent, South Kazakhstan *oblast*, 5 June 1998.

33. By using relatives in this way, the instructor could avoid appearances of soliciting bribes directly (author's field notes, Arys, South Kazakhstan *oblast*, 4 June 1998).

34. Interview, Nurbulat Masanov, professor of history, Almaty, Almaty *oblast*, 25 March 1998. Chapter seven details this process.

35. Gregory J. Kasza, "Quantitative Methods: Reflections on the Files of Recent Job Applicants," *PS: Political Science and Politics* (forthcoming).

36. John Waterbury, *The Commander of the Faithful: The Moroccan Political Elite—A Study in Segmented Politics* (London: Weidenfeld and Nicolson, 1970).

37. Clifford Geertz, "Thick Description: Toward an Interpretative Theory of Culture," in *The Interpretation of Cultures*, 6 (New York: Basic Books, 1973).

6 / CLAN METACONFLICT

The chapter's first epigraph is from Aleksei Iraklievich Levshin, *Opisanie kirgiz-kazach'ikh, ili kirgiz-kaisatskikh, ord i stepei* (1832; repr., Almaty: Sanat, 1996), 291.

1. Interview, Berik Abdugaliev, deputy director, Department of Internal Politics, Ministry of Information and Social Accord, Astana, Tselinograd *oblast*, 14 September 1998.

2. *Konstitutsiia Respubliki Kazakhstan*, art. 19, sec. 1, lines 1–3.

3. Interview, Aleksei Goncharov, journalist, Shymkent, South Kazakhstan *oblast*, 28 May 1998. His having the resources to pay travel expenses and court fees also separated him from more ordinary Kazakhstani citizens. For the 1999 state census, only one person in fifteen million did not indicate his or her ethnic background, according to official records (*Kratkie itogi perepisi naseleniia 1999 goda v Respublike Kazakhstan: Statisticheskii sbornik* [Almaty: Agenstvo Respubliki Kazakhstan po statistike, 1999], 11).

4. Interview, Kabyl Zhuraruly Duisenbi, deputy director, Department of Information and Public Accord, Shymkent, South Kazakhstan *oblast*, 6 June 1998. The original Russian was "*My nashli obshchee soglasiie nad vsemi.*"

5. Masanov's *Kochevaia tsivilizatsiia Kazakhov* (Almaty: Sotsinvest, 1995) echoes E. E. Evans-Pritchard's *The Nuer: A Description of the Modes of Livelihood and Political Institutions of a Niolitic People* (Oxford: Oxford University Press, 1940) in suggesting that segmentation was a necessary, functional response of nomadic societies to harsh ecological conditions.

6. Zamanbek Nurkadilov, *Ne tol'ko o sebe* (Almaty: Shartarap, 1996), 11.

7. Conversation with Bakhyt Murzhabekova, Almaty, Almaty *oblast*, 14 August 1998.

8. Shakarim Qudaiberdy-uly, *Rodoslovnaia Tiurkov, Kirgizov, Kazakhov i khanskikh dinastii*, trans. Bakhyt Kairbekov (Alma-Ata: Zhazushy, 1990).

9. Zaiyr Sadibekov, *Qazaq shezhiresi* (Tashkent: Uzbekiston, 1994); and Izturghan Sariev, *Ush zhuzding shezhiresi* (Almaty: Olke, 1997).

10. Baibota Serikbaiuly, *Qongyrat shezhiresi* (Almaty: Zhalyn, 1992)

11. Although women were often the transmitters of this knowledge

through early socialization, men were assumed to be the carriers of it, since family was understood patrilineally and living conditions defined patrilocally. I am unaware of any published *shezhire* by female authors.

12. Conversation with Gulnara Dadabaeva, Almaty, Almaty *oblast*, 3 March 1998.

13. *Qazaq adebieti*, 18 February 1998, 3. The original Kazakh was "*Tegin bilu — tektilikting belgisi.*"

14. Ibid.

15. Ernest Gellner, "Tribalism and the State in the Middle East," in Philip S. Khoury and Joseph Kostiner, eds., *Tribes and State Formation in the Middle East*, 109–27 (Berkeley: University of California Press, 1990).

16. *Tsentral'nyi Kazakhstan* (Zhezqazghan), 26 June 1993, 1

17. *Industrial'naia Karaganda* (Qaraghandy), 6 March 1997, 1

18. *Mestnoe vremia* (Aqtau), 9 December 1997, 3

19. A. Saduakasov and A. Bolgozhina, "Sokhranim sviaz' vremen," *Madeniet* (Semei), 15-28 February 1994, 11.

20. *Egemendi Qazaqstan*, 10 September 1992, 3.

21. Ibid., 17 September 1992, 4.

22. *Kazakhstanskaia pravda*, 31 October 1992, 2

23. Ibid., 14 August 1991.

24. *Tselinogradskaia pravda* (Astana), 8 June 1991.

25. *Egemendi Qazaqstan*, 22 June 1991. All indications are that at this event any scholarship on Bogenbai took a back seat to paeans sung in his honor.

26. The local newspapers indicate that the proposed location for a Bogenbai monument generated much controversy, with the authorities in much smaller Ermentau arguing his close ties to their small town, and those in larger Aqmola claiming that a monument there would have greater visibility.

27. *Tselinogradskaia pravda*, 23 May 1991.

28. Ibid., 12 June 1991, 1.

29. *Kyzylordinskie vesti* (Qyzylorda), 7 May 1992, 3.

30. *Akmolinskaia pravda* (Astana), 23 November 1993, 4.

31. *Mestnoe vremia* (Aqtau), 27 January 1998, 2.

32. Professor Masanov was more than willing to have his story told as an illustration of the political threat posed by subethnicity-based analyses.

33. Masanov, *Kochevaia tsivilizatsiia*. Masanov has pointed out that critics of his work in the past accused him of "geographical determinism" (personal communication, 5 July 1997).

34. Not surprisingly, Masanov's scholarship was in part a product of its time. In the 1970s and 1980s, Soviet scholars gradually began to interpret the Russian annexation of Kazakhstan as a positive development for the region, precisely because domestically generated social progress was understood as impossible where nomads could not accumulate significant capi-

tal. Masanov's emphasis was on geographic factors. See Ernest Gellner, foreword to Anatoly Khazanov, *Nomads and the Outside World*, 2nd ed., ix–xxv (Madison: University of Wisconsin Press, 1994) for a summary of this line of scholarship.

35. Nurbulat Masanov, "Kazakhskaia politicheskaia i intellektual'naia elita: klanovaia prinadlezhnost' i vnutrietnicheskoe sopernichestvo," *Vestnik evrazii* 1, no. 2 (1996): 46.

36. Ibid., 47.

37. See, for example, "Nurbolatqa ne daua?" *Ana tili*, 26 March 1998, 2. See also "Ozgeni dattap opa tappaq pa?" *Egemen Qazaqstan*, 22 July 1998, 4; and "Masanovty ne mazalaidy?" *Qazaq eli*, 28 March 1998, 3.

38. Masanov, "Kazakhskaia politicheskaia."

39. Ibid., 59.

40. *Kazakhstanskaia pravda*, 18 March 1998, 1.

41. Ibid. This was not Nazarbaev's first public reference to intraethnic divisions among Kazakhs. This was, however, the first time he referred to subethnicity-based analysis as tantamount to sowing division among Kazakhs.

42. Personal communication, 22 March 1998.

43. A fourth agenda supported, for various reasons, status quo political relationships. The business and financial elite was its central proponent, given the profound alliance between the regime and the economic sectors that emerged in the mid-1990s. Significant numbers of ordinary people supported Nazarbaev and the status quo. While the size of this group is impossible to gauge, it is certainly less than the 79.78 percent of the voting population that reelected Nazarbaev to a seven-year term in early 1999, since the elections were widely viewed as neither fair nor free. While public opinion appears to have turned against Nazarbaev, many still support his presidency by default. One informant claimed to support the president because "if we elect someone else, then he will steal his share [*khapnut' svoe*]. Nazarbaev has already stolen his share" (author's field notes, Almaty, Almaty *oblast*, 7 June 2002). The reference was based on the widespread conviction that high-level corruption has enriched, among others, the president.

44. Nurlan Amrekulov and Nurbulat Masanov, *Kazakhstan mezhdu proshlym i budushchim* (Almaty: Beren, 1994).

45. *Karavan*, 17 July 1998, 10

46. Nurlan Amrekulov, *Puti k ustoichivomu razvitiiu: razmyshleniia o glavnom* (Almaty, 1998), 128.

47. On these groups, see Bhavna Davé, "The Politics of Language Revival: National Identity and State Building in Kazakhstan" (Ph.D. diss., Syracuse University, 1996).

48. Interview, Khasen Qozhaakhmet, leader of the ethnonationalist movement Azat, Almaty, Almaty *oblast*, 26 March 1998.

49. These conclusions corroborate the intensive ethnographic work of Cynthia Werner, "The Significance of Tribal Identities in the Daily Life of Rural Kazaks in South Kazakhstan" (paper presented at the conference of the Association for the Study of Nationalities, Columbia University, New York, 24–26 April 1997).

50. Author's field notes, Almaty, Almaty *oblast*, 20 February 1998.

51. Interview, Russian member of the opposition, Almaty, Almaty *oblast*, 3 April 1998

52. *Konstitutsiia Respubliki Kazakhstan*, art. 20, sec. 3, lines 3–5.

53. *Karavan*, 20 March 1998, 37.

54. Author's field notes, Arys, South Kazakhstan *oblast*, 4 June 1998.

55. Akezhan Kazhegel'din, *Kazakhstan: pravo vybora* (Almaty: Qarzhy-Qarazhat, 1998), 55.

56. See V. N. Khliupin, *Imperskii sbornik No. 1: Respublika Kazakhstan — geopoliticheskie ocherki* (Moscow: Russkii Komitet pri Predsedatele Liberal'no-Demokraticheskoi partii Rossii, 1997). According to Zhirinovsky's one-page introduction to the work, later volumes would touch on other immediately neighboring states (Ukraine, Belarus, the Baltic states, the Caucasus), as well as thematic issues.

57. Ibid., 5.

58. Ibid., 122.

59. Ibid.

60. This metaphor comes from Atul Gawande, "The Cancer-Cluster Myth," *The New Yorker*, 8 February 1999, 37.

61. Anonymous local journalists in Shymkent provided these subethnic backgrounds in 1998.

62. Conversation with Gulnara Dadabaeva, Taraz, Zhambyl *oblast*, 25 January 1999.

63. Seken Dorzhenov and Bolat Babaquly, "Zhuzizm," *Aqiqat* 10 (1995): 73–77.

64. Abylai Aidosov, "'Zhuzism' atauynan aulaq bolaiyq," *Aqiqat* 3, 1996: 89

65. Institut Razvitiia Kazakhstana, *Kazakhskii traibalizm: sostoianie, osobennosti i puti preodoleniia* (Almaty: Institut Razvitiia Kazakhstana, 1995).

66. See, for example, Zhanash Nurmakhan, "Ru zhane rushyldyq," *Aqiqat* 3 (1993): 91–92.

67. *Karavan*, 15 May 1998, 37.

68. Tursun Sultanov, "The Kazakh Khanate and the Kazakh Zhuz," *Energiia Kazakhstana* 10 (1998): 89.

69. Interview, Erlan Abenov, director, Institut Razvitiia Kazakhstana, Almaty, Almaty *oblast*, 4 September 1998.

70. Seidakhmet Quttyqadam, "Rulyq sana zhane qazirgi zaman," *Aqiqat*

1 (1994): 12–18. The original Kazakh was *"zhanga zhaghdaidaghy zhanga erezheler."*

71. In interviews across the political spectrum, I was consistently warned that my topic was considered off-limits in official circles. Progress's stance on tribalism is mentioned in "V Shymkente obrazovan orgkomitet po sozdaniiu filiala dvizheniia Orleu," *Panorama*, 2 April 1999, http://www.panorama.kz.

72. *O bor'be s korruptsiei: zakon Respubliki Kazakhstan* (Almaty: Zheti zharghy, 1998), 27.

73. Interview, anticorruption official, 28 May 1998.

7 / A VICIOUS CYCLE?
KINSHIP AND POLITICAL CHANGE

The chapter's first epigraph is from Aleksei Iraklievich Levshin, *Opisanie kirgiz-kazach'ikh, ili kirgiz-kaisatskikh, ord i stepei* (1832; repr., Almaty: Sanat, 1996), 291.

1. Ian Murray Matley, "Industrialization," in Edward Allworth, ed., *Central Asia: 130 Years of Russian Dominance*, 3rd ed., 309–48 (Durham and London: Duke University Press, 1994).

2. In the sense of giving primacy to local identities, rural Central Asians were scarcely different from their rural counterparts in other parts of the Soviet state. See Ronald Grigor Suny, *Revenge of the Past: Nationalism, Revolution, and the Collapse of the Soviet Union* (Stanford: Stanford University Press, 1993).

3. On unveiling, see Gregory J. Massell, *The Surrogate Proletariat: Moslem Women and Revolutionary Strategies in Soviet Central Asia, 1919–1929* (Princeton: Princeton University Press, 1974). On census categories, see Francine Hirsch, "The Soviet Union as a Work-in-Progress: Ethnographers and the Category *Nationality* in the 1926, 1937, and 1939 Censuses," *Slavic Review* 56, no. 2 (1997): 251–78.

4. William Fierman, ed., *Soviet Cental Asia: The Failed Transformation* (Boulder, CO: Westview Press, 1991).

5. Teresa Rakowska-Harmstone "Soviet Legacies," *Central Asia Monitor* 3 (1994), http://www.chalidze.com/cam/41,3,4.htm (accessed 21 June 2000; site now discontinued).

6. Aleksandr N. Alekseenko, "Sel'skoe naselenie Kazakhstana 1920–1990 gg." (Kandidatskaia diss., Historical Sciences, Institut istorii i etnologii, Almaty, 1993), 182.

7. Michael Rywkin, *Moscow's Muslim Challenge: Soviet Central Asia*, rev. ed. (Armonk, NY: M.E. Sharpe, 1990), 52. Much depends on whether or not one considers the agricultural workers in the massive grain-producing enterprises of northern Kazakhstan's proletariat.

8. B. Ia. Dvoskin, N. F. Golikov, and M. D. Spektor, *Problemy rasseleniia naseleniia Kazakhstana* (Alma-Ata: Nauka Kazakhskoi SSR, 1989), 188–93.

9. Ajay Patnaik, "Agriculture and Rural Out-Migration in Central Asia, 1960–1991," *Europe-Asia Studies* 47, no. 1 (1995): 147–169.

10. Gregory Gleason, "Marketization and Migration: The Politics of Cotton in Central Asia," *Journal of Soviet Nationalities* 1, no. 2 (Summer 1990): 66–98.

11. Merle Fainsod, *Smolensk under Soviet Rule* (Cambridge, MA: Harvard University Press, 1958).

12. Pauline Jones Luong, *Institutional Change and Political Continuity in Post-Soviet Central Asia: Power, Perceptions, and Pacts* (New York: Cambridge University Press, 2002); and Nancy Lubin, et al., *Calming the Ferghana Valley: Development and Dialogue in the Heart of Central Asia* (New York: Century Foundation Press, 1999).

13. Ol'ga B. Naumova, "Nekotorye aspekty formirovaniia sovremennoi bytovoi kul'tury Kazakhov v mnogonatsional'nykh raionakh Kazakhstana," in A. Zhilina and S. Cheshko, eds., *Sovremennoe razvitie etnicheskikh grupp Srednei Azii i Kazakhstana*, 5 (Moscow: Institut etnologii i antropologii, 1992).

14. Interview, expedition participant, Almaty, Almaty *oblast*, 29 September 1998.

15. The main disadvantage of focus groups is that they remove participants from the everyday environment in which their identities normally find behavioral and symbolic expression. Their concerted use with other methodological strategies is thus particularly warranted. See Richard A. Krueger, *Focus Groups: A Practical Guide for Applied Research* (Thousand Oaks, CA: Sage Publications, 1994); and David L. Morgan, *Focus Groups as Qualitative Research* (Newbury Park, CA: Sage Publications, 1988). For details on my methodology, see the appendix.

16. Intensive ethnographic work is necessary to deepen our knowledge of identity politics, but the striking variation in cultural milieus makes the always-difficult level-of-analysis problem even more challenging to overcome. For an excellent study of largely mono-ethnic Shaulder in South Kazakhstan region, see Cynthia Werner, "Household Networks and the Security of Mutual Indebtedness in Rural Kazakhstan," *Central Asian Survey* 17, no. 4 (1998): 597–612; contrast Naumova, "Nekotorye aspekty," on a multi-ethnic region in West Kazakhstan.

17. Zhapar A. Zhambakin, "Pastbishchnoe zhivotnovodstvo Kazakhstana: proshloe, nastoiashchee, budushchee" (unpublished ms. of the general director, National Association of Farmers [Kazakhstan], Almaty, 1999), 8.

18. Anecdotal evidence suggests that urban agencies were the ones overwhelmed by migrants, whom they lacked the resources to count. Official data on rural unemployment probably better reflect actual levels than data on

urban unemployment. The observed migration may therefore have been even larger than is suggested here.

19. Natsional'noe statisticheskoe agenstvo Respubliki Kazakhstan, *Statisticheskii ezhegodnik Kazakhstana, 1994–1997* (Almaty: Natsstatagenstvo, 1998), 79–80, 93–95.

20. Zhulduzbek B. Abylkhojin, *Strana v serdtse Evrazii: siuzhety po istorii Kazakhstana* (Almaty: Qazaq universiteti, 1998).

21. Since clan identities are a Kazakh phenomenon, these focus groups concentrated on regions where Kazakhs numerically predominate. I did not examine regions where Kazakhs constitute a small minority: the Russian-dominated areas of northern and northeastern Kazakhstan.

22. A questionnaire listed nine categories of people with whom migrants were likely to have developed relationships. Participants were asked to rank the four top categories in answer to the question, "Which of the following types of people would be most likely in the future to help you in _____?" Participants gave separate rankings for each of the areas of potential assistance: employment, schooling, housing, and finances/credit. As work in network analysis shows, networks are a pervasive aspect of both rural and urban life, even if networks are qualitatively different in the countryside than in the city (John J. Beggs, Valerie A. Haines, and Jeanne S. Hurlbert, "Revisiting the Rural-Urban Contrast: Personal Networks in Nonmetropolitan and Metropolitan Settings," *Rural Sociology* 61, no. 2 [1996]: 306–25). Thanks to Igor Savin and Saulesh Esenova for their assistance in developing the categories for this questionnaire.

23. The categories given were not mutually exclusive. The relative, ordinal rankings given by participants were first given values. If the respondent offered four ranked choices, then the first choice received a score of 0.4, the second a score of 0.3, the third 0.2, and the fourth 0.1. A few respondents listed only three or two, and occasionally, only one ranked choice. As in the four-tiered ranking, in these cases the values given also added to 1.0. Thus, a three-tiered ranking received values of 0.5, 0.333, and 0.167. A two-tiered ranking received 0.67 and 0.33. A single ranking received a value of 1.0.

24. For an overview of the relationship between Islamic and ethnic identity in Kazakhstan, see Alma K. Sultangalieva, *Islam v Kazakhstane: istoriia, etnichnost', obshchestvo* (Almaty: Kazakhstanskii institut strategicheskikh issledovanii, 1998).

25. In this chapter, translations are from the Kazakh, unless otherwise indicated. The general language of discussion during these focus groups was Kazakh. A few participants preferred to use Russian, and many interspersed occasional Russian phrases in their spoken Kazakh. In those cases where a participant's use of a Russian word in an otherwise Kazakh sentence was a significant detail, I note the linguistic shift. Otherwise, I offer no such indication.

26. Zhumabek, Almaty focus group. I provide the first name and city of each participant quoted from the focus groups.

27. Timur, Almaty focus group.

28. In this project, I have largely bracketed Islamic identities as relatively unimportant for most Kazakhs. While there are some areas of southern Kazakhstan where the everyday practice of Islam approaches that of populations in Uzbekistan, these are the exception. For the most part, Islam penetrated far less deeply into nomadic culture than it did into sedentary culture.

29. Interview, Beisenbek Asanov, mullah, Shaulder, South Kazakhstan *oblast*, 31 May 1998.

30. Laura, Shymkent focus group. "Medicine" here refers to the belief that the societal prescription of exogamous marriage (and the concomitant norm to know one's genealogy) serves the purpose of minimizing genetic abnormalities.

31. See chapter one for an elaboration of the multilevel nature of segmentary identity among former nomads.

32. In 2000 the issue of the border between Uzbekistan and Kazakhstan led to tense relations between these two groups, even within Kazakhstan itself. See Sergei Borisov, "K granitse podtianuli tanki," *Obshchaia gazeta* (Moscow), 1 June 2000, http://www.eurasia.org.ru (accessed 1 June 2000).

33. Erqanat, Shymkent focus group.

34. One senior informant noted that, in spite of the traditional proscription on marriages within seven generations of common ancestry, the Zhetimder and Bozhbandar married each other rather often, a fact she attributed to their attending the same local school (conversation with Dildakul Tulgenova, Shaulder, South Kazakhstan *oblast*, 11 June 1998).

35. Naumova, "Nekotorye aspekty," 40. On the influence of Chinese nationalities policy on non-Han Muslim populations, see Dru C. Gladney, *Muslim Chinese: Ethnic Nationalism in the People's Republic* (Cambridge, MA: Council on East Asian Studies, 1991).

36. John F. Loncle, "Land Reform in Kazakhstan: Institutions and Lessons from Elsewhere" (unpublished paper, University of Wisconsin–Madison, 1999).

37. Interview, Nurbulat Masanov, professor of history, Almaty, Almaty *oblast*, 25 March 1998; and interview, Rakhat, Almaty, 11 August 1998. My collaborator in the Almaty focus group, Saulesh Esenova, conducted the latter interview for her own research. Thanks to her for permission to cite the interview.

38. Qanat, Almaty focus group.

39. Zhumabek, Almaty focus group.

40. Meiramgul, Atyrau focus group.

41. Author's field notes, Shymkent, South Kazakhstan *oblast*, 28 May 1998. On how uncritical acceptance of superficial informant responses affected ini-

tial research on Central Asia, see Deniz Kandiyoti, "Poverty in Transition: An Ethnographic Critique of Household Surveys in Post-Soviet Central Asia," *Development and Change* 30, no. 3 (1999): 499–524.

42. Meiramgul, Atyrau focus group. The original was *"Bir korgen—bilis. Eki korgen—tanys."* The word *bilis* suggests someone who is known. The word *tanys* suggests someone who is expected to provide help. Thanks to Cynthia Werner for helping with the translation (personal communication, 2 September 2003).

43. Aqmaral, Shymkent focus group.

44. The term *koke* is often used generically to refer to a male relative. In the context here, it refers to anyone who provides assistance or protection. It is a functional equivalent of the Russian term *kyrsha* [roof], which idiomatically refers to the protection—often for sale—that can provide coverage against "intrusions" by state or nonstate actors. In the Kazakh case, the language used is rooted in kinship, while in the Russian case it is not.

45. Anonymous, Shymkent focus group. Focus groups were audio recorded, not video recorded, since participants were less nervous about the former. From the audio recordering, it is occasionally not possible to discern who the specific speaker was.

46. Interview, NGO worker, Almaty, Almaty *oblast*, March 1998.

47. Interview, fisherman, rural South Kazakhstan *oblast*, 4 June 1998.

48. Participant in Soros Foundation Seminar on Political Science, Shymkent, South Kazakhstan *oblast*, 23 May 1998.

49. Werner, "Household Networks." If Werner's intensive ethnography of one rural site could be repeated at various other sites on this varied cultural landscape of rural Kazakhstan, it would establish these patterns with greater certainty.

50. Author's field notes, Arys, South Kazakhstan *oblast*, 4 June 1998.

51. Author's field notes, Shymkent, South Kazakhstan *oblast*, 1 June 1998.

52. Author's field notes, Shymkent, South Kazakhstan *oblast*, 7 June 1998. For a discussion of the *gap* in the Uzbek context, see Kandiyoti, "Poverty in Transition."

53. Saulesh Esenova, personal communication, 9 September 1998.

54. Interview, Serik Aidossov , director, Sociological Resource Center, Shymkent, Shymkent, South Kazakhstan *oblast*, 21 May 1998.

55. Conversation with Gulnara Dadabaeva, Almaty, Almaty *oblast*, 3 March 1998.

56. Torebek, Almaty focus group.

57. Anonymous, Shymkent focus group.

58. Anonymous, Atyrau focus group.

59. Erqanat, Atyrau focus group.

60. Saulesh Esenova, "'Tribalism' and Identity in Contemporary Cir-

cumstances: The Case of Kazakstan," *Central Asian Survey* 17, no. 3 (1998): 451.

61. Interview, Rakhat, 11 August 1998.

62. Meiramgul, Atyrau focus group.

63. Timur, Almaty focus group.

64. Chapter six details these events.

65. Zhyldyz, Almaty focus group.

66. Mary Douglas, *Purity and Danger* (New York: Praeger, 1966).

67. Zhumabek, Almaty focus group.

68. Author's field notes, Mikhailovka village, Shymkent, South Kazakhstan *oblast*, 24 May 1998.

CONCLUSIONS

1. Jacqueline Stevens, *Reproducing the State* (Princeton: Princeton University Press, 1999).

2. It may simplify the social world to assume "causal homogeneity," but to do so may distort more than it reveals. As Ragin shows, much social-scientific reasoning ignores the possibility of "causal heterogeneity"—that is, that similar end points can be reached through different causal paths. See Charles Ragin, *Fuzzy-Set Social Science* (Chicago: University of Chicago Press, 2000).

3. Thanks to an anonymous reviewer for suggesting this line of thinking.

4. Giuseppe Di Palma, *To Craft Democracies: An Essay on Democratic Transitions* (Berkeley: University of California Press, 1990), 4.

5. Mark R. Beissinger, *Nationalist Mobilization and the Collapse of the Soviet State* (Cambridge: Cambridge University Press, 2001).

6. Crawford Young, "The Dialectics of Cultural Pluralism," in Crawford Young, ed., *The Rising Tide of Cultural Pluralism: The Nation-State at Bay?* 3–35 (Madison: University of Wisconsin Press, 1993).

7. The classic debate about appropriate strategies is between Lijphart and Horowitz. See Arend Lijphart, "Consociational Democracy," *World Politics* 21, no. 2 (January 1969): 207–25; and Donald Horowitz, *Ethnic Groups in Conflict* (Berkeley: University of California Press, 1985), 601–80.

8. Thanks to Dennis Galvan for suggesting this line of inquiry.

9. Jennifer A. Widner, *The Rise of a Party-State in Kenya: From "Harambee!" to "Nyayo!"* (Berkeley: University of California Press, 1992).

10. Charles Taylor, "Nationalism and Modernity," in John A. Hall, ed., *The State of the Nation: Ernest Gellner and the Theory of Nationalism* (Cambridge: Cambridge University Press, 1998), 214.

11. Bernard Yack, "The Myth of the Civic Nation," *Critical Review* 10, no. 2 (Spring 1996): 193–211.

Bibliography

ENGLISH-LANGUAGE BOOKS AND JOURNAL ARTICLES

Akbarzadeh, Shahram, "Why Did Nationalism Fail in Tajikistan?" *Europe-Asia Studies* 48, no. 7 (1996): 1105–29.

Andaya, Barbara Watson, and Leonard Y. Andaya. *A History of Malaysia.* London: MacMillan, 1982.

Anderson, Benedict. *Imagined Communities: Reflections on the Origin and Spread of Nationalism.* London: Verso, 1983.

Anderson, John. *Kyrgyzstan: Central Asia's Island of Democracy?* London: Routledge, 1999.

Arendt, Hannah. *The Origins of Totalitarianism.* 1951. Reprint, New York: Harcourt Brace and Company 1979.

Arnason, Joanne P. "Communism and Modernity." *Daedalus* 129, no. 1 (2000): 61–90.

Bacon, Elizabeth E. *Central Asians Under Russian Rule: A Study in Culture Change.* Ithaca: Cornell University Press, 1966.

Baram, Amatzia. "Neo-Tribalism in Iraq: Saddam Hussein's Tribal Policies 1991–96." *International Journal of Middle East Studies* 29 (1997): 1–31.

Barth, Fredrik, ed. *Ethnic Groups and Boundaries: The Social Organization of Culture and Difference.* Boston: Little, Brown and Company, 1969.

Bauman, Zygmunt. *Modernity and the Holocaust.* Ithaca: Cornell University Press, 1989.

Beggs, John J., Valerie A. Haines, and Jeanne S. Hurlbert, "Revisiting the Rural-Urban Contrast: Personal Networks in Nonmetropolitan and Metropolitan Settings." *Rural Sociology* 61, no. 2 (1996): 306–25.

Beissinger, Mark R. "The Demise of an Empire-State: Identity, Legitimacy, and the Deconstruction of Soviet Politics." In Crawford Young, ed., *The Rising Tide of Cultural Pluralism: The Nation-State at Bay?* 93–115. Madison: University of Wisconsin Press, 1993.

———. *Nationalist Mobilization and the Collapse of the Soviet State.* Cambridge: Cambridge University Press, 2002.

——. "The Persisting Ambiguity of Empire." *Post-Soviet Affairs* 11, no. 2 (1995): 149–84.

Beissinger, Mark R., and Crawford Young, eds. *Beyond State Crisis?: Post-Colonial Africa and Post-Soviet Eurasia in Comparative Perspective.* Washington, DC: Woodrow Wilson Center Press, 2002.

Berger, Peter L., and Thomas Luckmann. *The Social Construction of Reality: A Treatise in the Sociology of Knowledge.* Garden City, NY: Doubleday, 1966.

Berger, Peter, Brigitte Berger, and Hansfried Kellner. *The Homeless Mind: Modernization and Consciousness.* New York: Vintage Books, 1974.

Berliner, Joseph. *Factory and Manager in the USSR.* Cambridge, MA: Harvard University Press, 1957.

Böröcz, József, and Caleb Southworth. "'Who You Know': Earning Effects of Formal and Informal Social Network Resources under Late State Socialism in Hungary, 1986–87." *Journal of Socio-Economics* 27, no. 3 (1998): 401–25.

Bose, Anuradha. "The *krug Prezidenta* or a Professional Civil Service in Kazakhstan?" Paper presented at the International Studies Association Conference, Washington DC, 16–20 February 1999.

Bremmer, Ian. "Nazarbaev and the North: State-Building and Ethnic Relations in Kazakhstan." *Ethnic and Racial Studies* 17, no 4 (1994): 619–35.

Bromlei, Yu. V. "A General Description of Ethnic Proceses." *Soviet Ethnographic Studies,* no. 3 (1983): 8–30.

——. *Theoretical Ethnography.* Moscow: General Editorial for Foreign Publications and Nauka Publishers, 1984.

Brower, Daniel. "Islam and Ethnicity: Russian Colonial Policy in Turkestan." In Daniel R. Brower and Edward J. Lazzerini, eds. *Russia's Orient: Imperial Borderlands and Peoples, 1700–1917,* 115–37. Bloomington: Indiana University Press, 1997.

Brubaker, Rogers. *Reframing Nationalism.* Cambridge: Cambridge University Press, 1996.

Central Intelligence Agency. *The World Factbook.* http://www.odci.gov/cia/publications/factbook/geos/kz.html.

Christie, Kenneth. "Introduction: The Problem with Ethnicity and 'Tribal' Politics." In Kenneth Christie, ed., *Ethnic Conflict, Tribal Politics: A Global Perspective,* 1–15. Surrey, UK: Curzon Press, 1998.

Collins, Kathleen. *Clans, Pacts, and Politics: Understanding Regime Transition in Central Asia.* Ph.D. dissertation, Stanford University, 1999, and book manuscript, 2002)

Colton, Timothy. *Transitional Citizens: Voters and What Influences Them in the New Russia.* Cambridge, MA: Harvard University Press, 2000.

Connor, Walker. *Ethnonationalism: The Quest for Understanding.* Princeton: Princeton University Press, 1993.

———. *The National Question in Marxist-Leninist Theory and Strategy.* Princeton: Princeton University Press, 1984.

———. "Nation-Building or Nation-Destroying?" *World Politics* 24, no. 3 (April 1972): 319–55.

Conquest, Robert. *The Harvest of Sorrow: Soviet Collectivization and the Terror-Famine.* New York: Oxford University Press, 1986.

Cooley, Alexander A. "Booms and Busts: Theorizing Institutional Formation and Change in Oil States." *Review of International Political Economy* 8, no.1 (Spring 2001): 163–80.

Cummings, Sally N. "Nursultan Nazarbaev and Presidential Power in Kazakhstan." Paper presented at the convention of the Association for the Study of Nationalities, Columbia University, New York, 15–17 April 1999.

Davé, Bhavna. "The Politics of Language Revival: National Identity and State Building in Kazakhstan." Ph.D. dissertation, Syracuse University, 1996.

Deutsch, Karl. *Nationalism and Social Communication: An Inquiry into the Foundations of Nationality.* New York: Wiley, 1953.

Deutsch, Karl. "Social Mobilization and Political Development." *American Political Science Review* 55, no. 3 (1961): 493–514.

Dienes, Leslie. *Soviet Asia: Economic Development and National Policy Choices.* Boulder, CO: Westview Press, 1987.

Dinello, Natalia. "Clientelism, Corruption and Clans in Hungary and Russia." Working paper, University of Pittsburgh, 1999.

Di Palma, Giuseppe. *To Craft Democracies: An Essay on Democratic Transitions.* Berkeley: University of California Press, 1990.

Douglas, Mary. *Purity and Danger.* New York: Praeger, 1966.

Durkheim, Emile. *The Division of Labor in Society.* Translated by W. D. Halls, with an introduction by Lewis A. Coser. 1893. Reprint, New York: Free Press, 1984.

Eisenstadt, S. N., and Luis Roniger. *Patrons, Clients, and Friends: Interpersonal Relations and the Structure of Trust in Society.* Cambridge: Cambridge University Press, 1984.

Emerson, Robert M., Rachel I. Fretz, and Linda L. Shaw. *Writing Ethnographic Fieldnotes.* Chicago: University of Chicago Press, 1995.

Esenova, Saulesh. "'Tribalism' and Identity in Contemporary Circumstances: The Case of Kazakstan." *Central Asian Survey* 17, no. 3 (1998): 443–62.

Evans, Peter. *Embedded Autonomy: States and Industrial Transformation.* Princeton: Princeton University Press, 1995.

Evans-Pritchard, E. E. *The Nuer: A Description of the Modes of Livelihood and Political Institutions of a Niolitic People.* Oxford: Oxford University Press, 1940.

Fainsod, Merle. *Smolensk under Soviet Rule.* Cambridge, MA: Harvard University Press, 1958.

Fierman, William, ed. *Soviet Central Asia: The Failed Transformation.* Boulder, CO: Westview Press, 1991.

Fish, M. Steven. "Mongolia: Democracy without Prerequisites." *Journal of Democracy* 9, no. 3 (July 1998): 127–41.

Fitzpatrick, Sheila. *Everyday Stalinism: Ordinary Life in Extraordinary Times—Soviet Russia in the 1930s.* London: Oxford University Press, 1999.

Forbes, H. D. *Ethnic Conflict: Commerce, Culture, and the Contact Hypothesis.* New Haven: Yale University Press, 1997.

Friedrich, Carl J. and Zbigniew K. Brzezinski. *Totalitarian Dictatorship and Autocracy.* Cambridge, MA: Harvard University Press, 1956.

Galvan, Dennis. *The State Must be the Master of Fire: Syncretism and Sustainable Development in Senegal.* Berkeley: University of California Press, forthcoming.

Ganev, Vanelin. "Postcommunism as an Episode of State-Building: A Historical-Sociological Approach." Working paper, Miami University, 2002.

Geertz, Clifford. "Thick Description: Toward an Interpretative Theory of Culture." In Clifford Geertz, *The Interpretation of Cultures,* 3–30. New York: Basic Books, 1973.

Gellner, Ernest. Foreword to Anatoly Khazanov, *Nomads and the Outside World,* 2nd ed., ix–xxv. Madison: University of Wisconsin Press, 1994.

———. *Nations and Nationalism.* Ithaca: Cornell University Press, 1983.

———. "Tribalism and the State in the Middle East." In Philip S. Khoury and Joseph Kostiner, eds., *Tribes and State Formation in the Middle East,* 109–27. Berkeley: University of California Press, 1990.

Gladney, Dru C. *Muslim Chinese: Ethnic Nationalism in the People's Republic.* Cambridge, MA: Council on East Asian Studies, 1991.

———. "Relational Alterity: Constructing Dungan (Hui), Uygur, and Kazakh Identities Across China, Central Asia, and Turkey." *History and Anthropology* 9, no. 4 (1996): 445–77.

Gleason, Gregory. "Marketization and Migration: The Politics of Cotton in Central Asia." *Journal of Soviet Nationalities* 1, no. 2 (Summer 1990): 66–98.

Goffman, Erving. *Strategic Interaction.* Philadelphia: University of Pennsylvania Press, 1969.

Granovetter, Mark S. "Economic Institutions as Social Constructions: A Framework for Analysis." *Acta Sociologica* 35, no. 3 (1992): 3–11.

———. "The Strength of Weak Ties." *American Journal of Sociology,* no. 6 (1973): 1360–80.

Hall, John A., ed. *The State of the Nation: Ernest Gellner and the Theory of Nationalism.* Cambridge: Cambridge University Press, 1998.

Hamzeh, A. Nizar. "Clan Conflicts, Hezbollah and the Lebanese State." *Journal of Social, Political and Economic Studies* 19, no. 4 (1994): 433–45.

Harty, Siobhan. "The Institutional Foundations of Substate National Movements." *Comparative Politics* 33, no. 2 (January 2001): 191–210.

Hirsch, Francine. "The Soviet Union as a Work-in-Progress: Ethnographers and the Category Nationality in the 1926, 1937, and 1939 Censuses." *Slavic Review* 56, no. 2 (1997): 251–78.

Hobsbawm, Eric, and Terrence Ranger. *The Invention of Tradition.* Cambridge: Cambridge University Press, 1983.

Hølm-Hansen, Jørn. *Territorial and Ethno-Cultural Self-Government in Nation-Building Kazakhstan.* Oslo: Norweigan Institute for Urban and Regional Research, 1997.

Horowitz, Donald L. *A Democratic South Africa?* Berkeley and Los Angeles: University of California Press, 1991.

———. *Ethnic Groups in Conflict.* Berkeley: University of California Press, 1985.

Hough, Jerry F. *The Soviet Prefects: The Local Party Organs in Industrial Decision-Making.* Cambridge, MA: Harvard University Press, 1969.

Huntington, Samuel P., "Clash of Civilizations?" *Foreign Affairs* 72, no. 3 (Summer 1993): 22–49.

Isaacs, Harold. *Idols of the Tribe: Group Identity and Political Change.* New York: Harper and Row, 1977.

Jones Luong, Pauline. "Economic Decentralization in Kazakhstan: Causes and Consequences." Working paper, Yale University, 2003.

———. *Institutional Change and Political Continuity in Post-Soviet Central Asia: Power, Perceptions, and Pacts.* New York: Cambridge University Press, 2002.

Jowitt, Ken. "Neotraditionalism." In Ken Jowitt, *New World Disorder: The Leninist Extinction*, 121–58. Berkeley: University of California Press, 1992.

Kandiyoti, Deniz. "Poverty in Transition: An Ethnographic Critique of Household Surveys in Post-Soviet Central Asia." *Development and Change* 30, no. 3 (1999): 499–524.

Karpat, Kemal. "Stages of Ottoman History." In Kemal Karpat, ed., *The Ottoman State and Its Place in the World History*, 79–98. Leiden, Netherlands: E.J. Brill, 1974.

Kasza, Gregory J. "Quantitative Methods: Reflections on the Files of Recent Job Applicants." *PS: Political Science and Politics* (forthcoming).

"Kazakh Customary Law." *Central Asian Review* 5, no. 2 (1957): 127–44.

Kazemzadeh, Firuz. "Russia and the Middle East." In Ivo Lederer, ed., *Russian Foreign Policy*, 489–530. New Haven: Yale University Press, 1962.

Khazanov, Anatoly M. *After the USSR: Ethnicity and Nationalism in the Commonwealth of Independent States.* Madison: University of Wisconsin Press, 1995.

Khazanov, Anatoly M. *Nomads and the Outside World.* 2nd ed. Madison: University of Wisconsin Press, 1994.

Khoury, Philip S., and Joseph Kostiner, eds. *Tribes and State Formation in the Middle East.* Berkeley: University of California Press, 1990.

Kolstø, Pål. "Anticipating Demographic Superiority: Kazakh Thinking on Integration and Nation-Building." *Europe-Asia Studies* 50, no. 1 (1998): 51–69.

Kondo, Dorinne K. *Crafting Selves: Power, Gender, and Discourses of Identity in a Japanese Workplace.* Chicago: University of Chicago Press, 1990.

Kornai, János. *Economics of Shortage.* Amsterdam: North-Holland, 1980.

Krueger, Richard A. *Focus Groups: A Practical Guide for Applied Research.* Thousand Oaks, CA: Sage Publications, 1994.

Kushlubayev, Vladimir. "Tribalism and the State Formation in Kyrgyzstan." Thesis, Central European University, 1995.

Laitin, David D. *Hegemony and Culture: Politics and Religious Change among the Yoruba.* Chicago: University of Chicago Press, 1986.

———. *Identity in Formation: The Russian-Speaking Populations in the Near Abroad.* Ithaca: Cornell University Press, 1998.

Landa, Janet Tai. *Trust, Ethnicity, and Identity: Beyond the New Institutional Economics of Ethnic Trading Networks, Contract Law, and Gift Exchange.* Ann Arbor: University of Michigan Press, 1994.

Landé, Carl B. "Kinship and Politics in Pre-Modern and Non-Western Societies." In John T. McAlister Jr., ed., *Southeast Asia: The Politics of National Integration,* 219–29. New York: Random House, 1973.

Ledeneva, Alena. *Russia's Economy of Favours: Blat, Networking and Informal Exchanges.* Cambridge: Cambridge University Press, 1998.

Lemarchand, René. "Political Clientelism and Ethnicity in Tropical Africa: Competing Solidarities in Nation-Building." In Steffen W. Schmidt, et al., eds., *Friends, Followers, and Factions,* 100–123. Berkeley: University of California, 1977.

———. *Burundi: Ethnocide as Discourse and Practice.* Cambridge and New York: Woodrow Wilson Center Press and Cambridge University Press, 1994.

Levitsky, Steven, and Lucan A. Way. "Elections without Democracy: The Rise of Competitive Authoritarianism." *Journal of Democracy* 13, no. 2 (April 2002): 51–65.

Lewis, I. M. *Blood and Bone: The Call of Kinship in Somali Society.* Lawrenceville, NJ: Red Sea Press, 1994.

———. *A Modern History of Somalia*. Boulder, CO: Westview Press, 1988.

Lewis, Robert A., Richard H. Rowland, and Ralph C. Clem. *Nationality and Population Change in Russia and the USSR: An Evaluation of Census Data, 1897–1970*. New York: Praeger, 1976.

Lieven, Anatol. *Chechnya: Tombstone of Russian Power*. New Haven: Yale University Press, 1998.

Lijphart, Arend. "Consociational Democracy." *World Politics* 21, no. 2 (January 1969): 207–25.

Lindholm, Charles. "Kinship Structure and Political Authority: The Middle East and Central Asia." *Comparative Studies in Society and History* 28, no. 2 (1986): 334–55.

Loncle, John F., "Land Reform in Kazakhstan: Institutions and Lessons from Elsewhere." Working paper, University of Wisconsin–Madison, 1999.

Lowenthal, David. *The Past is a Foreign Country*. New York: Cambridge University Press, 1985.

Lubin, Nancy, et al. *Calming the Ferghana Valley: Development and Dialogue in the Heart of Central Asia*. New York: Century Foundation Press, 1999.

Martin, Terry D. "An Affirmative Action Empire: Ethnicity and the Soviet State, 1923–1938." Ph.D. dissertation, University of Chicago, 1996.

Martin, Virginia. "Barimta: Nomadic Custom, Imperial Crime." In Daniel R. Brower and Edward J. Lazzerini, eds. *Russia's Orient: Imperial Borderlands and Peoples, 1700–1917*, 249–70. Bloomington: Indiana University Press, 1997.

———. "Law and Custom in the Steppe: Middle Horde Kazakh Judicial Practices and Russian Colonial Rule, 1868–1898." Ph.D. dissertation, University of Southern California, 1996.

Massell, Gregory J. *The Surrogate Proletariat: Moslem Women and Revolutionary Strategies in Soviet Central Asia, 1919–1929*. Princeton: Princeton University Press, 1974.

Matley, Ian Murray. "Industrialization." In Edward Allworth, ed., *Central Asia: 130 Years of Russian Dominance*, 3rd ed., 309–48. Durham and London: Duke University Press, 1994.

McGarry, John. "'Demographic Engineering': The State-Directed Movement of Ethnic Groups as a Technique of Conflict Regulation." *Ethnic and Racial Studies* 21, no. 4 (1998): 613–38.

Mead, George Herbert. *Mind, Self, and Society from the Standpoint of a Social Behaviorist*. Chicago: University of Chicago Press, 1934.

Merton, Robert K. *Social Theory and Social Structure*. Glencoe, IL: Free Press, 1957.

Migdal, Joel. *States in Society*. Cambridge: Cambridge University Press, 2001.

Moore, Barrington. *Social Origins of Dictatorship and Democracy*. Reprinted with a new foreword by Edward Friedman and James C. Scott. Boston: Beacon Press, 1993.

Morgan, David L. *Focus Groups as Qualitative Research*. Newbury Park, CA: Sage Publications, 1988.

Motyl, Alexander J. *Revolutions, Nations, and Empires: Conceptual Limits and Theoretical Possibilities*. New York: Columbia University Press, 1999.

Nekrich, Aleksandr M. *The Punished Peoples: The Deportation and Fate of Soviet Minorities at the End of the Second World War*. Translated by George Saunders. New York: Norton, 1978.

North, Douglass C. *Institutions, Institutional Change and Economic Performance*. Cambridge: Cambridge University Press, 1990.

Olcott, Martha Brill. "The Collectivization Drive in Kazakhstan." *Russian Review* 40, no. 2 (1981): 122–42.

———. *The Kazakhs*. 2nd ed. Stanford: Hoover Institution Press, 1995.

Patnaik, Ajay. "Agriculture and Rural Out-Migration in Central Asia, 1960–1991." *Europe-Asia Studies* 47, no. 1 (1995): 47–169.

Payne, Matthew J. "Turksib: The Building of the Turkestano-Siberian Railroad and the Politics of Production During the Cultural Revolution, 1926–1931." Ph.D. dissertation, University of Chicago, 1995.

Peletz, Michael G. "Kinship Studies in Late Twentieth-Century Anthropology." *Annual Review of Anthropology* 24 (1995): 343–72.

Pipes, Richard. *The Formation of the Soviet Union*. Cambridge, MA: Harvard University Press, 1954.

Poliakov, Sergei. *Everyday Islam: Religion and Tradition in Rural Central Asia*. Armonk, NY: M.E. Sharpe, 1992.

Putnam, Robert. *Making Democracy Work: Civic Traditions in Modern Italy*. Princeton: Princeton University Press, 1993.

Ragin, Charles. *Fuzzy-Set Social Science*. Chicago: University of Chicago Press, 2000.

Rakowska-Harmstone, Teresa. "Soviet Legacies." *Central Asia Monitor* 3 (1994), http://www.chalidze.com/cam/41,3,4.htm (accessed 21 June 2000; site now discontinued).

Roy, Olivier. *The New Central Asia: Creation of Nations*. New York: New York University Press, 2000.

Rubin, Barnett. "Russian Hegemony and State Breakdown in the Periphery: Causes and Consequences of the Civil War in Tajikistan." In Barnett R. Rubin and Jack Snyder, eds., *Post-Soviet Political Order: Conflict and State Building*. London: Routledge, 1997.

Rumer, Boris Z. *Soviet Central Asia: A Tragic Experiment*. Boston: Unwin Hyman, 1989.

Rywkin, Michael. *Moscow's Muslim Challenge: Soviet Central Asia*. Rev. ed. Armonk, NY: M.E. Sharpe, 1990.

Sabol, Steven. "Kazak Resistance to Russian Colonization: Kenesary Kasymov and His Revolt, 1837–1847." Paper presented at the meeting of the Association for the Study of Nationalities, Columbia University, New York, 15–17 April 1999.

Samatar, Abdi Ismail. "Destruction of State and Society in Somalia: Beyond the Tribal Convention." *Journal of Modern African Studies* 30, no. 4 (1992): 625–41

Schatz, Edward. "Framing Strategies and Non-Conflict in Multi-Ethnic Kazakhstan." *Nationalism and Ethnic Politics* 6, no. 2 (Summer 2000): 70–92.

———. "Notes on the 'Dog that Didn't Bark': Eco-Internationalism in Late Soviet Kazakstan." *Ethnic and Racial Studies* 22, no. 1 (1999): 136–61.

———. "The Politics of Multiple Identities: Lineage and Ethnicity in Kazakhstan." *Europe-Asia Studies* 52, no. 3 (2000): 489–506.

Schmidt, Steffen W., et al., eds. *Friends, Followers, and Factions*. Berkeley: University of California, 1977.

Schoeberlein-Engel, John. "Identity in Central Asia: Construction and Contention in the Conceptions of 'Ozbek,' 'Tajik,' 'Muslim,' 'Samarkandi' and Other Groups." Ph.D. dissertation, Harvard University, 1994.

Scott, James C. *Seeing Like a State: How Certain Schemes to Improve the Human Condition Have Failed*. New Haven: Yale University Press, 1998.

Shepsle, Kenneth A. "Studying Institutions: Some Lessons from the Rational Choice Approach." *Journal of Theoretical Politics* 1, no. 2 (1989): 131–47

Shnirelman, Victor A. *Who Gets the Past? Competition for Ancestors among Non-Russian Intellectuals in Russia*. Baltimore: Johns Hopkins, 1996.

Shryock, Andrew. *Nationalism and the Genealogical Imagination: Oral History and Textual Authority in Tribal Jordan*. Berkeley: University of California Press, 1997.

Slezkine, Yuri. "The USSR as Communal Apartment, or How a Socialist State Promoted Ethnic Particularism." *Slavic Review* 53, no. 2 (1994): 414–52.

Stevens, Jacqueline. *Reproducing the State*. Princeton: Princeton University Press, 1999.

Sultanov, Tursun. "The Kazakh Khanate and the Kazakh Zhuz." *Energiia Kazakhstana* 10 (1998): 82–89.

Suny, Ronald Grigor. *The Revenge of the Past: Nationalism, Revolution, and the Collapse of the Soviet Union*. Stanford: Stanford University Press, 1993.

Tapper, Richard. "Anthropologists, Historians, and Tribespeople on Tribe and State Formation in the Middle East." In Philip S. Khoury and Joseph Kostiner, eds., *Tribes and State Formation in the Middle East*, pp. 48–73 (Berkeley: University of California Press, 1990).

Taylor, Charles. "Nationalism and Modernity." In John A. Hall, ed., *The State of the Nation: Ernest Gellner and the Theory of Nationalism*, 191–218 (Cambridge: Cambridge University Press, 1998.

Thelen, Kathleen. "Historical Institutionalism in Comparative Politics." *Annual Review of Political Science* 2 (1999): 369–404.

Thelen, Kathleen, and Sven Steinmo. "Historical Institutionalism in Comparative Perspective." In Sven Steinmo, Kathleen Thelen, and Frank Longstreth, eds., *Structuring Politics: Historical Institutionalism in Comparative Analysis*, 1–32. Cambridge: Cambridge University Press, 1992.

Tilly, Charles. *The Formation of National States in Western Europe*. Princeton: Princeton University Press, 1975.

Tismaneanu, Vladimir. *Fantasies of Salvation: Democracy, Nationalism, and Myth in Post-Communist Europe*. Princeton: Princeton University Press, 1998.

United Nations Development Program. *Republic of Kazakstan: Human Development Report*. Almaty: United Nations Development Program, 1997.

Vaisman, Demian. "Regionalism and Clan Loyalty in the Political Life of Uzbekistan." In Yaacov Ro'i, ed., *Muslim Eurasia: Conflicting Legacies*, 105–21. London: Frank Cass, 1995.

Van Evera, Stephen. "Primordialism Lives!" *APSA-CP* 12, no. 1 (Winter 2001): 20–22.

Verdery, Katherine. *National Ideology Under Socialism*. Berkeley: University of California Press, 1991.

———. *What Was Socialism and What Comes Next?* Princeton: Princeton University Press, 1996.

Walder, Andrew G. *Communist Neo-Traditionalism: Work and Authority in Chinese Industry*. Berkeley: University of California Press, 1986.

Walzer, Michael. "The New Tribalism: Notes on a Difficult Problem." *Dissent* 3, no. 9 (Spring 1992): 164–71.

Waterbury, John. *The Commander of the Faithful: The Moroccan Political Elite—A Study in Segmented Politics*. London: Weidenfeld and Nicolson, 1970.

Weaver, Catherine. *The Hypocrisy of International Organizations: The Rhetoric, Reality and Reform of the World Bank*. Ph.D. dissertation, University of Wisconsin–Madison, 2003.

Weber, Max. *Economy and Society*. Vol. 3. Edited by Guenther Roth and Claus Wittich. Berkeley: University of California Press, 1968.

———. *From Max Weber: Essays in Sociology.* Translated and edited by H. H. Gerth and C. Wright Mills. New York: Oxford University Press, 1946.

———. *On Charisma and Institution Building.* Edited by Samuel N. Eisenstadt. Chicago: University of Chicago, 1968.

———. *The Theory of Social and Economic Organization,* translated and edited by A. M. Henderson and Talcott Parsons. New York: Free Press, 1947.

Werner, Cynthia. "Household Networks and the Security of Mutual Indebtedness in Rural Kazakhstan." *Central Asian Survey* 17, no. 4 (1998): 597–612.

———. "The Significance of Tribal Identities in the Daily Life of Rural Kazaks in South Kazakhstan." Paper presented at the conference of the Association for the Study of Nationalities, Columbia University, New York, 24–26 April 1997.

Widner, Jennifer A. *The Rise of a Party-State in Kenya: From "Harambee!" to "Nyayo!"* Berkeley: University of California Press, 1992.

Winner, Irene. "Some Problems of Nomadism and Social Organization Among the Recently Settled Kazakhs, part one." *Central Asian Review* 11, no. 3 (1963).

———. "Some Problems of Nomadism and Social Organization Among the Recently Settled Kazakhs, part two." *Central Asian Review* 11, no. 4 (1963): 355–73.

World Bank. *Kazakhstan: Transition of the State.* Washington, DC: The World Bank, 1997.

Yack, Bernard. "The Myth of the Civic Nation." *Critical Review* 10, no. 2 (Spring 1996): 193–211.

Young, Crawford. "Ethnicity and the Colonial and Post-Colonial State in Africa." In Paul Brass, ed., *Ethnic Groups and the State.* London: Croom Helm, 1985. Reprinted in John Hutchinson and Anthony D. Smith, eds., *Nationalism,* 225–31. London: Oxford University Press, 1994.

———. "The Dialectics of Cultural Pluralism." In Crawford Young, ed. *The Rising Tide of Cultural Pluralism: The Nation-State at Bay?* 3–35. (Madison: University of Wisconsin Press, 1993.

ENGLISH-LANGUAGE NEWS ARTICLES AND REPORTS

Gawande, Atul. "The Cancer-Cluster Myth." *The New Yorker,* 8 February 1999, 34–37.

Holos Ukrayiny, 13 October 1993. Translated by the Foreign Broadcast Information Service (FBIS-SOV-93-198).

Izvestiia, 11 February 1987. Translated by the Foreign Broadcast Information Service (FBIS-SOV-87-028).

LeVine, Steve. "Why Do Kazakhs Keep Trying to Ship MIGs to North Korea?" *New York Times*, 27 August 1999, A12.

New York Times, 16 December 1998, A19.

Pravda, 12 January 1987. Translated by the Foreign Broadcast Information Service (FBIS-SOV-87-007).

Radio Free Europe/Radio Liberty—Kazakh Service, Report on Kazakhstan, 20 January 1999.

Radio Free Europe/Radio Liberty, Report on Russia, Transcaucasia, and Central Asia, 12 February 1999.

Radio Free Europe/Radio Liberty, Report on Russia, Transcaucasia, and Central Asia, 4 December 1999.

Radio Free Europe/Radio Liberty, Report on (Un)civil Societies, 18 May 2000.

World Bank. "Economic Indicators." http://www.worldbank.org.kz/content/econ_ind_eng.html (accessed 30 June 2000).

RUSSIAN- AND KAZAKH-LANGUAGE BOOKS AND JOURNAL ARTICLES

Abdirov, M. *Khan Kuchum: izvestnyi i neizvestnyi*. Almaty: Zhalyn, 1996.

Abylkhojin, Zhulduzbek B. *Strana v serdtse Evrazii: siuzhety po istorii Kazakhstana*. Almaty: Qazaq universiteti, 1998.

Agenstvo Respubliki Kazakhstan po statistike. *Demograficheskii statezhegodnik Kazakhstana*. Almaty: Agenstvo Respubliki Kazakhstan po statistike, 2000.

———. *Demograficheskii ezhegodnik Kazakhstana*. Almaty: Agenstvo Respubliki Kazakhstan po statistike, 2002.

———. *Statisticheskii ezhegodnik Kazakhstana*. Almaty: Agenstvo Respubliki Kazakhstan po statistike, 1999.

Aidosov, Abylai. "'Zhuzism' atauynan aulaq bolaiyq." *Aqiqat* 3 (1996): 88–90.

Akhmetzhanova, G., and N. Makhanov. "Osnovnye napravleniia razvitiia bankovskoi sistemy Kazakhstana." In *Sbornik nauchnykh statei molodykh uchenykh*, 112–28. Almaty: Qazaqstan damu instituty, 1997.

———. "Sel'skoe naselenie Kazakhstana 1920–1990 gg." Kandidatskaia dissertation, Historical Sciences, Institut Razvitiia Kazakhstana, Almaty, 1993.

Alekseenko, Aleksandr N. "Sel'skoe naselenie Kazakhstana 1920–1990 gg." Kandidatskaia diss., Historical Sciences, Institut istorii i etnologii, Almaty, 1993.

Altmyshbaev, A. *Nekotorye perezhitki proshlogo v soznanii liudei v srednei azii i rol' sotsialisticheskoi kul'tury v bor'be s nimi*. Frunze, USSR: Academy of Sciences Kirgiz SSR, 1958.

Amrekulov, Nurlan. *Puti k ustoichivomu razvitiiu: razmyshleniia o glavnom*. Almaty: 1998.

Amrekulov, Nurlan, and Nurbulat Masanov. *Kazakhstan mezhdu proshlym i budushchim.* Almaty: Beren, 1994.

Artykbaev, Zh. O. *Kazakhskoe obshchestvo v XIX veke.* Qaraghandy: Poligrafiia, 1993.

Ashimbaev, D. R. *Kto est' kto v Kazakhstane.* Almaty: Credo, 2001.

Asylbekov, Askhat Z. *Kto est' kto v Respublike Kazakhstan: 1996–7.* Almaty: Izdatel'stvo "Respublika Kazakhstan," 1997.

Asylbekov, M. Kh. and A. B. Galiev. *Sotsial'no-demograficheskie protsessy v Kazakhstane (1917–1980).* Alma-Ata: Ghylym, 1991.

Bekmakhanov, Yermukhan Bekmakhanovich. *Kazakhstan v 20–40 gody XIX veka.* Alma-Ata: Qazaq universiteti, 1992.

Bromlei Yu. V., ed. *Etnicheskie protsessy v sovremennom mire.* Moscow: Nauka, 1987.

Chzhen, Kun Fu. *Geopolitika Kazakhstana: mezhdu proshlym i budushchim.* Almaty: Zheti zharghy, 1999.

Daniiarov, K. *Al'ternativnaia istoriia Kazakhstana.* Almaty: Zhibek zholy, 1998.

Dorzhenov, Seken, and Bolat Babaquly. "Zhuzizm." *Aqiqat* 10 (1995): 73–77.

Dvoskin, B. Ia., N. F. Golikov, and M. D. Spektor. *Problemy rasseleniia naseleniia Kazakhstana.* Alma-Ata: Nauka Kazakhskoi SSR, 1989.

Dzhunusova, Zhanylzhan Kh. *Respublika Kazakhstan: Prezident, instituty demokratii.* Almaty: Zheti zharghy, 1996.

Elebaeva, A. B., ed. *Razvitie mezhetnicheskikh otnoshenii v novykh nezavisimykh gosudarstvakh Tsentral'noi Azii.* Bishkek, Kyrgyzstan: Ilim, 1995.

Ergalieva, Gul'mira K. "Ekonomicheskaia rol' mestnykh gosudarstvennykh organov vlasti v Respublike Kazakhstan." *Saiasat* 7 (1996): 63–74.

Gosudarstvennyi komitet Kazakhskoi SSR po statistike. *Narodnoe khoziaistvo Kazakhstana za 70 let: statisticheskii sbornik.* Alma-Ata: Izdatel'stvo "Kazakhstan," 1990.

Gosudarstvennyi komitet SSSR po statistike, *Uroven' obrazovaniia naseleniia SSSR: po dannym vsesoiuznoi perepisi naseleniia 1989 g.* Moscow: Finansy i statistika, 1990.

Goskomstat Respubliki Kazakhstan. *Statisticheskii ezhegodnik Kazakhstana.* Almaty: Goskomstat Respubliki Kazakhstan, 1995.

Gumiliev, Lev N. *Drevnie Tiurki.* Moscow: Nauka, 1967.

Institut Razvitiia Kazakhstana. *Kazakhskii traibalizm: sostoianie, osobennosti i puti preodoleniia.* Almaty: Institut Razvitiia Kazakhstana, 1995.

Iudin, P. "Adaevskii bunt na poluostrove Mangyshlak v 1870 godu." *Russkaia starina* 7 (1894). Reprinted in F. M. Orazaev, *Tsarskaia kolonizatsiia v Kazakhstane: po materialam russkoi periodicheskoi pechati XIX veka,* 79–100. Almaty: Rauan, 1995.

Iuzefo, B. "O byte Kirgizov Turgaiskoi oblasti." *Russkii vestnik* (April 1880). Reprinted in F. M. Orazaev, *Tsarskaia kolonizatsiia v Kazakhstane: po materialam russkoi periodicheskoi pechati XIX veka,* 336–66. Almaty: Rauan, 1995.

Kazhegel'din, Akezhan. *Kazakhstan: pravo vybora.* Almaty: Qarzhy-Qarazhat, 1998.

Kenzhaliev, Z. Zh., et al., eds. *Qazaq adet-ghyryp quqyghynyng materialdary.* Almaty: Zheti zharghy, 1996.

Khliupin, V. N. *"Bol'shaia sem'ia" Nursultana Nazarbaeva: politicheskaia elita sovremennogo Kazakhstana.* Moscow: Institut aktual'nykh politicheskikh issledovanii, 1998.

———. *Imperskii sbornik No. 1: Respublika Kazakhstan—geopoliticheskie ocherki.* Moscow: Russkii Komitet pri Predsedatele Liberal'no-Demokraticheskoi partii Rossii, 1997.

Kiikbaev, N. *Torzhestvo leninskoi natsional'noi politiki v Kazakhstane.* Alma-Ata: Izdatel'stvo "Kazakhstan," 1968.

Kireev, F. N., and F. I. Kolodin, eds. *Rabochee i agrarnoe dvizhenie v Kazakhstane v 1907–1914 godakh: sbornik dokumentov i materialov.* Alma-Ata: Kazakhskoe gosizdatel'stvo, 1957.

Kliashtornyi, S. G., and T. I. Sultanov. *Kazakhstan: letopis' trekh tysiacheletii.* Alma-Ata: Rauan, 1992.

Komitet po statistike i analizu. *Regional'nyi statisticheskii ezhegodnik.* Almaty: Statkomitet, 1997.

Konstitutsiia Respubliki Kazakhstan. Almaty: Zheti zharghy, 1996.

Korbe, O. A. "Kul'tura i byt kazakhskogo kolkhoznogo aula." *Sovetskaia etnografiia* 4 (1950): 67–91.

Kratkie itogi perepisi naseleniia 1999 goda v Respublike Kazakhstan: Statisticheskii sbornik. Almaty: Agenstvo Respubliki Kazakhstan po statistike, 1999.

Kshibekov, D. *O preodolenii perezhitkov kapitalizma v soznanii i bytu.* Alma-Ata, 1957.

Kuchkin, Andrei Pavlovich. *Sovetizatsiia Kazakhskogo aula: 1926–1929 gg.* Moscow: Akademiia Nauk SSSR, 1962.

Kunaev, Dinmukhammed. *O moem vremeni.* Alma-Ata: Yntymaq, 1992.

Levshin, Aleksei Iraklievich. *Opisanie kirgiz-kazach'ikh, ili kirgiz-kaisatskikh, ord i stepei.* 1832. Reprint, Almaty: Sanat, 1996.

Makarova, O. K., M. P. Zhdanova, and E. A. Timofeeva. *Chislennost' i sostav naseleniia SSSR po dannym vsesoiuznoi perepisi naseleniia 1979 goda.* Moscow: Finansy i statistika, 1984.

Masanov, Nurbulat. "Kazakhskaia politicheskaia i intellektual'naia elita: klanovaia prinadlezhnost' i vnutrietnicheskoe sopernichestvo." *Vestnik Evrazii* 1, no. 2 (1996): 46–61.

———. *Kochevaia tsivilizatsiia Kazakhov.* Almaty: Sotsinvest, 1995.

———. "Migratsii v Kazakhstane: istoriia, problema i metod." Paper presented at Soros Foundation seminar on interethnic relations, Almaty, 25 March 1998.

Masanov, Nurbulat, and Igor Savin. *Mode'l etnopoliticheskogo monitoringa: Kazakhstan.* Moscow and Almaty: MOST, 1997.

Mendikulova, G. M. *Istoricheskie sud'by Kazakhskoi diaspory.* Almaty: Ghylym, 1997.

Mukanov, Marat Sabitovich. *Etnicheskii sostav i rasselenie kazakhov Srednego zhuza.* Alma-Ata: Nauka, 1974.

Namitov, A. *Perezhitki rodovogo byta i Sovetskii zakon.* Moscow: Gosizdatel'stvo, 1929.

Natsional'noe statisticheskoe agenstvo Respubliki Kazakhstan. *Demograficheskii ezhegodnik Kazakhstana.* Almaty: Natsstatagenstvo, 1998.

———. *Statisticheskii ezhegodnik Kazakhstana, 1994–1997.* Almaty: Natsstatagenstvo, 1998.

Naumova, Ol'ga B. "Materialy k izucheniiu etnicheskogo samosoznaniia omskykh i bel'agashskikh kazakhov." In Institut etnografii, ed., *Polevye issledovaniia instituta etnografii, 1978,* 107–11. Moscow: Nauka, 1980.

———. "Nekotorye aspekty formirovaniia sovremennoi bytovoi kul'tury Kazakhov v mnogonatsional'nykh raionakh Kazakhstana." In A. Zhilina and S. Cheshko, eds., *Sovremennoe razvitie etnicheskikh grupp Srednei Azii i Kazakhstana,* 5–50. Moscow: Institut etnologii i antropologii, 1992.

———. "Sovremennye etnokul'turnye protsessy u kazakhov v mnogonatsional'nykh raionakh Kazakhstana." Kandidatskaia dissertation, Institut etnologii i antropologii, Moscow, 1991.

Nauryzbai, Zh. "Etnokul'turnoe obrazovanie v Kazazkhstane." *Mysl'* 9 (1997): 65–75.

Nazarbaev, Nursultan. *Kazakhstan—2030: poslanie Prezidenta strany narodu Kazakhstana.* Almaty: Bilim, 1997.

———. *Piat' let nezavisimosti.* Almaty: Izdatel'stvo "Kazakhstan," 1996.

Nurkadilov, Zamanbek. *Ne tol'ko o sebe.* Almaty: Shartarap, 1996.

Nurmakhan, Zanash. "Ru zhane rushyldyq." *Aqiqat* 3 (1993): 91–92.

O bor'be s korruptsiei: zakon Respubliki Kazakhstan. Almaty: Zheti zharghy, 1998.

O iazykakh v Respublike Kazakhstan. Almaty: Zheti zharghy, 1997.

Omarov, Mukash. *Rasstreliannaia step': istoriia Adaevskogo vosstaniia 1931 goda; po materialam OGPU.* Almaty: Ghylym, 1994.

Orazbekov, N. *Kontsepsiia stanovleniia istoricheskogo soznaniia v Respublike Kazakhstan.* Almaty: Natsional'nyi sovet po gosudarstvennoi politike pri prezidente Respubliki Kazakhstan,1995.

Qudaiberdy-uly, Shakarim. *Rodoslovnaia Tiurkov, Kirgizov, Kazakhov i khanskikh dinastii.* Translated by Bakhyt Kairbekov. Alma-Ata: Zhazushy, 1990.

Quttyqadam, Seidakhmet. "Rulyq sana zhane qazirgi zaman." *Aqiqat* 1 (1994): 12–18.

Sabitov, N. S. "Obshchestvennaia zhizn' i semeinii byt Kazakhov-kolkhoz-nikov (po materialam Alma-Atiinskoi i Dzhambulskoi oblastei)." *Trudy instituta istorii, arkheologii, i etnografii* (1956): 190–230.

Sadibekov, Zaiyr. *Qazaq shezhiresi.* Tashkent: Uzbekiston, 1994.

Sariev, Izturghan. *Ush zhuzding shezhiresi.* Almaty: Olke, 1997.

Satpaev, D. "Tainye rychagi vlasti: lobbi i institut lobbizma v Kazakhstane." *Mysl'* 6 (1996): 31–36.

Savin, Igor. "O kategoriiakh gruppovogo soznaniia u kazakhov-kochevnikov." Working paper, Shymkent branch, Kazakhstan Academy of Sciences, 1998.

Serikbaiuly, Baibota. *Qongyrat shezhiresi.* Almaty: Zhalyn, 1992.

Sultangalieva, A. K. *Islam v Kazakhstane: istoriia, etnichnost', obshchestvo.* Almaty: Kazakhstanskii institit strategicheskikh issledovanii, 1998.

Tatimov, Maqash. *Qazaq alemi: qazaqtyng sany qansha?* Almaty: Atamura-Qazaqstan, 1993.

Tilegenov, Bekezhan. *Tuiyq omirding qupiiasy.* Almaty: Deuir, 1992.

Tileulesov, Temirtas. *Ordaly zhylan: korruptsiia turaly.* Shymkent, 1998.

Tolybekov, S. E. *Kochevoe obshchestvo Kazakhov v XVII-nachale XX veka.* Alma-Ata: Nauka, 1971.

Tulegulov, Askar Kumakovich. "Rekrutirovanie politicheskoi elity v uslovi-iakh transformatsii Kazakhstanskogo obshshestva." Kandidatskaia dissertation, Institut Razvitiia Kazakhstana, Almaty, 1998.

Tursunbaev, Abde Bochinovich. *Kazakhskii aul v trekh revoliutsiiakh.* Alma-Ata: Izdatel'stvo "Kazakhstan," 1967.

Tynyshpaev, Mukhamedzhan, "Genealogiia Kirgiz-Kazakhskikh rodov." 1925. Reprinted in Mukhamedzhan Tynyshpaev, *Istoriia Kazakhskogo naroda*, edited by A. Takenov and B. Baigaliev, 104–5. Almaty: Sanat, 1998.

Ustav o sibirskikh kirgizakh. In Aleksei Iraklievich Levshin, *Opisanie kirgiz-kazach'ikh, ili kirgiz-kaisatskikh, ord i stepei*, 399–428. 1832. Reprint, Almaty: Sanat, 1996.

Vagabov, M. V. *Kalym—vrednyi perezhitok.* Makhachkala: Dagestanskoe knizhnoe izdatel'stvo, 1975.

Viatkin, M. *Ocherki po istorii Kazakhskoi SSR.* Leningrad: Gospolitizdat, 1941.

Vostrov, V. V., and M. S. Mukanov. *Rodoplemennoi sostav i rasselenie Kaza-khov: konets XIX–nachalo XX v.* Alma-Ata: Nauka, 1968.

Zhambakin, Zhapar A. "Pastbishchnoe zhivotnovodstvo Kazakhstana: proshloe, nastoiashchee, budushchee." Unpublished manuscript of the general director, National Association of Farmers (Kazakhstan), Almaty, 1999.

Zhanuzakova, L. T. "Problemy vzaimootnoshenii akima oblasti s vyshestoiashchimi i nizhestoiashchimi organami ispolnitel'noi vlasti v uslovi-
iakh unitarnogo Kazakhstana." *Izvestiia Akademii Nauk RK* 4 (1997):
14–18.

RUSSIAN- AND KAZAKH-LANGUAGE
PERIODICALS

Kazakhstani Newspapers
(based in Almaty, unless otherwise indicated)

Akmolinskaia pravda (Astana)
Ana tili
Aq zhaiyq (Atyrau)
Dat
Dozhivem do ponidel'nika
Dzhezkazganskaia pravda (Zhezqazghan)
Egemen Qazaqstan
Egemendi Qazaqstan
Industrial'naia Karaganda (Qaraghandy)
Karavan
Kazakhstanskaia pravda
Kyzylordinskie vesti (Qyzylorda)
Madeniet (Semei)
Mestnoe vremia (Aqtau)
Novoe pokolenie
Panorama
Qazaq adebieti
Qazaq eli
Severnyi Kazakhstan (northern Kazakhstan)
Sotsialistik Qazaqstan
Tselinogradskaia pravda (Astana)
Tsentral'nyi Kazakhstan (Zhezqazghan)
Turkistan
XXI vek

Russian Newspapers

Argumenty i fakty
Literaturnaia gazeta
Nezavisimaia gazeta
Obshchaia gazeta

INTERVIEWS

Abdugaliev, Berik. Deputy director, Department of Internal Politics, Ministry of Information and Social Accord. Astana, Tselinograd *oblast*, 14 September 1998.

Abenov, Erlan. Director, Institut Razvitiia Kazakhstana. Almaty, Almaty *oblast*, 4 September 1998.

Aidossov, Serik. Director, Sociological Resource Center. Shymkent, South Kazakhstan *oblast*, 21 May 1998.

Aldamzherov, Gaziz K. Politician and business leader (later prominent in the Republican People's Party). Almaty, Almaty *oblast*, 1 April 1998.

Asanov, Beisenbek. Mullah. Shaulder, South Kazakhstan *oblast*, 31 May 1998.

Baltabaeva, Kulgazira Nurlanovna. Researcher, Department of Social and Humanitarian Sciences, Academy of Sciences. Almaty, Almaty *oblast*, 28 September 1998.

Editors of *Iuzhnyi variant* newspaper. Shymkent, South Kazakhstan *oblast*, 25 May 1998.

Erofeeva, Irina. Professor of history, Institute of History and Ethnography, Kazakhstan Academy of Sciences. Almaty, Almaty *oblast*, 1 October 1998.

Goncharov, Aleksei. Journalist. Shymkent, South Kazakhstan *oblast*, 28 May 1998.

Kairkhanov, Sabyr. Editor-in-chief of *Aq zhaiyq*. Atyrau, Atyrau *oblast*, 12 October 1998.

Kaletaev, Darkhan. Director, Department of Youth Policy, Ministry of Information and Social Accord. Astana, Tselinograd *oblast*, 14 September 1998.

Kelesbaev, Asan. Employee, television station Otyrar, Shymkent, South Kazakhstan *oblast*, 26 May 1998.

Kizatova, Toqzhan. Founder of labor movement at Tengizchevroil. Atyrau, Atyrau *oblast*, 25 October 1998.

Masanov, Nurbulat. Professor of history (later prominent in the Republican People's Party). Almaty, Almaty *oblast*, 25 March 1998.

Matyzhan, Kenzhekhan. Deputy, Department for the Development of Languages. Astana, Tselinograd *oblast*, 15 September 1998.

Mukanov, Marat Sabitovich. Professor of ethnography, Institute of History and Ethnography, Kazakhstan Academy of Sciences. Almaty, Almaty *oblast*, 16 March 1998.

Nurpeisov, Kenges Nurpeisovich. Professor of history, Institute of History and Ethnography, Kazakhstan Academy of Sciences. Almaty, Almaty *oblast*, 10 March 1998.

Qozhaakhmet, Khasen. Leader of the ethnonationalist movement Azat. Almaty, Almaty *oblast*, 26 March 1998.

Rakhat. Almaty, Almaty *oblast*, 11 August 1998. Conducted by Saulesh Esenova for her own research.

Shaimerdenov, Erbol. Director, Department for the Development of Languages. Astana, Tselinograd *oblast*, 15 September 1998.

Tekeev, Arykbai Amanovich. Businessman. Atyrau, Atyrau *oblast*, 14 October 1998.

Zhuraruly Duisenbi, Kabyl. Deputy director, Department of Information and Public Accord. Shymkent, South Kazakhstan *oblast*, 6 June 1998.

ANONYMOUS OR PSEUDONYMOUS INTERVIEWS

Anticorruption official. 28 May 1998.

Asqarov, Zhaqsylyq (pseud.). Rural South Kazakhstan *oblast*, June 2002.

Bakhyt (psued.). Shymkent *akimat*, South Kazakhstan *oblast*, 28 May 1998.

Besenov, Marat (pseud.). Rural South Kazakhstan *oblast*, June 2002.

Borisov, Pavel (pseud.). Shymkent, South Kazakhstan *oblast*, 5 June 1998.

Esenova, Beibit (pseud.). Shymkent, South Kazakhstan *oblast*, June 2002.

Expedition participant. Almaty, Almaty *oblast*, 29 September 1998.

Fisherman. Rural South Kazakhstan *oblast*, 4 June 1998.

Islam, Ozbekov (pseud.). Rural South Kazakhstan *oblast*, June 2002.

Ivanova, Natalia (pseud.). Shymkent, South Kazakhstan *oblast*, June 2002

Local journalist. Atyrau, Atyrau *oblast*, 16 October 1998.

NGO worker. Almaty, Almaty *oblast*, March 1998.

Qarataev, Zhyldyz (pseud.). Rural South Kazakhstan *oblast*, June 2002.

Russian member of the opposition. Almaty, Almaty *oblast*, 3 April 1998.

Tekenov, Nurlan (pseud.). Shymkent, South Kazakhstan *oblast*, June 2002.

Tulebaeva, Bakhyt (psued.). Shymkent, South Kazakhstan *oblast*, June 2002.

Zhandosov, Zhumabek (pseud.). Rural South Kazakhstan *oblast*, June 2002.

Zhdanova, Meiramgul (pseud.). Rural South Kazakhstan *oblast*, June 2002.

ADDITIONAL ETHNOGRAPHIC SOURCES

Conversations and Focus Groups

Anonymous local journalists. Shymkent, South Kazakhstan *oblast*, 27 May 1998.

Anonymous scholars affiliated with the Institute of History and Ethnography. Almaty, Almaty *oblast*, 1997–98.

Dadabaeva, Gulnara. Almaty, Almaty *oblast*, 3 March 1998; and Taraz, Zhambyl *oblast*, 25 January 1999.

Focus group participants. Almaty, Almaty *oblast*, 9 August 1998.
Focus group participants. Atyrau, Atyrau *oblast*, 21 October 1998.
Focus group participants. Shymkent, South Kazakhstan *oblast*, 2 June 1998.
Murzhabekova, Bakhyt. Almaty, Almaty *oblast*, 14 August 1998.
Open-forum meeting, Ukrainian national-cultural center. Almaty, Almaty *oblast*, 7 October 1998.
Participant in Soros Foundation seminar on political science. Shymkent, South Kazakhstan *oblast*, 23 May 1998.
Tulgenova, Dildakul. Shaulder, South Kazakhstan *oblast*, 11 June 1998.

Author's Field Notes

Almaty, Almaty *oblast*, 12 June 1997.
Rural South Kazakhstan *oblast*, July 1997.
Almaty, Almaty *oblast*, 20 February 1998.
Mikhailovka village, Shymkent, South Kazakhstan *oblast*, 24 May 1998.
Shymkent, South Kazakhstan *oblast*, 28 May 1998.
Shymkent, South Kazakhstan *oblast*, 1 June 1998.
Arys, South Kazakhstan *oblast*, 4 June 1998.
Shymkent, South Kazakhstan *oblast*, 7 June 1998.
Atyrau, Atyrau *oblast*, October 1998.
Almaty, Almaty *oblast*, 7 June 2002.

CENTRAL STATE ARCHIVES
OF THE REPUBLIC OF KAZAKHSTAN

Note: Post-Soviet archives are divided into *fondy* (f.), subdivided into *opisi* (o.), then into *dela* (d.), and finally into *listy* (l.).

f. 74, o. 1, d. 1, l. 53.
f. 74, o. 1, d. 129, l. 57.
f. 74, o. 11, d. 20.
f. 74, o. 11, d. 26, l. 4.
f. 74, o. 4, d. 6, l. 5.
f. 74, o. 4, d. 6, l. 78.
f. 74, o. 4. d. 133, l. 9.
f. 74, o. 4, d. 345.
f. 769, o. 1, d. 3, l. 3.
f. 769, o. 1, d. 3, l. 10.
f. 769, o. 1, d. 11, l. 86.

f. 769, o. 1, d. 66, l. 17.
f. 1380, o. 2, d. 12, l. 71.
f. 1380, o. 2, d. 200, l. 206.
f. 1380, o. 2, d. 200, l. 215.
f. 1380, o. 2, d. 242, l. 58.

Index

Abykaev, Nurtai, 99
Africa, ix, xix, 163; decolonization of, 7
agriculture, 28–29, 51
Akmolinsk region, 119, 120, 146
Aktobe region, 119
Aliev, Rakhat, 99
Almaty region, 117, 144, 157; assistance networks in, 147–49; Chemolgan village in, 124
Amrekulov, Nurlan, 126–27
Anderson, Benedict, 6
Arendt, Hannah, 48–49
Astana. *See* Kazakhstan
Atyrau region, 90, 104, 105, 106, 146; assistance networks in, 147–49

Baigel'di, Omirbek, 99
Balgimbaev, Nurlan, 103
Baltic states, 73
Barth, Fredrik, 23, 98
blat, 60, 61, 67–68
bribery. *See* corruption

causality, x, xxi. *See also* social science
Chechnya, xvi, 23
Cherdabaev, Ravil', 106
China, 60
Christie, Kenneth, 25
civicness, 172

clan, xviii, 25–27, 29; advantages of, xxv, 8, 70–71; barter and, 70; before Soviet rule, 27–37; behaviors associated with, 35, 43–45; celebrations, 155; clan-based histories, 118–21; concealable nature of, xxii, xxv, 14, 17, 70, 96, 165; criminalization of, 43–45; defined, 26; developmentally useful purposes of, 170; exogamous marriage and, 28, 134, 156; genealogies and, xxii, 58, 113, 132, 139, 157; information providers, 60, 70, 107, 113–15, 154; international norms and, 172–73; khans and, 31; local (*ru*), 27; metaphorical usage of, 26; multitiered nature of, 97–98, 170; networks, xxiii, xxiv, 17–19, 61–69, 99–103, 152–53; persistence of, xxiii, 12, 59–69; public stigma ascribed to, xxiii, xxv–xxvi, 17, 43, 55–59, 84, 113–14, 121–31, 172–73; relation to ethnicity, 116–21, 150, 158; shortage economy and, 16–18; state building and, xxiii, xxiv, xxvi, 8–9; trust and, 8, 9, 62, 70
clan politics: clan balancing and, 110–12, 167; and clan clientelism, 111–12; and clan conflict, 38–40, 95–112 passim; and clan meta-

clan politics *(continued)*
  conflict, xxiii, xxv–xxvi, 19–20,
  113–35 passim; distinctiveness
  of, xviii–xix, 97; and rational
  choice, 8. *See also* Kazakhstan
class divisions, 29–30; *bais*, 38; blackbone stratum, 30, 34–35, 38;
  whitebone stratum, 30
collectivization, xxiv–xxv, 18, 43
Collins, Kathleen, 9, 12
Commonwealth of Independent
  States, 78
Connor, Walker, 7
constructivism, xix, xx–xxi, 11–13
corruption, 8, 63, 64, 67, 107, 154–55;
  and anti-corruption campaigns,
  68, 135
Cossacks, 32, 101, 128

Democratic Choice of Kazakhstan,
  123
democratization. *See* political
  transition
Deutsch, Karl, 5
Di Palma, Giuseppe, 166
discourse, xxiii. *See also* clan politics
Douglas, Mary, 98
Durkheim, Emile, 22, 26, 97
Duvanov, Sergei, 89, 105

economic transition, 84–85, 89–90;
  barakholki and, 89; credit provision and, 90; and performance,
  89–90, 129, 144–45; implications
  for clans, 156; introduction of
  currency, 89; monetarization,
  153–54; possibility of "Dutch
  disease," 90; privatization, 90,
  152
education, xvii, 50–51, 65; ethnicity
  and, 80. *See also* modernization
Elder Umbrella Clan, 31, 34, 69,

98–99, 100–103, 132, 151; Akhsha
  subdivision, 59; Alban, 58; Dulat,
  59, 105, 124; Kozhai (Qozhai) subdivision, 59; Qangly, 32; Sha-
  prasht, 124; Shymyr subdivision,
  59; Taz subdivision 58; Zhanys
  subdivision, 105
emic perspectives. *See* ethnographic
  methods
Esenberlin, Ilias, 57–58
Esimov, Akhmetzhan, 99
ethnicity, xix, 23–25, 146; defined,
  23; international norms and, 172;
  language and, 23–24, 79–81;
  markers of, 24; purity and, 160;
  Soviet Union's promotion of, 54,
  74
ethnic redress. *See* Kazakhstan
ethnocultural expeditions, 83–84,
  143
ethnographic methods, xxi , 175–77;
  and ethnographic "present," 6.
  See also social science
Eurasianism, 75–78
Eurasian Union, 78
Evans-Pritchard, E. E., 27
exchange of goods, xxii, 62, 96, 105,
  153, 155, 169

Geertz, Clifford, 112
Gellner, Ernest, 4–5
genealogies, xxii, 26, 27–28; promo-
  tion of, 117. *See also* clan
Genghis Khan, 30
Germans, 78
Goffmann, Erving, 22
Gumiliev, Lev, 76

habitus, 73
historical institutionalism, xx, 20.
  See also identity
Hobbes, Thomas, 22

Homo sovieticus, 54, 76. *See also*
  Soviet Union
Horowitz, Donald, xix, 24
Huntington, Samuel, 22

identity modernization, 4, 20, 140,
  164
identity, 22–23, 149–50; change, xx;
  defined, 23; and mechanisms
  of reproduction, xx–xxii, xxiii,
  xxiv–xxv, 13–14, 59–69; multiple
  levels of, 164, 172; persistence
  of, xx, 47
identity politics, xix. *See also* clan;
  clan politics; constructivism;
  ethnicity; primordialism
Indonesia, 25, 99
insider perspectives. *See*
  ethnographic methods
institutional syncretism, xxii
Iraq, 9
Islam. *See* Muslim identity

Jordan, 10

Kasymov, Kenesary, 35
Kasza, Gregory, 109
Kazakh Khanate, 30, 31
Kazakhs: demographic position of,
  24–25; emergence of ethnic identity among, 31–32; ethnic unity
  of, 134; ethnonationalists among,
  127–28; forced resettlement of,
  49; hospitality of, 39, 63; mutual
  assistance among, 66; mythologi-
  cal progenitor of, 27; stereotypes
  among, 145; urban migrants,
  143–50
Kazakhstan: demographic policies
  in, 81–82; environmental conditions, xxiv, 18; ethnic relations in,
  75–84, 115–16, 142–43, 146; mod-

ernization of, 15, 141–43; political
  appointments in, 81, 99–103; as
  nationalizing state, 74–84; political institutions in, 85–89; relocation of capital city, 76–77, 87, 102,
  132, 134; state building in, 37–40;
  statehood and, 82–83. *See also*
  clan politics; Soviet Union
Kazhegel'din, Akezhan, 85, 101, 130
Kenya, 171
kinship. *See* clan
Korbe expedition, 58
korenizatsiia policy. *See* nativization
Kornai, János, 60–61
Koshchi Union, 39–40
Kuchkin, Andrei Pavlovich, 39
Kunaev, D. A., 69, 98–99
Kurds, 78
Kyrgyzstan, xvi–xvii, 9, 72

Laitin, David D., 9, 24
land: competition for, 35–36; People's
  Commissariat on Land, 41; Soviet
  reform efforts, 40–43
Lande, Carl H., xv
Lebanon, 9
Ledeneva, Alena, 61
legitimacy: competing notions of, 9;
  traditional, xxii
Levshin, Aleksei Iraklievich, 27, 113,
  139
Lindholm, Charles, 3
literacy, xvii, 36. *See also* modernization
local administration, 88, 106–7

Malaysia, 79, 116
Mangystau, 28, 104, 119, 120
marketization. *See* economic
  transition
Martin, Terry, 54
Marx, Karl, 54

Masanov, Nurbulat, 160; scholarship of, 28, 122–23; subethnic criticism and, 122–25

Mead, George Herbert, 22

media: language used by, 80–81; limits on freedom of, 88–89, 134–35

metaconflict, clan, xxiii, xxv–xxvi, 19–20, 113–35 passim

Middle East, ix, xix, 5; and Palestinian identity, xxi

Middle Umbrella Clan, 31, 34, 58, 65, 98, 100–103, 151; Abylai Khan, 34; Arghyn, 32, 105, 124; Bozhbandar subdivision, 151; Mangytai subdivision, 151; Naiman, 32, 124; Qanzhygaly subdivision, 119; Qongyrat, 65, 118, 124, 151; Qulan-Qypshaq, 106; Qypshaq, 65, 106; Sanghyl subdivision, 151; Uzyn subdivision, 106; Zhetimder subdivision, 151; Zhoghary-Shekty subdivision, 105

Migdal, Joel, 46

modernism: discourse of, xxvi, 47–48; failures of, 16

modernity, xv–xvi; nation-state and, xv

modernization, 165; aspects of, 4; consequences of, 4–7; defined, 7; paradigms of, ix, 166

Mongolia, 72

Moore, Barrington, 21

Morocco, 4, 9, 111, 163

mundane behaviors, xv, xx

Musaev, Al'nur, 99

Muslim identity, 149; relation to clan, 149–50

national-cultural centers, 77–78

national-cultural revival, 79, 82–84

nation building, 7–8, 9

nativization, 37

Nazarbaev, Nursultan, xviii, 69, 95, 116; and allegations of corruption, 87–88; clan network of, xxv, 98–99, 124; clan balancing by, 111; depiction of Kazakhstan by, 18; Eurasianism and, 76–78; intelligentsia and, 124–25; opposition to, 121–31; portrayal of clans by, 133–35; powers of, 85–89, 104–5; and pro-Nazarbaev parties, 86

Nazarbaeva, Dariga, 99

nepotism. *See* corruption

networks, xxv, 17, 60–62, 97; types of, 147–49

nomadism, xvii, 32, 45; attachment to territory and, 29; migrations, 28

opposition. *See* Nazarbaev, Nursultan

patrimonialism, xix

Pavlodar region, 104

political transition, 72–73; limited extent of, 85–89

post-Soviet state: capacity of, xvii, 161–62

poverty: implications for clan, 170. *See also* economic transition

press. *See* media

primordialism, xix, xx–xxi, 11–13, 15, 140, 143, 149, 162

Qaraghandy region, 119, 144, 157

Qostanai, 39, 41, 146

Qozhaakhmet, Khasen, 127

Qozybaev, Manash, 84

quasi-state actors, 115–21. *See also* regions

qumys (fermented mare's milk), 40

Qunanbai, Abai, 65
Qyzylorda region, 119, 120, 146

rational choice approaches, 15, 24, 96
regions: governors (*akims*) of, 88, 105; *maslikhat* in, 88; and regionalism, 103–4; turnover of governors in, 88, 104. *See also individual names of regions*
Regulations on the Siberian Kyrgyz, 34
Republican People's Party, 85, 86
residence permits, 144
ru. See clan; *individual clan names*
Russia: colonial administration, 34; expansion of empire, xxi, 33–37; imperial census of 1897, 36; Liberal Democratic Party, 130–31; political factions in, 25
Russians, 23; emigrants from Kazakhstan, 82, 108; fourth "umbrella clan," 108–9; migration to Kazakhstan, 33, 36, 41–42, 54, 142; and kinship, 67–68; possible separatism among, 76, 101, 103; subethnic criticism and, 128–29

Sabol, Steven, 36
Sarsenbaev, Altynbek, 99
Scotland, 12
Scott, James C., xxii
sedentarization, xxiv–xxv, 18, 35; forced, 42–43
Semei region, 119
shezhire. See genealogies
Silk Road, 33, 76
social science: assumptions of, xxi; categories used, 11; focus on observable phenomena, xxiv, 7, 109, 131–33; lack of attention to clans, 3–4, 20; inductive

approaches in, ix–x; postmodern turn in, 22
social structure: segmentation, 26; traditional, xxi–xxii, 6
Solzhenitsyn, Aleksandr, 130
Somalia, 3, 9, 10, 111
South Kazakhstan region, 83, 106, 107, 116, 132, 146; Arys district, 129; assistance networks in, 147–49; Mikhailovka village, 160; Saizaq district, 106; Shaulder village, 150, 151; Shymkent, 40, 66, 106–7, 153
Southeast Asia, xix; decolonization of, 7
Soviet Union: coercive capacity of, xxii; collapse of, xvi, 46, 59, 166; command economy of, 59–60; desirable professions in, 62–63; "grey" market economy, xxii, 60, 62; internationalism, 54, 75; legacies of, xxv, 73–91; modernization project of, xviii, 16–17, 48, 50–59, 141–43; nationalities policy in, 53–55, 74; penetration of society in, 48; and popular mobilization in Central Asia, 73; promotion of ethnicity in, 16; propaganda of class warfare in, 37–38, 41; Russification in, 55–56, 121, 145, 157; use of terror in, 49
Sovietization, x, 37–45; resistance to, 38
Stalin, Josef, xxiv
state: building, xxiii, xxiv, xxvi, 8–9, 165–67; capacity in Kazakhstan, 161–62; failure, 9; role in promoting clan, 156–62; unintended consequences of, action, 15–16, 59; transparency of, institutions, 167–69

stateless populations, 21
Stevens, Jacqueline, 20
structural-functionalism, 6
subethnicity, 25–27. *See also* clan
Sudan, 27
Svoik, Piotr, 86, 129
Syr Darya, 28, 34

Tajikistan, xvii, 163
Taldy-Qorghan region, 119, 151
Taylor, Charles, 171–72
technocrats, 130
Tengiz oil field, 90
Tereshchenko, Sergei, 101
Tismaneanu, Vladimir, 72
Torghai region, 41, 105
totalitarianism, xvii
transitology. *See* political transition
tribalism, xviii, 25, 66, 133, 135, 159–60
Tshanov, Amalbek, 105
Turkestan autonomous republic, 41

Umbrella Clan, xviii, 30
urbanization, 50–51, 142; ethnicity
    and, 146–47. *See also*
    modernization

Uyghurs, 78
Uzbekistan, xvi, 9
Uzbeks, 31

Verdery, Katherine, 59, 95
Virgin Lands, 142

Weber, Max, xix, 163; and concept
    of social closure, 11, 96, 110; and
    concept of state, xxiii, 8, 10
West Kazakhstan region, 146

Younger Umbrella Clan, 31, 33, 65,
    66, 98, 100–103, 151; Abulkhair
    Khan, 33; Adai, 32; Alimulin,
    124; resistance to state authority
    among, 104; Vaiulin, 124; Zhan-
    galbaily, 65; Zhetiru, 105, 124

Zhakiyanov, Galimzhan, 104
Zhambyl region, 105, 149
zheti ata. See genealogies
Zhezqazghan region, 119
Zhirinovsky, Vladimir. *See* Russia
*zhuz. See individual umbrella clan
    names*; umbrella clan

Library of Congress Cataloging-in-Publication Data

Schatz, Edward.
Modern clan politics : the power of "blood" in
Kazakhstan and beyond / Edward Schatz.
p.   cm.
Includes bibliographical references
and index.
ISBN 0-295-98446-5 (hardback : alk. paper)
ISBN 0-295-98447-3 (pbk. : alk. paper)
1. Ethnology—Kazakhstan.
2. Kinship—Kazakhstan.
3. Clans—Kazakhstan.
4. Politics and culture—Kazakhstan.
5. Kazakhstan—Ethnic relations.
6. Kazakhstan—Politics and government.
I. Title.
DK907.S34 2004   306.2'095845—dc22   2004013607